That Night in the Garden

That Night
in the Garden

Great Fights and Great Moments
from Madison Square Garden

Jim McNeill

ROBSON BOOKS

Once again, for Jacqueline and Frank

First published in Great Britain in 2003 by Robson Books, The Chrysalis Building, Bramley Road, London, W10 6SP

An imprint of Chrysalis Books Group plc

British Library Cataloguing in Publication Data
A catalogue record for this title is available from the British Library.

ISBN 1 86105 692 3

Typeset by SX Composing DTP, Rayleigh, Essex
Printed by Butler and Tanner Ltd , Frome and London

'It was only a four-round bout, where I'd been fighting six-rounders already, but this was the Garden. This was the big top of fighting, where Barney Ross fought and Jimmy McLarnin, Henry Armstrong and Joe Louis, Mickey Walker and Tony Canzoneri.'

Rocky Graziano

Champion and Garden hero

'I don't care who they are. When they walk down the aisle to that Garden ring, they choke up. Especially the first time. It does something to them inside, something that can't be explained.'

Al Weill

Manager and Garden matchmaker

CONTENTS

Introduction

Madison Square Garden . . . the Garden . . . that marvellous New York arena that has seen Pavarotti, Sinatra and Streisand, Elvis, Elton and The Stones all hold centre stage; a venue that has hosted the very best of ice hockey and basketball, wrestling, athletics and cycling; and which, well over one hundred years after P T Barnum's elephants first danced in Madison Square, still houses an annual circus treat. But despite all this, a name that will forever be synonymous with boxing.

The late Harry Markson, a one-time president of MSG Boxing, loved to recall a 1968 visit to Rome where, along with middleweight champion Nino Benvenuti and his family, he was granted an audience with Pope Paul VI. When he was introduced as 'Harry Markson of Madison Square Garden' the Pope smiled and exclaimed, 'Ah, Madison Square Garden – boxing.' His Holiness had got it in one!

From John L Sullivan to Lennox Lewis, the story of boxing has been fought out under the hot lights over the Garden ring. Of course, such was the public demand for tickets that many fights were staged outdoors, and today the casinos, particularly in Las Vegas, offer stiff competition in their unceasing efforts to lure the high rollers. But no fight centre will ever come close to capturing the magic that still is the Garden.

There have, in fact, been four Gardens, erected on three different sites. The crazy roller coaster adventure first got underway when Phineas T Barnum cast a speculative eye on a derelict property on the north-east corner of Madison Square, previously the depot for the New York, New Haven and Hartford Railroad Company.

Phineas T was an extraordinarily imaginative entrepreneur who today would have been right up there with the major players – the Donald Trumps and the Donald Kings, and the faceless guys who control the entertainment industry and decide what we are going to like next. In 1873 Barnum leased the property, then spent considerable sums on building what was at that time a spectacular arena. On April 27, 1874 he unveiled the modestly titled Barnum's Monster Classical and Geological Hippodrome, offering wide-eyed New Yorkers such spectacles as chariot racing, performing wild animals and a huge collection of sideshow freaks.

His venture was an instant hit, but drawing in the punters month after month and discovering fresh attractions was always going to be a problem. Before very long Barnum succumbed to his wanderlust and took his giant carnival on the road, but not before he auctioned off his Madison Square lease.

The top bidder was one Patrick Sarsfield Gilmore, another bold showman. He took over in 1875, immediately dubbed the arena Gilmore's Garden and, in an audacious bid to attract the New York sports, started to promote boxing despite a state law that threatened jail for anyone participating in a 'contention of fists'. Gilmore walked a fine line, advertising his contests as 'exhibitions' and billing his pugs as 'professors'. But he found the going extremely hard and was probably relieved when the Vanderbilt family, who still owned the site, decided to reassert control and launch into the entertainment business.

And so, on May 31, 1879 the venue reopened under yet another name – Madison Square Garden.

Just like his predecessors, William Vanderbilt quickly became familiar with the kingsize headache of trying to unearth a steady flow of major crowd-pullers. And eventually, like Gilmore before him, he resolved to go for broke and stage boxing. Unlike Gilmore, however, he could call upon an established star, a guaranteed box-office smash – none other than John L Sullivan, the Boston Strong Boy, who on February 7, 1882 had won the heavyweight championship by knocking out Paddy Ryan with bare knuckles in Mississippi City.

On July 17, 1882 Madison Square Garden featured its first world champion fighter when Sullivan faced an Englishman who some-times appeared as Joe (Tug) Wilson, sometimes as Joe Collins. That night in the Garden he was Tug, and he was delighted to box under the terms of John L's challenge to any opponent: if Wilson was still upright after four rounds he would pocket $1,000 plus half the gate receipts. Not surprisingly, the slippery Wilson grabbed and held at every opportunity, took a count at the slightest excuse, and easily survived the twelve minutes.

A milestone, if not much of a spectacle, but the house had been packed and many thousands had been turned away. Vanderbilt was eager to promote more Sullivan fights; the police were less enthusiastic.

In his second Garden appearance on May 14, 1883, having survived a first-round knockdown, Sullivan was well on top against another Englishman, Charlie Mitchell, when police captain Alexander Williams halted proceedings in the third round, claiming the stoppage came 'just short of murder'. Even worse, the following year the cops arrested the Strong Boy in the second round of a match against Alf Greenfield. The complaint: 'Fighting in a cruel and inhuman manner and corrupting public morals'.

And when on January 19, 1885 the gendarmes stepped in before the end of the first round as Sullivan reopposed Paddy Ryan in front of 11,000 customers, boxing was effectively dead in that first Garden.

Barnum's building would last just four more years before Vanderbilt decided to start again and build from scratch. He gathered together a wealthy syndicate including the banker J P Morgan and our old friend Phineas T himself; demolition work began in July 1889 and just eleven months later a brand-new Garden was ready for business.

The construction was the talk of New York. Architect Stanford White's creation covered a full square block. There was an auditorium which could hold more than 10,000; there was a 1,200-seater theatre and a 1,500-capacity concert hall; there was an enormous restaurant and a roof-garden cabaret; there was a 320-foot tower, and on top of the tower stood a statue of the goddess Diana.

There was also a mortgage as breathtaking as any of Stanford's wonders. MSG2 cost anything up to three million dollars, incredible money for the time, but the new building had not answered the old teaser – how to make it pay for its keep.

Boxing in New York was still off-limits, though James J Corbett did appear at the Garden on February 16, 1892 without police intervention, going through the motions against three opponents. Just over six months later, Gentleman Jim would take the title from Sullivan – but in New Orleans, because New York law prevented the Garden from making a bid for the historic fight.

Without boxing, Madison Square Garden was a white elephant. The company stumbled into the new century, changed owners, and eventually became the property of the mortgage holders, the New York Life Insurance Company. It seemed a safe bet that sooner rather than later the company would convert the building into office space, or just about anything else that might guarantee a return . . . until along came a gambler and promoter of P T Barnum proportions to bail them out. His name was George Rickard, Tex to his many newspaper cronies and political pals.

Tex Rickard was 45 when he arrived in the Big Apple to give fresh hope to the New York Life. He had been a teenage cowboy in Montana, a town marshal in Texas, a gold prospector and hotelier in Alaska, a rancher in South America, and a brilliant promoter of boxing in Nevada. Quite a track record.

In 1906 he had cleaned up after laying out a purse of $35,000 to stage the Joe Gans–Battling Nelson lightweight title clash at Goldfield; he brought off an even greater coup four years later when he got the money together to promote Jack Johnson's heavyweight title defence against Jim Jeffries in Reno. Now, with a more benign attitude to boxing prevailing in New York, Rickard reckoned the time was right to switch his operation to the big city.

Under the Frawley Law, boxing was now legal in the state – at least halfway legal. No official decisions could be rendered but this oddball ruling was circumvented by the fans and especially the gamblers who relied on the verdicts published in specific newspapers – a set-up open to all sorts of skulduggery, but one that did not trouble Rickard.

He leased the Garden from a grateful New York Life and on March 25, 1916 promoted new heavyweight champion Jess Willard's first title defence against Frank Moran. Willard earned the newspapers' nod after a lousy fight; Tex attracted a record gate of $152,000 for MSG2's first world championship fight, the owners breathing a huge sigh of relief. But their relief did not last long.

The following year the Frawley Law was rescinded. Boxing was again outlawed in New York state, and Rickard was forced to travel elsewhere to showcase his new sensation, a blue-chinned hardcase from Manassa, Colorado, called Jack Dempsey. On Independence Day 1919, Dempsey annihilated Willard in three rounds in Toledo, and Tex had his heavyweight champion. Next business was to find a way back to New York and the Garden.

Rickard had a powerful ally in a sharpshooter called James J Walker, a future mayor of New York, but at that time the Democratic leader in the state assembly. Jimmy Walker loved a good time and he loved a good fight. In 1920 he introduced the bill – the Walker Law – that once and for all legalised boxing in New York. Tex did not hang about: two months after the law was passed he signed a ten-year lease at $200,000 a year with New York Life. At long last boxing had found a safe house on Madison Square.

That first year, Dempsey defended his title in MSG2 with a twelfth round knockout over Bill Brennan; the fabulous light-weight Benny Leonard emerged as an enormous attraction; New Yorkers, defying prohibition and often packing hip flasks, flocked to see such wonderful talents as Jack Britton and Ted Kid Lewis, Harry Greb, Mickey Walker and Gene Tunney. Of course, Rickard was delighted to host all sorts of other events, from rodeos and circuses to political conventions. But boxing had been established as the big earner.

In 1924, New York Life, perhaps relieved to have recouped so much of its money, controversially announced plans to demolish the Garden and build their main offices on the site, and on May 5, 1925 the arena at Madison Square staged its last fight when Sid Terris outpointed Johnny Dundee before the wrecking crews got busy. Tex Rickard, however, had not been idle either.

Backed by a team of heavyweight investors, he had discovered a new locale which had been the home for New York's trolley cars. His dream arena on Eighth Avenue between 49th and 50th Streets was constructed in just 249 days, could seat around 19,000 for boxing, and Tex insisted that the building should retain its predecessor's name. Madison Square Garden would live on. With scarcely a pause, the fights resumed on December 11, 1925, Paul Berlenbach successfully defending his light-heavyweight title, thanks to a split decision over Jack Delaney.

Rickard, however, would not live long to enjoy his role as

president of the Garden corporation. On January 6, 1929 he died in Miami Beach, a victim of acute appendicitis, and his body was transported to New York to lie in state in the arena that he had built. Thousands more than just the hardcore boxing crowd filed into the Garden to pay their last respects.

A black day for boxing and a black day for the Garden, but before the end of the year, there were to be even blacker days for everyone. On October 24 – Black Thursday – the crash hit Wall Street and few escaped the resulting squeeze. After recording a million-dollar profit in 1927, six years later, the Garden's boxing department had slumped into the red.

An Englishman called Jimmy Johnston, known along Broadway as The Boy Bandit, was now the main man, but he had stiff competition. A rival promotional outfit calling itself the Twentieth Century Sporting Club, fronted by a shrewd operator called Mike Jacobs and supported by the powerful Hearst newspaper organisation, was enjoying increasing success, especially when in 1935 Jacobs secured the exclusive rights to promote a young Detroit heavyweight named Joe Louis.

And when on June 22, 1937 Louis knocked out Jimmy Braddock to win the title in Chicago, the Garden bowed to the inevitable and signed a deal with Jacobs that would endure until 1949.

A New Yorker, Mike Jacobs had been the archetypal street hustler from a very early age. Nobody appreciated the value of a dollar better than Uncle Mike, and few could gauge public demand so accurately. He made a fortune buying up blocks of tickets for all types of major events, and selling them on at a considerable profit. He may have been the original ticket tout and he was seldom left with unsold bundles. Jacobs also earned healthy sums investing in Rickard's promotions, and when he took over control at Tex's house he knew exactly how to promote the talent he had on tap.

And what talent!

Not only did Jacobs have Louis – who would defend his title eight times in the Garden – he also had signed the phenomenal Henry Armstrong, a whirlwind package of energy and aggression who electrified the fans as he bludgeoned opponents from feather- to middleweight, winning three world titles in the process. And he could call on the lightweight demon Beau Jack who sold out the Garden three times in just over a month. There was the young

Sugar Ray Robinson and the indestructible Jake La Motta; there was wonderful Willie Pep, fearsome Sandy Saddler and murderous Rocky Graziano . . . headliners dreamed about getting their chance in the Garden; managers scuffled just to wangle a slot on the undercard for their latest prospect.

Truly a golden age for boxing and Madison Square Garden, but all good things . . .

In 1946 Jacobs suffered a stroke and passed control to his cousin Sol Strauss; the career of the great Louis began to grind to a melancholy close; and in 1949 a newly formed group called the International Boxing Club took charge of the fights in the Garden – and not only there, but at venues in all the major cities throughout the country.

The IBC figurehead was Jim Norris, a millionaire whose family owned such important sporting venues as the Detroit Olympia, the Chicago Stadium and the St Louis Arena. Despite his immense wealth, Norris proved to be naive in the extreme – or worse. Right from the start, his outfit was badly compromised by criminal influences, particularly by the machinations of a notorious mafioso called Frank Carbo, and after the IBC's ten-year reign, a federal court deemed it a monopoly which tied up the championships and ordered that the company be wound up.

Harry Markson, who enjoyed a clean reputation, became chief executive and the Garden continued to attract the best fighters and fights. The Norris era had featured the rise of Rocky Marciano, the ever-popular Kid Gavilan and the emergence of new attractions like Carmen Basilio and Joey Giardello. Under Markson, the arena turned the spotlight on a fresh crop of stars – excellent practitioners such as Emile Griffith and Dick Tiger, Nino Benvenuti, Jose Torres and Carlos Ortiz. And the young man who started out life as Cassius Clay.

Muhammad Ali, along with Joe Frazier, would provide the Garden with its most memorable occasion ever – but in yet another brand new building.

As far back as 1960 plans were being made for this latest move when MSG president Irving Felt outlined the blueprint for the fourth Garden, which would be located on Seventh Avenue above Pennsylvania Station. Demolition of the old station started in 1963 and the building was completed in 1968. The tab? Somewhere in the region of $116 million.

Benvenuti and Griffith fought the last title fight in the Eighth Avenue Garden; on March 4, 1968 the same two fighters, alongside Joe Frazier and Buster Mathis, headlined the renewal of boxing in MSG4. There would be many more sensational nights ahead, but somehow the glory that was the Garden of Rickard and Jacobs could never quite be recaptured.

The fight business in New York was about to go into serious decline. There was the relentless competition from casinos, eager to splash out astronomical sums to snare top attractions; heavy state and city taxes further hobbled the promotions; saddest of all, the Garden chiefs no longer seemed to care. Madison Square Garden, which had relied so heavily on boxing to keep its doors open, no longer considered boxing a priority.

In 1993 MSG officially wound up its boxing department, but the controlling company were still prepared to negotiate with independent promoters interested in staging major fights in the historic arena. A far cry, of course, from the wonderful years when the house was crammed every Friday to see Beau Jack or Willie Pep or Rocky Graziano. But somehow the Garden will never be able to gain a total divorce from the fights and the fighters.

There are champions, mega rich, who feel unfulfilled because they never had a date in the Garden; fans from all over the world still regard a visit as a pilgrimage; even an old softie like Don King enjoys a special kick when he is promoting at the Garden – the unique institution that Graziano liked to call 'the big top'. The magic lingers on.

The fights highlighted here have been chosen to recapture some of that magic, but of course, this can only be a personal selection. Many of the battles will never be forgotten; some, sadly, are all but forgotten; perhaps there are a few that boxing would prefer to forget. But the fights and the boxers, managers, cornermen and referees involved all played their part in the ongoing story of sport's most famous and enduring venue.

For fans and fighters alike, there should always be a good reason to hark back to That Night in the Garden.

'. . . And New Champion!'

Today, thanks to the bewildering number of sanctioning organisations and weight divisions, winning a world title is not such a big deal. And yet, no matter how tawdry the championship belt, or how spurious the governing body, nobody should grudge any fighter that special moment when he is declared a champion.

The title is often won in a local hall and televised to a public, bleary from a weekly diet of seeing yet another belt being fastened around another waist. But for the new champ, his family and his friends, this is still a night to remember. And rightly so.

So just try to imagine that extraordinary thrill, that wonderful buzz when the new king is crowned before a roaring crowd in the home of boxing. An unforgettable moment!

CHAPTER ONE

Carl (Bobo) Olson
v Randolph Turpin

WEDNESDAY, OCTOBER 21, 1953

For Randolph Turpin, this surprise return to the Garden was a welcome respite from the life of debt, drudgery and depression that haunted him back home in England. Twelve long and increasingly desperate years had passed since he had last stepped into the famous ring, squaring off against Bobo Olson for the vacant middleweight championship and a very healthy purse. This time he was on expenses only, but he would not have to take any punches, and for a fleeting few days in New York, the old Leamington Licker could shake off his troubles, particularly the ever hostile correspondence from a posse of taxmen.

His one-time rival, Bobo, was also there, along with Gene Fullmer and Carmen Basilio . . . three other fine holders of the 160lb title. All had been invited to the Garden by matchmaker Teddy Brenner to help pay tribute to their former common opponent, the legendary Sugar Ray Robinson, considered by many to be the greatest pound-for-pound boxer of all time.

The date was December 10, 1965 and Robinson, after a career that had spanned more than a quarter of a century, was formally announcing his retirement. That night the serious fighting was provided by Emile Griffith and Manuel Gonzalez, Emile readily retaining his welterweight belt, but the loudest cheers from the 12,146 aficionados were for Sugar Ray and Bobo, Gene, Carmen and finally Randolph, as one by one they were introduced into the ring.

3

With Robinson standing centre ring, immaculately garbed in a thigh-length white robe, the warriors marched from the four corners to greet him. As they embraced, posing for the cameras, acknowledging the rapturous reception one last time, the five old pros must have been brimful of conflicting emotions . . . warm memories of their glory nights; injustices, real or imagined, that still niggled in some dark corner of the mind; a shared wish that somehow they could turn back the clock; a shared question: where had all the dough gone?

When they had last met in New York neither Randolph Turpin nor Carl Olson had any apparent reason to be too preoccupied with money. They were big earners, about to box for Robinson's vacated title; they employed managers to haggle with the promoters, and the managers employed accountants and lawyers to take care of the mundane business of keeping the books straight and life simple. Didn't they?

In reality, life was anything but simple for either Bobo or Randy.

Back in 1953 America had yet to discover that Olson conducted a bizarre double life, somehow juggling his time between wife Helen and their kids, and his girlfriend Judy Crabbe and another fast-growing family, the ladies blissfully ignorant of one another, despite the fact that Bobo had transported his two loves and their broods on the same ship from Hawaii to the States. In England Turpin had already made headlines following an acrimonious divorce from his first wife Mary; he was barely managing to keep the lid on his new passion, Gwen Price, who would become the second Mrs T; and he was about to co-star with a Harlem beauty called Adele Daniels in a sensational court battle. Scarcely humdrum.

But everything appeared fine, and as they prepared in wildly contrasting fashion for their October 21 confrontation there must have been a long queue of lesser mortals who would have gladly swapped roles with Bobo and Randy.

This was Coronation year in Britain and one celebration followed another. New Zealander Edmund Hillary planted the Union Jack on Everest; Gordon Richards rode his only Derby winner at the 28th attempt; and ageing soccer idol Stanley Matthews finally collected an FA Cup winner's medal.

Yet Turpin still reigned as the country's super-hero, and that June he gave the Brits another reason to rejoice when he outpointed

France's Charles Humez before a sell-out crowd at London's White City for what promoter Jack Solomons optimistically billed as the vacant world middleweight championship. Full marks to Solomons for front, but in reality only Turpin's European title was at stake, and even wily Jack appreciated that Randy would have to beat America's best to warrant universal recognition.

Meanwhile in the States the society bash of the year saw 36-year-old senator Jack Kennedy wed society beauty Jacqueline Bouvier; new heavyweight king Rocky Marciano demolished the old champ Jersey Joe Walcott inside one round; on both sides of the Atlantic the bunting fluttered to mark the end of the Korean War; and just ten days after Turpin beat Humez, Bobo Olson became the US middleweight champion after outpointing rugged Paddy Young in a hard-fought fifteen-rounder in the Garden.

The stage was set for the international showdown.

Though totally different in ring style, Bobo and Randy had many similarities. Both were 25, Turpin being the elder by a month; at 5ft 10½", Olson had a fractional height advantage, although Turpin always looked an immense middle; Bobo was in his ninth year as a pro, Randy in his eighth, but he had fought just six fights fewer; both had run up unbeaten sequences after losing to Sugar Ray; and both had been throwing punches since their wild teenage days on the streets.

Olson was born in Honolulu, Hawaii on July 11, 1928. His father was Swedish-American, his mother Portuguese-Hawaiian, and years before the Japanese bombed the island and wrecked Pearl Harbor, Master Bobo was a formidable street scrapper. At fourteen he was good enough to box against seasoned pros in the gym, and a year later – with a brace of tattoos designed to make him look older – he was fighting for money, becoming a popular performer at the army and navy bases scattered throughout the island.

That was an exceptionally severe schooling for the youngster. His career stalled briefly when the authorities discovered that he was under-age, but four months after his seventeenth birthday Bobo officially became a professional, stopping one Art Robinson in four rounds in San Francisco.

He was managed by Sid Flaherty, a leading light on the West Coast who had seen Olson fight in Hawaii. Flaherty gave Bobo few easy jobs, but the teenager progressed, gathered a following, and by 1950 he was regarded as one of the best 160lb fighters in the world. True, that year he lost his two biggest fights – being outpointed by the excellent Australian Dave Sands in Sydney and knocked out in twelve by the great Sugar Ray in Philadelphia – but Bobo was now a well-established headliner.

Robinson would forever give Olson nightmares: all told, the Sugarman beat him four times, Bobo coming closest in a 1952 title challenge in San Francisco where he lost a close decision. But when Ray announced his first retirement at the close of that year, the Hawaiian emerged as the clear top choice to keep the championship in the States.

In the build-up to facing Turpin he had put together a sequence of ten wins, more workmanlike than spectacular, but good enough to hearten the home support. His training had gone according to plan, but staying strong at 160lb was becoming an increasing concern within Bobo's camp. The Americans, however, could gain some cheer from the fact that Turpin would also have to keep a close eye on the pounds and ounces. Before facing Humez, Randy had required three trips to the scales before weighing in right on the limit with only ten minutes to spare. Olson–Turpin was fast shaping up as the battle of the weight-watchers.

Just like his opponent, there was never much doubt that Turpin was destined to earn his money from the ring. Born in Leamington Spa, Warwickshire, on June 7, 1928, he was the son of a British Guianan (now Guyana) father and an English mother; life for a mixed-race family in the Midlands was not without its problems, and the five kids – the two girls as well as the boys – quickly learned to take care of themselves. Dick was the oldest and would win the British and Empire middleweight titles, bringing down the shameful colour barriers that had been maintained for far too long by the British Board of Control; Jackie developed into a busy and talented featherweight; but Randolph, the baby of the family, was always considered somebody special.

Twice British amateur champion, he turned pro aged eighteen, with manager George Middleton who also did the business for his brothers and it was soon apparent that he was too good for the domestic crop. A stunning puncher, he was also an awkwardly smart boxer and very powerful; British, then European titles were won with the minimum fuss; and he had lost only twice in 43 contests when promoter Solomons negotiated a world title chance against Sugar Ray, then doing a grand tour of Europe.

Few outside the Turpin clan expected the battle to last more than a handful of rounds, but on July 10, 1951, before a crowd of 18,000 in London's Earl's Court, Randolph kept his cool, remembered his boxing, and used his tremendous strength to outrough and outpoint a champion who might have regarded him too lightly and gone easy in training. Britain went bananas! But for just 64 days.

In the mandatory September return in New York's Polo Grounds, Robinson – marginally ahead going into the tenth but visibly tiring and badly cut – produced a sensational right to drop the Englishman flat on his back. Although Turpin regained his feet, he threw no punches as Ray swarmed all over him, pounding him on the ropes. Referee Ruby Goldstein rightly intervened with just eight seconds remaining in the round.

Since that night Turpin had gone undefeated, had even stepped up to light heavy to win the British and Empire titles from Don Cockell, but in his eight fights before Olson his work had lacked the chilling ferocity that had made him such a stand-out. And when he arrived at Grossinger's, his training head-quarters in the Catskills, the word quickly spread that morale in the Turpin camp was low.

The first signs of unrest came on the voyage to New York, Randolph bickering about his preparation – or lack of it – with manager Middleton and brother Dick. Always a headstrong character and never at ease with strangers, he largely shunned the sizeable travelling press corps and soon a flood of negative stories was being filed from first the *Queen Elizabeth* and then Grossinger's. The Brit insisted that he had completed the bulk of his sparring work in England, but experienced observers like the old heavyweight contender Tommy Farr and respected hacks like Peter Wilson and George Whiting would not buy any of that.

In the Catskills, Turpin's training sessions bordered on farce and in his infrequent rounds in the ring he was lethargic and offered absolutely no threat to his workmates. He was bad-tempered and petulant, and at one stage even threatened to pack his bags and head home. Not surprisingly the odds on an Olson win strengthened from 8/5 to 11/5.

Perhaps there would have been some late money for Turpin had the news leaked out that Bobo had been forced to sweat off the last few pesky pounds in a steam room on the morning of the fight.

Remember, unlike today, the weigh-in was held on the same day as the fight and a drained boxer had only a few hours to recharge his batteries. Last-minute reductions could be significant.

Olson, however, passed the scales first time with a half pound to spare. The gasps came when Turpin's weight was announced at 157lb – a full 3lb below the limit. Somebody had miscalculated badly, and all the evidence pointed straight to the boxer himself.

Frank Algar, a former navy mate of Randolph's, had been the nominal boss of training in the camp though, curiously, he did not even hold a licence in Britain; for back-up the extremely knowledgeable American Jimmy August was on hand, but he was given little chance to prove his expertise and wound up taking care of the sparring partners; the advice of Turpin's brothers and manager Middleton went ignored. Randolph was running the show, but there have been very few fighters who have successfully trained themselves. Even the gifted and the great require either constant cajoling or relentless bullying. Turpin would stand for neither.

So how had he contrived to weigh so light? This was a guy who had almost flunked the scales before his last contest four months earlier yet this time he had treated his training with disdain. It is not unreasonable to conclude that Turpin's troubled mind throughout his stay at Grossinger's was just as likely to have caused the weight loss as any exertions in the gym. He was anxious to keep new love Gwen a secret from the media; the assault charges initiated by Adele Daniels were just a few days away from making the headlines – not too far-fetched to suggest that women troubles had worried the weight off Randy! Olson, despite his own peculiar domestic arrangements, remained focused on the job ahead.

He had the support of the bulk of the 18,000 who packed into the Garden, and all the better if the British guy had sleepwalked through training and got hung up on dames. The fans provided receipts of $167,651 with another sixty grand from television thrown into the pot – mere expense money by today's standards, but very serious dough back then. No question, Olson–Turpin was the international sporting event of the year.

In those final few minutes in the dressing room, waiting for the call to the ring, boxers often silently reflect on how honest they have been in their preparation or secretly curse having cut so many corners. This is just one of the many moments of truth on fight night, and having gone through the routine on 53 previous occasions Turpin must have been agonisingly aware that he had cheated himself and also those who believed in him. And possibly that prompted him to gamble, banking everything on an early stoppage, looking to land his heavy shots right from the first bell.

The tactic may have been born of desperation but there was logic to reinforce it. Bobo always took time to find his rhythm, and in the opening three minutes he was quickly under fire as Turpin scored heavily with both hands. A hard right to the head, followed by a left hook to the body sent shudders through the Hawaiian, and just before the bell, a fierce right to the jaw underlined just how much the outsider had dominated the exchanges.

There was more of the same in rounds two and three as Randolph continued to control the action from long range, using his powerful jab to excellent effect, and catching Olson with solid follow-up hooks and crosses. On his best night, Turpin was a better boxer and a harder puncher than Olson, and now the strange tales from the Catskills were looking as unreliable as the long odds bet on the American. Turpin just could not miss him, and going back to his corner at the end of the third Bobo looked a very ordinary fighter, totally lacking in inspiration.

But that inspiration arrived in the minute's break when, for the first time, manager Flaherty and trainer Syd Gold started earning their wages, loudly spelling out the strategy that would bring about Turpin's downfall: Olson would continue to get murdered if he stayed on the outside; boxing at long range was making the Englishman look like a million dollars; Bobo must get in close, beat him up around the belly, and only then switch to the head.

In later years Olson would claim that Turpin was the strongest man he ever fought, but Flaherty and Gold had done their research: Randolph was not nearly so effective fighting inside and a close-quarters battle was sure to tax his suspect stamina.

There was an immediate and dramatic turnaround in fortunes. Obeying his corner's instructions, Olson started to score for the first time; almost immediately Turpin began to wilt. Bobo was no great puncher but he could cut and bruise, was always busy, and his instant success gave him a tremendous boost. The Turpin who had manhandled Sugar Ray so readily just could not cope with the barrage.

During the following three rounds – in a complete reversal of the opening nine minutes – he was driven all over the ring, absorbing a steady if unspectacular beating from a fighter who was taking strength from his opponent's weakness. There was little that was flashy in the Hawaiian's work, and many of his best shots were missed by fans just a few rows back. But they were not missing Randy.

In the British corner hopes soared briefly in the eighth when a full-blooded Turpin right almost toppled Olson, but he failed to find another good shot and by the close of the round Bobo had regrouped and had resumed his assault. The remainder of the fight was to be painful for the proud and game Englishman, and almost as painful to watch for those who had seen him on his all-conquering march to the championship. His talent had deserted him and all that was left was courage.

The bell signalled the end of the ninth with Randolph rising from the canvas following an Olson assault, cut and swollen around his left eye and looking thoroughly beaten. From the ring apron, commission doctor Vincent Nardiello looked closely at the distressed fighter but he made no recommendation to referee Al Berl. The Englishman was still groggy coming out for the tenth and Olson quickly slapped him down again, this time for a nine count, and when he rose there was blood leaking from his nose and mouth.

Turpin was as beaten as any fighter could be, and in an eerie replay to the second Robinson fight he retreated to the ropes and stood up under a sustained battering from the American. Bobo should have applied the finisher, but he lacked the terrific power and expertise of a Sugar Ray, and the packed tiers began to barrack the homeboy for his failure to put Turpin on the canvas again, and to cheer the Brit every time he tossed a shot in reply. There were precious few of these, but Turpin stayed upright to the final bell, actually taking the last round on some cards when, fighting from memory, he brought the fans to their feet with a remarkable rally.

Of course, this came far too late to sway the decision, even though judge Arthur Susskind scored the fight as close as eight rounds to seven. Susskind, a popular figure in New York when boxing as Young Otto, clearly did not give his countryman due credit for his work on the inside and the two knockdowns. Judge

Charley Shortell scored a much more emphatic 11–4 for Olson and referee Berl also had Bobo a clear winner at 9–4 and two rounds even. Unanimous. The crown was staying in the States, the fans were happy, and as announcer Johnny Addie raised the new champion's arm, an overcome Olson burst into tears. Perhaps he was thinking of his two families and what the title would mean to them. He was only 25, but this had been a long haul.

Standing beside him, a tired and marked Turpin produced something approaching a smile for the cameras. Almost wistful. Better than anyone, he knew that with proper preparation he could easily have been champion again. Perhaps he was just glad that the sorry business was over and he could return to England and Gwen; perhaps he was already dreading the fall-out of his stormy affair with Adele Daniels.

He had first met Daniels when he was in New York to box Robinson, and she was there to greet him off the boat when he returned to fight Olson. But this was no match made in heaven, more like one made by Teddy Brenner.

On the day before he was due to sail home he was arrested and charged with the rape and assault of the 24-year-old Harlem girl. The following morning she sensationally withdrew the charges, but would instead sue the boxer for $100,000. Turpin was granted permission to sail, but first he had to deposit $10,000 as security in case he should be recalled to the States to face civil charges.

Turpin could not escape the front pages. This was payback time for the British sports writers who slammed Randolph's shoddy preparation and sorry showing; Board of Control secretary Teddy Waltham initiated an inquiry into Turpin's training routine, and the newshawks fed on stories of both Adele and Gwen.

But two years passed before he returned to New York to face the music and the vitriol of Daniels' lawyer, a headline-grabber called Raymond Sala. The case, made memorable mostly for Mr Sala's vivid antics, bubbled along for four days, then on day five Miss Daniels unexpectedly accepted a settlement – a miserly £1,250 – much to Sala's outrage and Turpin's relief. By this time, however, he was a spent force as a fighter.

In 1954 Italy's Tiberio Mitri had knocked him out inside one round in Rome to take his European middleweight title. Despite the machinations and lofty pronouncements of promoter Solomons, who still saw him as box-office, he was finished as a serious title challenger. He would struggle on for another four years and could still attract the crowds, right up to a sad finale when Trinidad's Yolande Pompey, another good fighter on the slide, knocked him out in two rounds before 15,000 curiosity seekers in Birmingham.

He had dropped bundles on an ambitious hotel venture and to a long line of spongers; stints on the wrestling circuit and labouring in a scrapyard scarcely met the bills. There were bankruptcy hearings, incessant tax demands, and the crushing boredom of serving behind the counter in Gwen's transport café in Leamington. Only the invitation to meet up with his old pals Sugar Ray and Bobo provided a brief respite from his despair.

On May 17, 1966, just over five months after he last heard the cheers in the Garden, Turpin put an end to his torment. In a bedroom above the café, he wounded his baby daughter then turned the gun on himself. Two bullets, head and chest, from a .22. He was 37.

Bobo would survive to almost twice that age. Once he had wiped away those tears in the Garden and realised he was the new middleweight champ, he got busy. There were so many mouths to feed. Despite an increasing struggle to make 160lb, he packed in three defences in 1954, beating the fine welterweight champion Kid Gavilan, the durable Rocky Castellani and the French hope Pierre Langlois. A bumper year for earnings, but 1955 was to prove a disaster.

He challenged Archie Moore for his light heavyweight belt. Not only did many give him a good chance against The Mongoose, there were headbangers suggesting that this would be a stepping stone to a showdown against Rocky Marciano. Old Archie snuffed those pipedreams in three rounds.

Before the end of the year Olson again suffered the torture of boiling down to 160lb to defend against Sugar Ray, now on a comeback. Robinson caught him flush in the second and in the return, six months later, Ray applied the finisher in the fourth. Robinson would always be Olson's jinx, but by now the scales were an equally dangerous opponent. At the weight, his punch resistance had vanished.

Sugar Ray would be Olson's last venture at middleweight and his last crack at a world title. For the next ten years he tackled light heavies and heavyweights, fighting good-calibre opponents and winning far more than he lost until he called it quits following a points defeat against Don Fullmer on November 22, 1966 in Oakland. He wound up with a record of 99 wins and two draws from 117 fights. More than all right.

Between the final two Robinson knockouts, Olson's complex double life at last hit the headlines and for a time Bobo jokes were the staple of every club comedian from New York to his home in San Francisco. There was an expensive divorce from Helen and he married Judy, but there were still all those kids to support – the final tally was 6–4 in favour of Judy. And like old foe Turpin, he was deep in hock to the taxman. Manager Flaherty had been granted power of attorney over his finances. Sid claimed he trusted others more qualified to invest the dough for Bobo; the investments bombed. A familiar tale.

And so Olson could never enjoy a financial cushion at the end of his career, but he and Judy did their best and life could still be a laugh until his closing years which were plagued by Alzheimer's. He died on January 18, 2002, aged 73.

Randolph and Bobo – so alike and yet so unalike, and by no means the greatest middleweights ever to grace the Garden, but courageous, talented and crowd-pleasing performers nonetheless. Olson's reputation will always suffer from those four Robinson defeats; Turpin, on the other hand, will always be a hero, at least in Britain, for that shock win over Sugar Ray in London.

Winners and losers. Sometimes it is hard to tell one from the other.

CHAPTER TWO

Roberto Duran
v Davey Moore

THURSDAY, JUNE 16, 1983

Boxing's million-dollar brainteaser. When is the hot young prospect ripe for his shot, his crack at the big money, maybe even a chance at a title belt? Twenty fights? . . . more? . . . less? Generations of trainers, managers and promoters have agonised over this defining moment which, with one scrawl of a signature on a contract, can ruin years of patient planning and incredibly hard graft, or rocket everyone concerned straight into the funny money.

The team conducting the affairs of a promising welterweight called Davey Moore experienced no such angst. Moore had fought only eight times – all wins, five inside the distance – but powerful forces were about to take a hand in his destiny. In its November 1981 ratings, the World Boxing Association inexplicably put him at number ten in their light middleweight list; shortly after, this curious manoeuvre was taken a stage further when, without having faced a ranked light middle, Moore was offered a chance to challenge the reigning WBA champion Tadashi Mihara on his home turf in Tokyo. Team Moore jumped at the opportunity, and Davey jumped all over the Japanese, winning in the sixth.

After only nine pro appearances the boy from the South Bronx was a world champion. Brilliant strategy or just blinding good luck? Nobody was soul-searching, and certainly there was nothing lucky about the manner in which he set about his first three challengers who were summoned with an almost indecent haste and who survived a total of just nineteen rounds.

This kid could really fight and serious money was beginning to flow into the coffers.

Davey Moore was flying high, more lucrative matches beckoned, yet in boxing terms he was still a mere babe. But promoter Bob Arum and manager Leon Washington did not dwell overlong on such a detail when they agreed the next defence, this time against a legend, albeit a slightly tarnished one . . . the remarkable Roberto Duran. Moore was only a week past 24 when he stepped into the ring with Roberto; the Panamanian, celebrating his 32nd birthday, planned an extra-special Garden party on June 16 by becoming a champion at three different weights.

Roberto Duran, the eccentric, magnetic, marvellously talented wild man who teased and tormented both boxers and beasts with an equal lack of compassion.

The scary Duran stories. The tales of Roberto strutting the streets of Panama City, a suitably cowed lion on a leash; the day he knocked out a horse with one savage punch to collect a bet of two bottles of whisky; the sickening episode recalled by American boxing analyst Alex Wallau when Duran allegedly scooped up a cat, twirled the animal around his head, then threw it against a wall. All fact or all fiction? Perhaps a soupçon of both, but the young Duran never tried to hide his vicious streak, and in the ring he gloried in being the bad guy.

Nasty or not, there could be no arguments over his prodigious exploits. Long before he fought Moore, and an incredible nineteen years before he would finally announce his retirement, Duran's name was written large in the history of the fight game.

One of eight children, he was born into the squalor and slums of Guarare on June 16, 1951 and was soon a pint-sized street bandit, scraping a living and battling for the hell of it. Inevitable that he would soon find directions to a gym, and at the grand old age of sixteen the bantamweight Roberto was turned loose on the professionals, capturing a four-rounds points win over a guy called Carlos Mendoza. Carlos could not have been too bad because Duran's next eight opponents failed to come out for the second round. His patron was a wealthy countryman, Carlos Eleta, who had long cornered the market in Panama's top fighters. Realising he had unearthed someone exceptional, he decided to spare no effort or expense and so contacted his New York friend Ray Arcel.

Arcel died in 1994, but his name lives on as one of the brainiest and most articulate trainers of all time, a true professor who, with first Whitey Bimstein and then Freddie Brown, worked with a host of great champions and near-champs. His association with Eleta stretched back to the 1950s and a decent boxer called Frederico Plummer, but Arcel had been retired from the business for almost twenty years when the Panamanian again called on his help.

In Boston in the early 1950s Arcel had been the victim of an assault with a lead pipe outside his hotel. At the time he had been staging promotions that were screened on ABC television and providing competition to the all-powerful International Boxing Club and its television interests. The lead pipe? Frankie Carbo? Who knows? Arcel, however, took the hint and dropped out of boxing.

Eleta's call rekindled his interest. The Panamanian wanted Ray to help coach his fighter, Alfonso (Peppermint) Frazer, then preparing to challenge Nicolino Loche for his junior welterweight title. Arcel regarded the trip as a one-off and with some shrewd tactical advice and his mere presence in the corner, Frazer won the championship. Shortly after, Eleta showed him Duran and the old trainer was hooked.

On June 26, 1972 Arcel and Brown formed Duran's corner team in the Garden when Roberto took the lightweight title from the brilliant Scot Ken Buchanan in round thirteen. Buchanan was embittered for years because he was never granted a rematch and he was a notable exception as Duran steamrollered his way to an impressive twelve defences, only Edwin Viruet lasting the full trip. Then he relinquished the title, moved up to welter, and produced his finest performance ever, outpointing Sugar Ray Leonard over fifteen rounds for the championship in Montreal.

Arcel, however, never tried to take credit for making Duran into a great fighter. He told author Ronald K Fried, 'Nobody had to teach Duran how to fight. The first day I saw him – not in New York, I saw him in Panama – I told everyone around him, "Don't change his style. Leave him alone. I don't want anyone to ever tell him what to do. Let him fight," I said. "He'll carry the whole gang of us." He knew how to fight.'

But the veteran did suggest minor adjustments that improved his left jab and tightened his defence, and, most important of all, in the gym the wild man transformed into a pussycat around Brown and especially Arcel. They had gained his respect and he obeyed their commands.

The Leonard victory in Montreal was the highpoint of their partnership; the return five months later in New Orleans brought an abrupt end to the association. That was the infamous night when Duran – the epitome of macho – well behind and on the brink of humiliation, turned away with a dismissive wave of his glove and said: 'No mas' – 'No more'. Ray Leonard could scarcely believe his eyes; a shellshocked Arcel was so distraught that he ended a relationship that had developed a father-son quality. Duran had rocked the world but for all the wrong reasons.

There were parallels with Sonny Liston's meek capitulation against the young Cassius Clay. Liston claimed a bad shoulder, Duran blamed stomach cramps for his downfall but few were buying that one. However, a loyal fan base remained in Panama and the country's leader General Omar Torrijos sent him a telegram of support; but in the States his rehabilitation would prove tortuous.

Returning as a beefy light-middle, he shaped no better than so-so when outpointing Nino Gonzales and Luigi Minichillo, and the years appeared to have caught up with him in January 1982 when he lost a unanimous decision to the extremely accomplished WBC champion Wilfred Benitez in Las Vegas. Eleta advised him to retire, Duran ignored the advice, and they parted company. Worse was to follow when he was outpointed by the unheralded Nottingham welter Kirkland Laing in Detroit, and when he could only sleepwalk to a points victory over another Englishman, Jimmy Batten, in Miami, the word went out that Roberto was most definitely past tense.

He desperately needed a major success, and at last appreciating the gravity of his situation, for the first time since Arcel's departure he began to work seriously in the gym.

He rediscovered his pride and his enthusiasm and exactly a year after the Benitez defeat, and in his best condition since the first Leonard fight, he became the ferocious Roberto of old. Before a crowd of 16,824 in the Los Angeles Sports Arena he completely outclassed a Mexican hero, the former welterweight champion Pipino Cuevas, scoring two knockdowns before the referee intervened in the fourth.

In New York, however, the cynics were not convinced, nor was the Moore camp particularly impressed. The consensus was that both Duran and Cuevas were used up; that Roberto was the better of two shot fighters and had smashed little more than a shell. Odds against him beating Moore soared as high as 3/1 before settling at 5/2. The price seemed an insult to the memory of a once-great champion.

Davey Moore had come such a long way in such a short space of time. Born on June 9, 1959, he escaped trouble at school, was a bright pupil and an excellent athlete, discovering boxing when taking a look around the Morrisania Youth Center in the Bronx where he was introduced to the Center's boxing guru, Leon Washington.

Moore and Washington developed a rapport. The kid was a fast learner, quickly became a headliner in the amateurs, and wound up a four-time New York Golden Gloves champion (1977–9). At 5ft 10″, he was rugged and aggressive with an assortment of damaging punches. And after a career of only six losses from 96 bouts, Davey turned pro with Washington doubling as manager and trainer. But not even in the South Bronx was there any great fanfare, nor were there any lucrative sponsorship deals or cosy long-term contracts.

Moore made his debut on November 1, 1980 with a six-rounds points win over Chuco Saucedo at Lake Tahoe. He was more adequate than sensational, but Washington kept him busy and the steady improvement was encouraging. After three distance victories, he followed up with five successive stoppages, the most notable being a seven-rounds win over Cus D'Amato disciple Kevin Rooney in Atlantic City. Moore was going places, but few could have guessed that he would go as far as Tokyo.

Tadashi Mihara was no superman but no mug either. The 26-year-old was a stiff puncher, unbeaten in fifteen contests, and had travelled to the States to outpoint Rocky Fratto for the vacant WBA belt in Rochester. Moore was being served up as the traditional offering, the well-paid uncomplicated first defence on home ground, but on February 2, 1982, the American ruined that scenario, scoring four knockdowns in halting Mihara in the sixth. He was a champ after boxing only 46 professional rounds.

Part of what was obviously a complex deal to clinch the title shot included a stipulation that Moore must make a prompt defence against the South African Charlie Weir in Johannesburg. So, just over two months later, Davey again found himself the underdog on foreign soil. He was under no illusions that the masterplan was to see Weir crowned champion; there was additional pressure from civil rights activists, in particular Jesse Jackson, for him not to travel to South Africa; but the Reverend was not offering him $300,000 to stay at home. Once again, Davey Moore rewrote the script. Before a shocked 45,000 crowd in Ellis Park, he dismantled Weir, scoring five knockdowns and completing the job with a classic right hand in the fifth.

He was on a tremendous roll and another defence was pencilled in for three months later, but yet again, nobody was offering him an easy shift. This time the nominated challenger was a former champion, the Denmark-based Ugandan, Ayub Kalule, beaten only once in 41 starts – in nine rounds by none other than Sugar Ray Leonard.

The African's confidence had been restored with four wins back in Denmark and he was still considered lively and dangerous, but at least this time Davey was boxing back in the States and on July 17, 1982 at Bally's Casino in Atlantic City, he again proved his mettle. He had to survive several rocky passages against a fiercely determined opponent, but in the tenth, a volley of twenty unanswered punches forced the referee to rescue the Ugandan.

The first seven months of 1982 had been a sharp and exhausting learning curve and he was given a deserved break from the gym while negotiations opened for a mega-match against another unbeaten *wunderkind*, the Texan Tony Ayala. Just about the hottest property in the business, Ayala would have been many people's choice to beat Moore, but all the excited speculation became hypothetical when he was found guilty of rape, burglary and possession of a knife and was packed off to prison where he would languish for the next sixteen years. Promoter Arum decided that on the strength of the win over Cuevas, Duran would prove an equally attractive alternative.

On the same evening that Roberto crushed Pipino in Los Angeles, Moore completed a hat-trick of successful defences, stopping a fair fighter called Gary Guiden in Atlantic City, coincidentally in the fourth.

Again he looked the business, and the lopsided odds on him taking Duran's scalp reflected the growing belief that the apprentice champion had grown into a tough and skilled tradesman, ignoring the downside that he had boxed professionally only twelve times and had never fought past the tenth round. The Garden showdown, of course, was scheduled for the traditional fifteen.

We are told that the odds layers in Las Vegas employ a network of informants to update them on the welfare of the participants in the countdown to every major sporting event that is likely to attract betting interest. No detail or piece of gossip is considered irrelevant or too minute to matter; if a guy sneezes, there may be an adjustment of a fraction of a point . . . anyway, that's the story. But the Las Vegas intelligence from the camps of both champion Moore and challenger Duran was either abysmal or went ignored.

Being unimpressed with Duran's performance in Los Angeles can be ascribed to faulty judgement; disregarding the tremendous condition that Duran had achieved was remiss; failing to chart Roberto's movements after he had done with Cuevas was just plain negligence.

The norm for the playboy from Panama had always been to go off on a monumental bender after a fight; the release from the hated discipline of training had always signalled a celebratory consumption of gallons of booze and mountains of food, and to hell with the weight and the waistline. But not this time. He had slaved to get himself into wonderful shape and was determined not to waste all that sterling work in the bars and restaurants. This time the partying was limited to mild excess and he was soon back in the gym and pounding the roads; this title meant so much to him and there could be no distractions. A fortnight before fight night his weight was perfect; come his birthday he had the scent of blood and was looking to crack skulls.

If there were any spies in the Moore camp, they must have decided to stay quiet and cash in on Duran's great price: the guys in Vegas certainly would have got busy had they been aware of the problems piling up for the champion, who was having anything but a trouble-free preparation.

For a start, Moore and his manager were scarcely speaking. Both Washington and his fighter had prospered from a close relationship which spanned the best part of a decade, but now there was increasing friction which could lead to repercussions in the corner. Davey's schedule had been interrupted because of a sprained ankle and then just three days before the fight, the champ required two hours' dentistry to have two teeth extracted, and the stitches were removed only on the eve of the fight. Quite incredible! Washington allegedly claimed later that he had no knowledge of the visit to the dentist; if true, that illustrated the gulf that existed between the boxer and his principal cornerman.

Thursday, June 16, and a vast, noisy crowd crammed into the Garden. Davey may have been the homeboy from the Bronx, but by far the bulk of the 20,061 (the largest Garden attendance since the Ali–Frazier return in 1974) had forked out their cash to wish Roberto many happy returns. This was his patch, the ring where he had first stopped poor Benny Huertas in a round, and where he had overcome great champions like Buchanan and Palomino to the delight of his huge support.

Moore had his backers, but they were drowned in the sea of nostalgia that swept through the arena.

New York's favourite fighter of all time, the old Manassa Mauler, Jack Dempsey, had passed away just two weeks earlier aged 88, leaving so many fond memories for the fight regulars. Jack had fought – and been booed! – in the second Garden; he had performed as a cornerman and a referee in the third Garden, and he was also sure to get the biggest cheer when he was introduced ringside at Garden Four. Tonight, Muhammad Ali would be the principal target for the gladhanders, the autograph hounds, and the acclaim of the fans.

Davey Moore may have been shocked by the overwhelming reception given Duran and he was allowed no time to settle any nerves once the bell sounded for round one. The champion was about to become the victim of a dreadful mugging, witnessed by thousands.

Pre-fight strategists were convinced that Moore's youth, his three-inch height advantage, his strength and his punching power would prove far too much for the birthday boy to handle. Duran rubbished those theories in the opening three minutes thanks to his speed and his dazzling combinations. Moore could not get his own shots off, and when Roberto, drawing on the experience of hundreds of street battles and eighty ring recitals, decided to give the champion a lesson in the darker arts, he was left bewildered and seriously hurt.

An elbow, a shoulder, a brush across the face with the spiky jet hair. The Panamanian was playing by his own rules but, of course, the thumb that speared Davey's right eye before the bell rescued him for the end of round one just might have been accidental.

Duran had been both brilliant and brutal and the Garden was in an uproar as Moore took an uncertain path back to his corner.

Davey had never encountered this brand of violence in the gym, in the ring, or even on the mean streets of the Bronx. On his stool, he used his one good eye to squint across at his challenger who seemed to be sneering and the frantic advice from his corner went unheard. Moore was in deep, deep trouble.

Later, he would claim, 'The thumbing was intentional, no doubt about it. There's no way that thumb wasn't aimed for my eye. I knew he was a filthy guy but I didn't expect to get it in the first round.'

Expect anything from Duran apart from mercy.

In the second, he continued to dish out the grim chastisement, scoring with spectacular combinations to the head, digging heavy hooks to the body, relishing his work against a one-eyed opponent, already outclassed in everything bar courage. The champ was being paid one million dollars, but that was beginning to look small change considering the battering he was having to absorb. After six minutes of hell, the favourite backers were already resigned to their fate.

Many years later, *Boxing Monthly* writer Graham Houston would remember, 'Moore was given one of the most one-sided beatings I can recall for a fighter who came into the ring as a favourite. It was no contest, man against boy.' He went on to quote *New York Times* correspondent Michael Katz, 'The famous hands of stone were hands of quicksilver as they constantly beat Moore to the punch.'

And there would be so many more punches, for Duran was enjoying himself and was in no hurry. Moore was being made to suffer for all that garbage about the great Roberto being all washed up. This was vintage Duran.

Nothing could have prepared the New Yorker for the ferocity and the sheer expertise of the onslaught: his glittering amateur career counted for zilch, and the Tadashi Miharas and Charlie Weirs had been choirboys compared to this guy. Davey was in fathoms over his head: aside from the tightly closed right eye, now there was blood pouring from a burst nose and a torn mouth. But there was nothing wrong with his heart, and in the fourth and fifth he actually landed a few token replies, but not nearly enough to give him a squeak.

And when he crashed to the canvas in the seventh following another sensational barrage, he should have been rescued from his torment. Sadly, his cornermen had other ideas, and he was allowed out for the eighth, only to soak up further needless abuse until at last the towel was tossed into the ring and the referee stopped the slaughter with 58 seconds left in the round.

The triumphant Duran was once again a champion, a three-time champion, and as his handlers hoisted him aloft, the packed tiers sang, 'Happy Birthday, Roberto'. The man they called Hands Of Stone said it all, 'I've returned to be Robert Duran.' Few noticed Davey Moore's pain-racked journey back to the haven of his dressing room.

Nine months would pass before Davey would fight again, and for the first few weeks, a red spot remained in his right eye to remind him of Roberto. The split with Washington became permanent, and Davey told *Ring*'s Doug Blackburn, 'I got mugged. Still, I know why I took the fight when I did, even if I wish now that I hadn't. I knew I couldn't get a million dollars fighting anybody else.'

Back in the ring, his spirits soared when he made short work of the faded former champion Benitez in Monaco, but his dreams were shattered in the unlikely setting of Juan Les Pins, when on August 24, 1986 he was stopped in the tenth by fellow country-man Buster Drayton in a challenge for the IBF belt. Davey, however, was not convinced, and he was struggling to put together another campaign (two wins, two losses) when, in 1988, fate delivered the killer blow.

A rainy June day in Holmdel, New Jersey, and Davey Moore, six days short of his 29th birthday and attending to some chores outside his house, spotted the unoccupied Dodge truck in his driveway start to roll towards him. He raced to halt its momentum, slipped on some wet leaves, and the truck rolled over him. As cruel and crazy as that. He left a wife, two children and a mortgage.

A vehicle also brought an end to the career, but happily not the life, of Roberto Duran. And not before he thrilled and chilled and earned and squandered several more fortunes. There were still to be many big nights, both great and grim.

The noble points loss to the outstanding middleweight champion Marvin Hagler five months after the Moore win; the stunning two-rounds blowout against Hitman Tommy Hearns; the incredible evening in Atlantic City in 1989 when he became a champion in four divisions by outpunching and outgaming tough Iran Barkley before millions of awestruck television fans; the anticlimactic defeat against Ray Leonard in Vegas; the final title fight when, aged 47, he was stopped in three by WBA middleweight champion William Joppy.

But he just would not quit. He still loved throwing punches, and he was savvy enough to avoid any serious harm. Unrecognisable from the sleek, lightweight marvel of the 1970s, he was still an attraction for the curious, and he was fifty when he fumbled to a points defeat against another long-faded star, Hector Camacho, in Denver. Any decisions to box on, however, were taken out of his hands when in October 2001, three months after the Camacho appearance, he survived a car smash in Argentina where he was a guest at Diego Maradona's farewell to soccer. Duran suffered a punctured lung, eight broken ribs and a broken hand – the Hands Of Stone had finally cracked. Still he stalled making his official retirement announcement until March 2002, and he claims he has sufficient funds to ensure a comfortable lifestyle for himself and his dependants who include eight children. Let us hope so.

Roberto Duran may well have been the best lightweight of all time, he was also a magnificent welter the night he beat Leonard in Montreal; and when fit at the heavier weights only the very best could beat him. Sadly for Davey Moore, he had not been granted the time to reach that status when he clashed head-on with reality that night in the Garden.

CHAPTER THREE

Bernard Hopkins
v Felix Trinidad

SATURDAY, SEPTEMBER 29, 2001

More than two weeks had flashed past, and around the world the horror that was the Twin Towers refused to abate. The outrageous attack on New York's World Trade Center was being run and rerun on every news channel. Despite the grim evidence of the body count, the harrowing stories from eyewitnesses, the remarkable tales of heroism, and the heartbreak of those still searching for missing friends and relatives, the endless hours of television played more like a disaster movie that had no end. This was life in the new millennium and things could never be the same again.

Fear and fury, utter bewilderment, and increasingly urgent calls for swift retribution jammed the airwaves. In New York, however, the anger, the defiance and the heartache were being matched by a growing swell of self-esteem. And thanks largely to one man.

Rudolph Giuliani had first earned his headlines as a hard-nosed prosecutor who had packed off a truckload of mafia heavyweights to spend life behind bars. Now as the city's mayor, he somehow discovered all the right words to calm and comfort his people, and instil in them a massive pride in their firefighters and their cops. New York and New Yorkers may have been terribly scarred but nobody had defeated them, and as Rudy Giuliani gently insisted, life must go on.

For Don King, getting on with life means promoting fights and fighters, and he had big business scheduled for the Garden.

A round-the-clock hustler of awesome imagination and gall, The Don has made himself one of the most recognisable faces in the world: a self-appointed flag-waver for the States whose outward buffoonery and bonhomie disguise a cold heart and a calculator for a brain. He has been responsible for the deaths of two men and served time for the manslaughter of one of them – pint-sized Sam Garrett. That was back in April 1966 when King was a young blood in the rough Cleveland numbers racket and in the roller coaster years after his release, thanks to a unique combination of brains and braggadocio, and despite investigations by the FBI and the IRS, plus seemingly endless lawsuits from a gang of disgruntled fighters, managers and rival promoters, King continues to call the shots.

His personal wealth is huge, his legal bills alone would be the envy of many a Third World exchequer, and even in his seventies and not always in the best of health he thrives on growing old disgracefully. King is still a seriously dangerous old dude, but for all his so-called trickeration, many fighters and managers have been forced to concede that The Don is the guy who can make things happen, and who invariably comes up with the best deal – even allowing for his notorious deductions. Quite simply, Don King is the world's best promoter of boxing.

The less charitable will be quick to claim that after September 11, only an obsessive such as King would be so eager to get back earning. A bum rap. Initially, he had booked the Garden for a middleweight showdown between Felix Trinidad and Bernard Hopkins on September 15, and a two-week postponement seemed just about right. On the big night a crowd of 19,075 agreed with him.

As King explained, 'The mayor and the governor have been urging everyone to get back to normality, which is hard under the present circumstances. But we want to play our part and having this fight might lift the spirits of the people.'

Whether The Don was more concerned with profit than the people is a matter for individual conjecture, but King's 'return to normality' was being staged in Madison Square Garden, and for well over a century the Garden has been held dear by all New Yorkers. Where better to start all over again?

The clash between Trinidad and Hopkins promised to be a special occasion and an excellent match. For far too long the ever-increasing number of sanctioning organisations has only served to cheapen boxing's titles and confuse the fans, but recently there have been encouraging signs that, at last, the television pay-masters are starting to see sense, searching out quality fights, looking for the best against the best. Early in 2001, King, perhaps scenting a change in the air, devised a fight-off in the 160lb division involving the holders of the WBC, WBA and IBF belts, and also the reigning IBF light middleweight champion. Three fights leading to one champion: a welcome return to sanity and the grand old days of Marvin Hagler.

Of course, King had not suddenly discovered altruism in his dictionary. He had contractual agreements with three of the participants – William Joppy (WBA), Keith Holmes (WBC) and Trinidad (IBF light middle) – and that obviously kindled his enthusiasm for the project. The independent was Hopkins who had racked up twelve defences of his IBF title, but who had yet to earn in big numbers. He could not afford to be left out.

Even before his unification tournament had got underway, King was already formulating ambitious plans to stage a super-fight involving the winner. The promoter was banking heavily on the Puerto Rican, Trinidad, to emerge the outright victor, and he aimed to shoot for the jackpot with the undefeated young man that they called Tito. Technically and commercially, he was by far the most attractive of the quartet, and as the new and undisputed middleweight champion, the pay-per-view figures would be breathtaking for a fight between Trinidad and the outstanding light heavyweight kingpin, Roy Jones. But there were two fights for Tito to win before he could begin thinking about Jones.

The handsome Trinidad was at ringside when the series opened on April 14 with Hopkins paired against Holmes, the IBF and WBC belts being up for grabs. Holmes, a tall, slick southpaw from Washington DC, was given a chance by several good judges, but on the night he just failed to produce, appearing more interested in survival. Hopkins was efficient rather than exciting, but he won unanimously by wide margins and he was in the final. Possibly the most significant aspect of the fight was the venue, the Garden's cosy Theater complex which attracted a crowd of 4,223.

There could be no such intimate atmosphere for Trinidad's semi. Hopkins was just one of a roaring crowd of 18,235 packed into the main arena on May 12, when Tito squared off against the 30-year-old Joppy from Maryland. Some experts surprisingly opted for William because he was a decent puncher and Tito could be caught and knocked down. But not this time. A left hook floored Joppy near the end of the first; a repeat dose did the trick in the fourth; in the fifth, Joppy took another count, this time from a right, and he was dazed and beaten when referee Arthur Mercante Jr stepped in with 35 seconds remaining.

Despite the hysterical acclaim of his Garden fans, for Felix the crushing defeat of Joppy was just another big win in front of another big crowd for another big paynight; not really anything memorable, considering that he had been boxing for world championships ever since he had knocked out lanky Maurice Blocker for the IBF welter belt back in 1993. In fact, of his twenty wins since Blocker, he had been allowed the luxury of just one non-title bout, and that lasted less than a round against Troy Waters.

For Hopkins, however, this was shaping as the day of reckoning, a career-defining contest that could guarantee him the seven-figure purses that had been denied him for so many years; the opportunity finally to earn the respect that he felt was his due; the chance to be rated alongside boxing's handful of true superstars.

The journey to the Garden confrontation had been a painfully long, hard haul for the man billed as The Executioner. He had survived the dangerous streets of Philadelphia, and the even tougher confines of Graterford Prison. He had overcome the trauma of a losing pro debut and then the frustration of a marathon court battle against promoter Butch Lewis. There were other wars with other promoters, and in the business he gained the reputation of being a suspicious hardhead, a real pain at the negotiating table. Victory over Trinidad would be a vindication.

Bernard Hopkins was born on January 15, 1965 and reared in the Germantown housing projects. There were three brothers, four sisters, and just a mother to ride shotgun, and perhaps it was inevitable that he should follow a depressingly familiar path that took him to Graterford to serve a five stretch for armed robbery.

Bernard can count himself one of Graterford's success stories. Early into his sentence, two sheriffs escorted him in shackles from the prison to attend the funeral of one of his brothers, an eighteen-year-old who had been shot dead in a street dispute. Hopkins was allowed ten minutes at the funeral home, just long enough to look down on his dead brother and hear the anguished cries of his mother. The utter helplessness and humiliation accompanied him back to his cell; the memories remained painfully sharp; and finally, he learned the lesson that so many jailbirds choose to ignore.

Since his release in 1988, Hopkins has become a model citizen who makes only celebrity guest returns to prison where he is now welcomed as an inspiration to the inmates. He has a wife, a former para-legal called Jeannette, and a daughter, Latree, a comfortable home and a healthy bank balance: everything a million miles from exchanging high fives with lifers in the joint.

On coming out, there were few career options and like so many other ex-cons, he chose boxing as an escape route. He had shown talent in an amateur career often disrupted by hassle, and he was fortunate to have an excellent coach in Philadelphia veteran Bouie Fisher who had picked up plenty from another Philly gym professor, Quenzell McCall. Bernard, however, came unstuck first time out when, boxing as a light heavy, he dropped a four rounds decision to Clinton Mitchell in Atlantic City.

After that nightmare debut – October 11, 1988 – The Executioner got his act together and ran up a sequence of 22 wins (only six going the distance) until he was outpointed by Roy Jones for the vacant IBF middleweight title in May 1993. No disgrace losing to a brilliant performer like Jones, and Hopkins was now an established name. But backstage all was not well.

Bernard has an inquiring mind, a suspicious nature, and a short fuse. After studying the accounts following the Jones loss, he exploded. According to Hopkins, there were serious dis-crepancies, and he pointed the finger at his promoter, Butch Lewis, yet another flamboyant character who had made his name and his fortune advising light heavy and heavyweight champion Michael Spinks. Eventually the bust-up led to litigation, the court case dragging on for ten months before judge Wynita Brodie ruled in favour of the fighter. A thumb in the eye for boxing's establishment, and a warning that this was one middleweight who could haggle almost as well as he could hook.

Hopkins had again demonstrated the steely resolve that had served him so well during his prison years, and through his rise through the 160lb ranks. In fact, by the time his contract with Lewis was officially ended, The Executioner had become the holder of the IBF belt.

On his second try for the title, which was again vacant, he came back from two knockdowns in Quito, Ecuador, to scramble a draw with the local hero, Segundo Mercado. It was a different story in the return four months later in Landover, Maryland, where Hopkins handed Mercado a severe beating before referee Rudy Battle halted the action in the seventh. A champion at last, but just one of a handful of middleweights who could call themselves champ.

He earned reasonable money – but no mega-purses – from his title, and going into the war with Trinidad, the Philadelphia hardcase had recorded thirteen IBF defences which was just one short of Argentinian Carlos Monzon's record tally for the 160lb division. He had proved that he had the technical know-how to match his heavy hitting; he had beaten off dangerous challengers like Holmes and Antwun Echols and John David Jackson; and he was being advised by Lou Di Bella, the former guru for HBO's boxing department. But, aged 36, time was not on his side.

Everything, or so it seemed, appeared to be on Trinidad's side. This was a man who had been bred to box. He was an idol in Puerto Rico; had moved smoothly up the divisions without serious mishap; and he could finish off an opponent with one chilling left hook. No surprise that going in against Hopkins, the 28-year-old Tito was a raging hot 3/1 on favourite.

Felix was born on January 10, 1973 in Cupey Alto which remains his home base. His father, Felix Sr, had held the Puerto Rican featherweight title, and before he was nine, Junior was attracting applause in the gym. Possibly because of his youth, there were few stoppages in a 57-fight amateur stint, but by the time he turned pro as a seventeen-year-old with a two-round knockout over Angel Romero on March 10, 1990 in San Juan, he had already developed into a ferocious puncher.

Aside from his father, Tito was advised by a crafty veteran called Yamile Chade whose history stretched back over fifty years to the days when he was co-managing another great welter, the Cuban Kid Gavilan. In truth, neither Chade nor Trinidad Sr had to perform miracles to promote young Felix. His exciting style and tremendous punching guaranteed a rapid rise and he was in only his twentieth contest when he poleaxed Blocker in San Diego to land his first world championship. The million-dollar purses and high-profile showdowns were just a few rounds away.

And though he had experienced some scary seconds on the canvas on his journey to the top, Tito tackled the very best and was still unbeaten when he stepped into the ring to face The Executioner.

Hope for all prospective Trinidad opponents came from the established fact that he could be caught and knocked over. England's Kevin Lueshing, Oba Carr from Detroit, and the powerful Mexican puncher Yory Boy Campas had all dropped him in the second round; the rugged Argentinian Alberto Cortes had floored him twice in Paris, both knockdowns coming in the second. For some strange reason, Tito was at his most vulnerable in round two but he was also at his most dangerous coming back from a count, and none of the guys who got lucky survived to the final bell.

Then there were the Trinidad blockbusters . . . the Vegas nights when he beat Hector Camacho and Oscar De La Hoya and David Reid and Fernando Vargas; and the New York appearances when he took care of Pernell Whitaker and, most recently, William Joppy. He had been involved in an extremely close call with De La Hoya in September 1999, when many ringsiders were convinced that Oscar's safety-first tactics in the late rounds cost him the decision rather than anything that Trinidad had done. But the bottom line was that Tito had fought a smart fight and earned the nod from two judges (the third scored a draw); of equal significance, the fight attracted a whopping 1.3 million pay-per-view customers. No arguing with those figures.

On his last outing in 2000, Felix had produced his finest performance when he outboxed, outpunched and outstayed the dangerous Vargas, dropping his challenger three times in the final round before referee Jay Nady stepped in. He had not been asked to dig nearly so deep against Joppy, and now the odds reflected a growing belief in his invincibility.

Typically, Bernard Hopkins announced that he had bet $100,000 on himself to prove everybody wrong.

King would have no problems packing the Garden, but a hard sell is usually required to capture the vital but discerning pay-per-view market, and it has become the custom for the principals to tour the major cities, entertaining the media and generally drumming up interest. The more pay-per-view buys, the more dough for everyone: a boring, but necessary and normally harmless exercise, unless the participants happen to be Lennox Lewis and Mike Tyson.

Hopkins, however, basked in the pre-fight hype. The Philadelphia fighter always dons an executioner's leather mask and the accessories when going into the ring, and for many, his contrived stage entry comes uncomfortably close to the shenanigans of the wrestling heroes. On the promotional tour Bernard lived the role of baddie. At the New York reception, he stunned and offended the Trinidad faction by throwing the Puerto Rican flag on to the floor. Further disrespect followed in San Juan, but this time when he insulted the flag he was attacked by an enraged mob and following a car chase to the airport, he was fortunate to get back to the States in one piece.

This was no publicity hoax dreamt up by King; Hopkins was freelancing and back in New York, a concerned Athletic Commission warned the fighter about his conduct. The commissioners feared a violent reaction in the Garden, possibly a riot, but after 9/11, nobody was in the humour to play the fool. Hopkins behaved himself.

He had been running in Central Park when the Trade Center was struck; like so many millions of others, Felix watched the horror unfold on his hotel television. He remained in the city throughout the postponement – Hopkins went home to Philadelphia – and stressed that his preparation had not been affected.

'I'm in 100 per cent condition,' Trinidad declared. 'The wait isn't going to make any difference to the fight. I'm ready. My hands are strong. I'm a big puncher and just feel I can knock him out.'

Extremely upbeat. But Tito had little to say when quizzed about his domestic woes: a mistress who was five months pregnant; a wife and two daughters awaiting an explanation. And there was no respite from Bernard's relentless goading: 'I'm going to take him into the alley and give him an old-fashioned Philly butt whipping. I'm going to show him a little Gypsy Joe Harris, a little Jersey Joe Walcott, a little Bennie Briscoe.'

Nobody had ever spoken about Tito like that, and there was further unsettling aggravation when, in the Trinidad dressing room, Hopkins' representative objected to the way Tito's hands were being bandaged and won the battle to force Felix Sr to do a rewrap. The Philadelphia camp had been clear winners of the psychological exchanges Bernard also stole the thunder entering the ring, demonic in his red leather mask, his red trunks sporting adverts for a casino, a further plug for the gambling house stencilled on his back. Trinidad, pristine in his country's colours, appeared relaxed and ready for business.

The 19,000 customers had filed through heavy security, including metal detectors, and seemed subdued in comparison to other carnival nights at the Garden. There was a warm cheer for legendary referee Arthur Mercante Sr, aged 81 and handling his last title fight – an IBF light flyweight match in which the excellent Ricardo Lopez knocked out Zolani Petelo. Old Arthur had refereed all the great ones over six decades and deserved his ovation. But still, the atmosphere was not that of a regular MSG party night.

There may have been many customers wondering if they had done the right thing buying a ticket, and an extremely tentative opening round from both fighters did nothing to shift the mood. At 6ft 1½″, The Executioner had a 2-inch height advantage, but Tito had a slight edge in reach and, at 158½lb, he was the heavier. Hopkins, however, impressed as by far the more powerful, even to an untutored eye.

Round two . . . always a dodgy round for Felix, and this time he survived without touching down. But he was being made to chase a cool, controlled Hopkins and one hard right from the Philadelphian sent a shiver down through his legs. Rounds three and four saw Hopkins in command, spearing Trinidad with ramrod lefts, banging home hard rights, boxing beautifully and well within himself. In comparison, Tito lacked a game plan, and in the fifth he was swinging and missing while Bernard scored heavily with both hands. By now the action was beginning to live up to the hype and they exchanged hard shots after the bell, the huge Puerto Rican contingent at last waking up and making themselves heard.

And finally Trinidad responded. He burst into life in the sixth, scoring with his pet left hook, but Bernard was unfazed and came straight back with a fast right. Referee Steve Smoger warned Felix for using his elbow, but no question, he now upped his workrate, and he returned to a relieved corner.

Hopkins had bossed the majority of the first six rounds, but never forget, scoring a fight is a most subjective exercise. Two of the judges – South African Stanley Christodoulou and Anek Hongtonkam from Thailand – had each given Trinidad three rounds; the third judge, New Yorker Don Ackerman, had awarded only the tame opener to Felix.

But following his big effort in the sixth, Trinidad's supporters had every reason to remain optimistic. Their man had finally found his rhythm, had come from behind before, and nobody could have forecast that Tito would not win another round on any of the cards.

In the seventh it was Hopkins who stepped up the tempo and Trinidad was unable to go with him: one of boxing's brightest was being made to look a dunce by a tough guy, an exceptionally smart tough guy, who was always two or three moves ahead of the favourite.

By the ninth the normally silk-smooth Tito was ragged and increasingly desperate, and in the tenth he threw everything at Hopkins. He landed flush with the left hook – the pay-off punch that had always served him so well – but instead of going down, Bernard repaid him with terrific counters off the ropes, and just before the bell he delivered the best shot of the fight, a crunching right that effectively ruined the Puerto Rican. Hopkins followed up with a couple of late digs before referee Smoger separated the boxers, and Trinidad was in Noddyland, wobbling back to his corner.

The only surprise remaining was that he managed to stumble through the three minutes of the eleventh: his legs had gone on strike; he flopped down from a push; then he somehow stayed upright under a four-punch barrage; and yet he was considered fit to answer the bell for round twelve. No more than the gesture of a gladiator. Hopkins dropped him for a nine count from yet another right; he was helpless and totally beaten; and his father was already ducking through the ropes as Smoger intervened after 78 seconds.

Hopkins was the undisputed champion of the middleweights, and how he savoured the moment!

He found the energy to perform a somersault before stretching out on the canvas to delight in his ultimate moment . . . the huge bet that he had won, the mega-bucks that awaited him from King. The Trinidads were in shock; the ringside experts were equally stunned – *Boxing News* editor Claude Abrams and veteran writer and historian Bert Randolph Sugar were two of a select few who had tipped The Executioner. But all were unanimous that the new three-belt champ had been a revelation. His performance had been that of a master.

In the ring, Don King's beam was genuine. Sure, he had just seen his plans scuppered for the Trinidad–Jones bonanza, but Jones against Hopkins – this brilliant, born-again Executioner – could be even bigger. And Tito? He could go home to Cupey Alto, rest up, sort out his marital troubles, then recharge his career. There were still fortunes to be earned in a return with De La Hoya or a revenge joust with Hopkins . . . maybe Roy Jones could still figure in his future long-term. There were many avenues for The Don to explore.

But this is boxing, and in boxing sanity can prevail only for so long. And soon after King started talking terms for his dream fight, he no longer required a stylist to encourage his hair to stand on end.

Roy Jones had always been a tricky guy to pin down to a contract. He negotiates from a position of great strength and total independence, and if his demands are deemed unreasonable (which they often are) then he will go elsewhere to find another deal. And Hopkins, even when he was a 'mere' $500,000 IBF champion, could induce palpitations in the hearts of the hardest of promoters. Now he could bargain with three belts, and King, or anyone else, had to talk serious money before Bernard was prepared to do business.

He was offered six million dollars to face Jones, but Bernard held out for another four million. Not a chance. As the defending light heavyweight champion, Jones, not unreasonably, was demanding a 60–40 split, but Hopkins was insisting on parity. Then there was the matter of the weight. The Executioner wanted Jones to trim down to 168lb – 7lb lighter than the light heavy-weight limit – and once again it was no dice. The Philly fighter had negotiated himself out of a fortune and the proposed superfight was transferred to limbo.

Who was advising him? Certainly not former HBO chief Lou Di Bella. There had been an acrimonious fall-out between the pair who had apparently been so tight just a few months earlier, and when Di Bella sued for defamation, Hopkins was once again knee-deep in litigation. In November 2002 a New York court awarded Lou $610,000 in damages. And, even more sadly, the middleweight split with his longtime trainer, Bouie Fisher, allegedly over the increasing involvement of Fisher's son in the training set-up. Further court dates are pending.

Sloan Harrison took charge of Bernard's training for his only ring appearance in 2002. After all the hot air and mega-buck deals that failed to materialise, he engaged in a fairly low-key affair in Reading, Pennsylvania, in February when he wore down Carl Daniels to win in the tenth. He did not earn his dream dough, nor did he look particularly awesome. Small consolation that he recorded a landmark fifteenth defence of his IBF belt.

Three months after Hopkins' return, Trinidad made his eagerly awaited reappearance in a ten-rounder in San Juan on May 11. Almost 10,000 adoring fans went home happy after Tito outclassed Frenchman Hacine Cherifi in four rounds, scoring three knockdowns along the way. Again the big offers flooded in but on July 3 Trinidad issued a press release more stunning than his hardest left hook. He announced his retirement.

The initial reaction was that this was no more than a cynical ploy to hurry Hopkins into granting Felix a speedy return; then rumours about his health did a grand tour of the gyms; insiders just could not believe that with only one loss in 42 starts, he could simply walk away from the offered mountains of money. But as the months pass, Tito shows no signs of performing an about-face. From time to time his father issues bulletins, knocking back yet another offer, and stressing just how much Tito is enjoying life away from the ring. The best of good luck to both of them.

At the time of writing, Don King is still striking fantastic deals and making millions. And Roy Jones has beaten the WBA heavyweight champion John Ruiz and is now eyeing more mega purses and Bernard Hopkins is still chasing rainbows. And New Yorkers go about their business and try not to think about another terrorist outrage.

As Rudy Giuliani said, 'Life must go on.'

Let's Do It Again!

Almost one hundred years ago, there was a gang of great black boxers who fought one another so often, they could do it from memory. Legends such as Joe Jeannette, Harry Wills, Sam McVey and Sam Langford were forced to face one another time and again simply because so few white fighters wanted to know them. Shameful and sad, but part of the evolution of the sport.

More curious was the twenty-fight feud between Jack Britton and Ted Kid Lewis which spanned seven years and saw the welter title swap back and forth. Likewise the fans never tired of watching Sugar Ray Robinson and Jake La Motta. Final score: 5–1 for Ray.

Two and three-part serials are more the norm, often producing extraordinary tales of the unexpected. Of course, the Garden has played host to some of the greatest.

CHAPTER FOUR

Lou Ambers *v* Tony Canzoneri

THURSDAY, SEPTEMBER 3, 1936

The States were in high good humour, with the exception, of course, of those sinister backwaters where the Klan chapters sneaked out at night to plant their crosses and lynch their fellow Americans. The nation was still rejoicing after a glorious August which had seen the incredible Jesse Owens win four gold medals at the Berlin Olympics; not only that, Owens had rained on Hitler's great propaganda parade, and Adolf had not been amused. That a black man could go to der Führer's capital and make mugs of the Master Race!

For the majority of Americans, Jesse's wonderful achievements more than atoned for the seismic stunner of two months earlier when the seemingly invincible Joe Louis had been battered and beaten up by Max Schmeling in New York's Yankee Stadium. That June night The Bomber had been exposed as mortal, and Schmeling – never a card-carrying Nazi – had unwittingly become a symbol of Aryan supremacy, thanks to the energetic PR of Joseph Goebbels.

Owens had restored American honour and black pride. But at 919 Eighth Avenue, New York, the celebrations had been muted. True, Owens had been terrific, a real shot in the arm for the country. And granted, Louis had shaken off the Schmeling disaster just a few weeks back, flattening the former champ, Jack Sharkey. But for the gentlemen who every day huffed and puffed up the steep stairs at 919 in order to discuss this and that, 1936 had been a lean year, one when it had been very hard to make a buck.

The wooden stairs led into a large hall, dominated by two regulation-size boxing rings, and an iron staircase spiralled up to a gallery where an assortment of punchbags and punchballs stubbornly resisted the bad intentions of the young men pounding on them. The windows were thick with grime, the air heavy with cigar smoke. The soundtrack was that of leather hitting leather and leather hitting flesh, the slap-slap-slap of skipping ropes, the tommy gun rattle of the speedballs, the urgent chorus from the line of telephone booths, the bell that tolled every three minutes, sporadic outbursts of laughter, indignant voices raised in desperate haggle. This was Stillman's Gym, the throbbing pulse of big time boxing.

Lou Stillman's clientele recognised that the business needed a great heavyweight champion. Louis could still be the man, but that Schmeling stoppage had been a real bummer. Everyone had a nice word for Jimmy Braddock, but Jim was no superman. And the other champs? Difficult to get into a lather over John Henry Lewis or Marcel Thil or Petey Sarron or Sixto Escobar. Thank God for the lightweights and the welters: a gang of wonderful fighters and hugely popular attractions like Barney Ross and Jimmy McLarnin, Lou Ambers, Tony Canzoneri and Pedro Montanez.

These were the little men who were keeping the game afloat.

The Garden had not staged a championship promotion since way back in March when the light heavy Lewis had unanimously outpointed Britain's Jock McAvoy, yet nobody was getting too excited about this upcoming lightweight clash between Canzoneri and Ambers. They were both fine fighters with crowd-pleasing styles, but first time around Tony had handled Al Weill's young contender so convincingly that it was all but impossible to forecast a reversal.

The betting action had been snail's pace and an additional title fight had been included on the programme to encourage ticket sales – Mike Belloise defending his New York version of the featherweight belt in a return with the Englishman, Dave Crowley. A strong enough bill, but hardly one to put the ticket touts on standby.

There was at least one man, however, who would have been prepared to pay well over the odds to sit ringside on September 3: Signor Salvatore Lucania, noted fight buff and notorious gangster. The outbreak of the Spanish Civil War may have been the major event of the year, but in New York that summer the tabloids all led with Salvatore's month-long battle with State prosecutor, Tom Dewey, in Manhattan's New York Supreme Court. Charged with organising the city's lucrative prostitution racket, Lucania, more familiar in the headlines as Lucky Luciano, lost a disputed decision.

Now he was languishing in Dannemora, a top-security facility upstate, serving the first months of the thirty to fifty years that Justice Philip J McCook had deemed an appropriate punishment. Charley Lucky loved to be seen ringside on the big fight nights, and occasionally he liked to place a bet, especially if an Italian was involved. On September 3, there would be two Italians in the ring because, like Canzoneri, Ambers was a *paisan*.

Lou Ambers was born Luigi Giuseppe D'Ambrosio on November 8, 1913 in Herkimer, New York. The fifth of ten children born to Anthony and Louise D'Ambrosio, Luigi, a cocky, aggressive, but likeable youngster, lived above his father's saloon, enjoying a fairly stress-free childhood until the crash of 1929 wiped out the family fortune.

Like millions of others across the country, the teenager had to start scrambling to bring home a dollar. He had been a terror in the schoolyard, had boxed in the local gym, and so, encouraged by his friend Joe Sanginetti, who became an unofficial first manager, the sixteen-year-old D'Ambrosio took to the road and became a bootleg fighter.

Bootleg boxing was supervised by neither the amateur authorities nor the professional commissions – it was more like a rough and ready and rather dangerous halfway house. The wages might be anything between five and ten bucks a fight, and the dollars were hard-earned: reputations spread by word of mouth rather than press cuttings, and with the collapse of the economy, the competition was fierce just to get a booking.

Young Luigi, sometimes accompanied by Sanginetti, hopped freight trains and bummed rides all over the state; the boy slept on park benches and in bus stations and once fast-talked his way into enjoying for a night the luxury of a cot in a police cell. Harsh times for precious little reward, but the experience was to prove an excellent apprenticeship. At the ripe old age of eighteen, and with more than eighty bootleg fights under his belt, Luigi decided he was ready to tackle the real professionals for real money. He brought in a part-time manager called Nick Rafael, and on

June 16, 1932 he made his first appearance as a fully fledged pro, knocking out somebody called Frankie Curry inside two rounds.

The partnership with Rafael would survive an unbeaten run of thirteen fights, winding up with a six rounds points decision over Tony Scarpati at the Coney Island Velodrome on June 27, 1933. Scarpati would play a tragic role in the youngster's future career; a chubby, cigar-chomping man sitting near the ring would mastermind that career.

Al Weill was already a major-league manager with a sharp eye for talent. The Vest, as he was known to his associates, was impressed by the way that young Luigi handled Scarpati, introduced himself after the fight and offered to take over his management. As simple as that, and Rafael did not get rich on his pay-off.

Al Weill never won any awards for his manners and flunked his courses at charm school. He could be rude, short-tempered, greedy, sly and suspicious, but nobody knew more about the machinations of bigtime boxing and Ambers would become his first world champion. Others would follow, like the featherweight Joey Archibald and a smart, brave welter called Marty Servo. He eventually lived every manager's dream when he guided Rocky Marciano to the heavyweight championship. Ambers, however, would forever remain Weill's favourite fighter.

Many years after his career was over, Lou gave his opinion of the great man. 'Getting along with Al was no secret. You just had to understand one thing: he was the boss and his word was law. Once you respected that, he treated you like a son.'

The Vest's first command was that Luigi D'Ambrosio must get a new name. D'Ambrosio, he decided, was too ethnic and too unwieldy: Lou Ambers would look far smarter on the posters and fit far better into the headlines. There would be plenty of posters and many more banner headlines: in the space of two years and with a record of 48 fights with only a solitary loss (a six-rounder against Steve Halaiko in Syracuse) the 21-year-old had been manoeuvred by Weill into a shot for the vacant lightweight belt.

Ambers had been carefully matched but he had impressed New Yorkers with a fifteen rounds win over Sammy Fuller, and the cautious Weill decided that he was finally ready to challenge for the championship vacated by the brilliant Barney Ross.

There was just one problem. The guy in the opposite corner would be Tony Canzoneri, and Tony just happened to be Lou's idol and a hero to thousands of immigrants and sons of immigrants living in the Italian enclaves scattered throughout the big cities and towns. Little Tony with the fast hands, the concussive right, and the chin of granite. He was a phenomenon.

Tony broke rules to break records. Before he was nineteen, Canzoneri had twice challenged for the bantamweight title; New York regulations decreed that he was under-age when he won the featherweight championship; he was just turned 22 yet was having his 92nd contest when he first won the lightweight belt inside one round; he became a triple champ when he won the junior welter crown. Though the fabulous Ross twice outpointed him, Canzoneri remained a tremendous draw and a match for the very best.

Tony was born on November 6, 1908 in Slidell, Louisiana, perhaps an unlikely birthplace for a future ring legend, but he had not reached his teens when he was hustling dimes and quarters as a shoeshine boy in New Orleans, and raising eyebrows in Gayosa's Gym, thanks to his precocious ability. Two of the eyebrows that shot skywards belonged to the reigning bantamweight champion, Pete Herman, who befriended the youngster and started passing on some of the moves that had made him a standout. Even allowing for Herman's valuable input, there was no doubt that Canzoneri was naturally gifted and it was no surprise that by the time he was fifteen, this extraordinary bundle of energy who never grew taller than 5ft 5″, could call himself the amateur flyweight champion of New Orleans.

Herman became so excited about his prospect that he began talking about Tony striking out for New York where there would be greater opportunities, and he contacted his manager Sammy Goldman, a well-known face around Stillman's and the Garden offices. The upshot was that the entire Canzoneri clan – father, mother, three brothers and a sister – headed north, and only months passed before Tony won the New York State amateur bantamweight title. A pragmatist, Goldman figured that if the boy was good enough, then he was old enough and on July 24, 1925, aged sixteen, Tony Canzoneri made his professional debut, knocking out Jack Gardner in a round in Rockaway, New York.

Even by the demanding standards of that era, Canzoneri was forced to work hard and learn fast. In his initial sixteen months, he crowded in 31 appearances before suffering his first reverse – ten rounds on points to Davey Abad in New York. He had been gathering an enthusiastic support in the city, but in 1927 Chicago was the site for the first of many title battles when he boxed a draw with Bud Taylor for the vacant NBA bantam championship, and in the rematch three months later, again in the Windy City, the extremely capable Taylor earned the decision.

The Canzoneri connections were not too disappointed as Tony was already outgrowing the 118lb division. And before the end of the year he officially moved up to feather, capturing his first world championship on October 24 when unanimously outpointing Johnny Dundee in the Garden.

In New York, a boxer was barred from championship fighting until he was 21, but the ever-resourceful Goldman had simply doctored Tony's licence to make him two years older. Following the fight, however, Sammy's deception was discovered and though the commissioners huffed and puffed, they took no action: censuring a champion for being too young might have proved tricky. And strangely, Canzoneri was still under-age when, eleven months later, and again in the Garden, he lost the title to André Routis from Bordeaux.

Tony, still filling out, was now a natural lightweight, and for the next nine years he flourished, facing some of the best fighters who ever lived, winning, losing and regaining titles, earning top dollar and the adulation of a public that was not easily fooled.

In 1929 – around the time Ambers was setting out on the bootleg trail – Canzoneri beat Routis with no title at stake, but lost to Sammy Mandell in a bid for the title. In 1930 he lost to Kid Berg and Billy Petrolle, but on November 14 – eight days after his 22nd birthday – he knocked out Al Singer in the first round to become the lightweight king. Singer, as any aficionado will delight to tell you, distinguished himself by winning then losing his title in the opening round.

In 1931 Tony scored a chilling revenge knockout over Kid Berg to land the junior welter belt, and before the close of the year again beat Berg and also the brilliant Cuban Kid Chocolate. In 1932, he dropped his junior welter title, twice losing to Johnny Jadick on Jadick's home turf of Philadelphia, but back in New York he was still boss of the lightweights, successfully defending against Petrolle. He was a magic money machine.

The sheer pace of his schedule was fearsome, as was the quality of the opposition. In 1933 he rewon the junior welter title, beating

Battling Shaw back home in New Orleans, but just a month later he lost both the championships when Barney Ross beat him in Chicago. Goldman and Canzoneri screamed 'hometown decision' but three months later, at New York's Polo Grounds, Barney was again awarded the verdict, and this time the squawks were less shrill.

Around the gyms, the message was that all those hard fights had finally taken their toll on a fine little champion: the Ross return had been his 119th contest, and it was hard to remember that he was still just 24. Burn-out time?

Naturally, neither Goldman nor Canzoneri entertained such thoughts. Tony enjoyed a sabbatical – all of six weeks – and was then back as busy as ever. And when Ross relinquished the title to step up to welter, Canzoneri was to value his nomination as one of the contenders for the vacant championship. But no more so than Ambers, Weill's ambitious young tiger.

The record books will tell you that their three-fight series got underway in the Garden on May 10, 1935, but the boys were already familiar with one another both in and out of the ring. In fact, their shared early experiences would play a significant role in their first night in the Garden, and had a knock-on effect that influenced the return. Despite the fifteen-month interval, those first two battles fuse into one thirty-rounder, a roller coaster that fooled the bookmakers and did nothing for the reputations of the experts.

But first we must consider their time spent together at Madame Bey's, a holiday camp in Summit, New Jersey, which became a favourite hangout for the fight crowd. Madame Bey was a Turkish lady who realised the publicity potential of having famous boxers at her camp and managers regarded it as a perfect retreat for their fighters, far from the distractions of the big city.

Those smart enough to squeeze some expenses from the tight pockets of a promoter sent their champions and their contenders out to Summit to breathe in a brand of fresh air unknown in the malodorous oven that was Stillman's. Later, Louis and Sugar Ray would make Greenwood Lake and Pompton Lakes fashionable, and later again, Marciano would put Grossinger's on the map. But in the first half of the 1930s, Madame Bey's was the camp which attracted the cream.

In the summer of 1933 Ambers was thrilled to be invited to

Summit. Still no more than another raw hopeful, scrapping in prelims, Lou was considered a bright enough student to work out with Canzoneri. Free board, not to mention $75 a week, was a terrific inducement, and the experience of sparring with the champ would be invaluable. All of this was a far cry from his days squatting in Central Park.

Much thought goes into the selection of sparring partners. Some are engaged only because of their ability stoically to absorb considerable punishment, and, not surprisingly, there is a large turnover in this breed; others are hired because they are gifted enough to copy the style of their employer's next opponent, and they are in great demand. A kid like Ambers was useful because he was still fresh and ambitious enough to ensure Canzoneri's mind stayed on the job.

For six weeks, the pair worked together and relaxed together, and Lou satisfied his masters, especially as he did nothing in the ring to embarrass the champ. Canzoneri always played the boss, Ambers the grateful hired hand, in awe of the star and eager to please.

Eighteen months later, and the 21-year-old Ambers, now dubbed the Herkimer Hurricane, bubbled with self-belief, but the fond memories of Madame Bey's were still fresh in his mind: as far as he was concerned, Tony remained the greatest. Although there were only five years separating the pair, the punters had latched on to youth to conquer experience and Lou was a strong favourite to become the new champion. But the layers and the 17,433 who paid into the Garden on May 10, 1935 were unaware that Ambers was suffering from a bad dose of hero worship, aggravated by the lingering traces of sparmate syndrome.

Canzoneri jumped all over him. In the dressing room, Lou had endured an uncharacteristic attack of nerves, and when the first bell rang he found himself replaying the role of sparring partner, treating Tony as the governor. Canzoneri, however, had erased the memories of their friendship at Madame Bey's. No lightweight had ever regained the championship and he wanted to be the first; Ambers was just another pug in his path and he came out fast.

Tony could scarcely believe just how easily Ambers could be caught with a right, and in rounds one and two Lou, boxing as if in a daze, soaked up a continuous stream of heavy shots. Worse was to follow for the youngster in the third, when Canzoneri twice dropped him with vicious rights, and the stunned fans prepared for an early exit. This was vintage Canzoneri, their great Tony. Ambers? Just an over-rated bum.

Weill, never the calmest man in the corner, was having fits; trainer Whitey Bimstein, a godsend in a crisis, set about reviving his shellshocked fighter. Both were screaming desperate advice into Lou's ears, but Ambers was not receiving.

Only his tremendous fitness and courage enabled him to negotiate the fourth, but in the following round the Herkimer Hurricane began to snap out of his bad dream, and in the seventh he brought the crowd off their seats as he battered Canzoneri with both hands, sending him reeling across the ring. At last he was fighting like a contender and not a sparring partner, but he had handed Tony a big lead which he was not about to squander. Canzoneri never lost his cool, and, boxing brilliantly, stayed one step ahead. Coming out for the fifteenth he was still in charge. Deciding to grandstand, he opened up again with both hands and had Ambers in dire trouble once more. A unanimous decision.

Back in the dressing room, Weill was disgusted, Bimstein furious at the gift of so many early rounds, but Ambers remained upbeat for the press post-mortem. All three were convinced that the result would be different next time around. Time to fast forward to September 3, 1936.

Canzoneri had made nonsense of the prophecies of doom. Far from being on the slide, he had added another eleven wins, including a successful defence against Al Roth, and on his most recent outing in May, he had looked as good as ever when outpointing Jimmy McLarnin. Ambers, however, had suffered nightmares.

He had won all his fourteen fights, but at a considerable cost. Weill did not line up an easy comeback after the Canzoneri loss, and less than two months later in Pittsburgh Lou outpointed rough Fritzie Zivic, but he had to survive the last three rounds with a broken jaw. Agony would turn to tragedy seven fights later when he boxed Tony Scarpati in Brooklyn – the same Scarpati who had lost to Ambers when Weill first came into his life. This time, Lou won in the seventh, but poor Scarpati failed to recover and died three days later.

Like all fighters, Ambers knew the dangers of his profession but that did not ease the trauma. The shrewd Weill quickly brought him back, and less than a month had elapsed before he outpointed Pete Mascia in Brooklyn, in a benefit for the Scarpati family. Being able to contribute something did little to alleviate the anguish, and many years later he would recall that in several subsequent fights he would look across the ring and suddenly see Tony Scarpati sitting on the opposite stool. 'Like a picture' was how he remembered the eerie sensation.

But by now he had responsibilities. He had a wife, Margaret, and he had bills to pay. Canzoneri remained a pal, but no longer an object of hero worship. His training had gone smoothly and he was in the best shape of his life – Bimstein always claimed that of the thousands of fighters that had passed through his care, Ambers caused the fewest problems. Lou was growing up; Tony was growing old.

The 18,026 who turned up at the Garden expected to see the scintillating champion who had dazzled Ambers the first time and who had looked so sharp outpointing the popular McLarnin just back in May. But this night in the Garden, Canzoneri transformed into a tired old man. The experts had been out in their forecasts of doom and deterioration by fifteen months and the same number of fights. In the parlance, Tony was 'gone'.

From the opening bell Ambers commanded the centre of the ring and controlled the action: textbook boxing with stiff left hands keeping Tony off balance, and vicious right uppercuts which rocked the veteran when he did get in close. From very early on, it was Canzoneri who had become the sparring partner.

For a fight to become great there must be at least one or two dramatic switches in fortune; electrifying seconds when the trailing fighter suddenly launches back and threatens to rewrite the script. But Canzoneri had left his pen and his dynamite right hand in the dressing room or in the training camp. Who can tell where and when Tony's magic went for that final walk? The fans, however, were far from bored. They were seeing a champion who would never concede and there was always the slim chance that he might land flush with the right that caused such damage in the first encounter. Ambers was never able to relax, but Bimstein had schooled him well on how to nullify the threat, and Canzoneri never got close.

As round followed round, the challenger's lead extended. The champion was cut under the eye and bleeding from the nose and mouth; gasping, trying to fill his lungs, his attacks becoming increasingly desperate; but as early as the eleventh, miracles were required and the crowd knew that the title was about to change hands.

In fact, aside from Canzoneri, just about the only man in the Garden who would not accept that the result was inevitable controlled the Ambers corner. The Vest never counted his chickens, always feared a double cross from the judges and forever fretted about that one lucky punch. Lou was only minutes away from giving Al his first champion, but Weill was still a bundle of nerves.

Before the final round he implored Ambers to 'get in there and fight'. At the same time, he was advising caution! Bimstein simply told the fighter to do what he had been doing all night, and so there was no grandstand finish. Nor had the judges been nobbled and the decision was unanimous and wide. Tony may have won three rounds.

Canzoneri, as always, was gracious in defeat, but like all exceptional talents, he searched for the reasons for the upset. He reckoned the humidity in the Garden had seriously affected him; the four months out of the ring after beating McLarnin had been a mistake; he would be better next time around. His friend, the former lightweight idol Benny Leonard, was far more realistic, 'Youth licked Tony tonight. After all, he's been tossing leather for eleven years.'

Leonard's unsentimental appraisal was borne out just a month later when Canzoneri again finished badly marked-up after McLarnin avenged the May defeat. Only his marquee name earned him his third meeting with Ambers, and on May 7, 1937, he appeared in his last championship bout, but he had nothing left. Lou burst him up, closed both Tony's eyes, and the decision was again embarrassingly lopsided. Still, he was not convinced, and he boxed for another two years before Al Davis retired him with a brutal three-rounds knockout on November 1, 1939. He was just days away from his 32nd birthday and that was his only kayo loss in 175 fights.

A great, great champion at three weights, Canzoneri was also one of the most popular sportsmen of his time, and he remained in the spotlight. He had small parts in films, became popular as a nightclub entertainer, ran a successful restaurant, and from

time to time invested money in a Broadway show. His picture
still appeared in the papers; writers printed his opinion on forthcoming fights; and not just the fight mob was stunned when he
died of a heart attack in a New York hotel on December 9,
1959, aged 51.

Right to the end, little Tony did everything ahead of schedule.

For hungry new champion Ambers and even hungrier manager
Weill there were several hiccups before they really got their show
on the road. In fact, the new champ lost his first two fights –
non-title bouts – against Eddie Cool and the great McLarnin,
and in 1937 he dropped a disputed decision to Pedro Montanez.
The third Canzoneri championship fight restored any waning
confidence, and in the September of an eventful year he successfully defended again, gaining revenge over the Puerto Rican
Montanez, and earning a record $82,500 which put a smile on
the face of The Vest.

More big money followed, but it was earned the hard way. He
lost and regained the title in two memorably bloody and bitterly
fought battles against the extraordinary Henry Armstrong. Those
fights left their mark and, struggling now to make the weight,
Ambers was a soft target on May 10, 1940, when the Texan
puncher Lew Jenkins stopped him in three rounds to take the title.
Ignoring the advice of both Weill and Bimstein, he insisted on a
rematch and this time Jenkins did the business in the seventh. The
date was February 28, 1941, and it would be Lou's last fight.
Weill would see to that.

The Vest was a hard man with a soft spot for Ambers. After
the second Jenkins beating, he conned Lou into signing a
contract that stipulated that he would not box again for ten
years; nobody broke a contract with Al. And so Lou and
Margaret, whose partnership lasted 56 years, were able to enjoy
a comfortable life, settling in Phoenix, Arizona, where they
raised two sons and a daughter.

And, ever tough and durable, he survived until he was 81, dying
on April 24, 1995.

Canzoneri and Ambers were outstanding fighters in a division
and at a time when there were many tremendous performers
around that weight. They earned not only the recognition of an
extremely knowledgeable public, but also a warm affection, of a
kind we just do not see any more. And if there is a regret about

their careers, then it must be that they both did not box at their peak on the same night in their three jousts in the Garden. Now, that would have been some fight!

CHAPTER FIVE

Beau Jack *v* Bob Montgomery

FRIDAY, NOVEMBER 19, 1943

They are an elegant couple, seated front row ringside, right on the aisle, and within easy hailing distance of *New York Daily Mirror* columnist Dan Parker who is dwarfing the fabled Nat Fleischer, owl-like and peeking over the ring apron. The gentleman is extremely distinguished, silver-haired, buttonhole in his lapel, upright in his seat; the lady is in her finery, perhaps a mite genteel for the Garden, but none the worse for that.

They watch with a cool fascination as the big and rather cumbersome Cuban Nino Valdes bounces an uncoordinated Tommy (Hurricane) Jackson all over the Garden ring before scoring a second-round stoppage.

You can view the pair again, captured forever on film, and in the same prime seats, as the exceptional light heavyweight champion Archie Moore gets off the canvas eventually to dismantle Harold Johnson in round fourteen. The lady's concerned expression suggests she may just have invested her wardrobe allowance on the challenger from Philadelphia. And we can catch them once more, just a few feet from the action, gazing approvingly, like satisfied patrons, as teenager Floyd Patterson hammers out an eight-round decision over the tough and brave Jimmy Slade. They are aficionados.

Those fights all took place during 1954 and, evidently, an evening at the ringside, followed perhaps by a late snack at Jack Dempsey's to maintain the buzz, was still highly popular within the social clique. But times had changed: no longer was Friday the traditional night for boxing in the arena at 49th Street and Eighth Avenue (both the Valdes and Moore triumphs were staged on

Wednesdays) and there were other significant departures from the wonderful days of just a decade before, when every New Yorker knew that Friday night was Garden night.

Following a long illness, Uncle Mike Jacobs, notoriously tight with a dollar but a genius when organising the third Garden's most memorable galas, had died in January 1953 and now the increasingly shady International Boxing Club was calling the shots, not only in New York, but also in most of the major cities throughout the States. Veteran observers bemoaned the dearth of talent as old-timers are wont to do: they yearned for a return to the fabulous forties when names like Louis, Armstrong, Graziano and Pep were up there in lights; and how they longed to see a remake of the unforgettable four-part serial featuring Beau Jack and Bob Montgomery which played to packed houses for its fifteen-month run.

Bob Montgomery, the super-smart Bobcat from Philadelphia, and the amazing Beau Jack . . . two sensational lightweights whose styles were made for one another.

Most unlikely that our well-dressed, well-heeled couple ever managed to see The Bobcat and The Beau in their prime: probably the gentleman was busy directing his troops in the Pacific or planning strategy in Washington; the lady would have been preoccupied organising Red Cross benefits.

But for thousands of other New Yorkers, those battling lightweights provided a welcome release from the daily realities of wartime. And Beau Jack in particular punched his way not only into the record books but also into the hearts of the city's sporting legions.

Beau Jack, the shoeshine boy from Georgia who was booked into the Garden on no fewer than 27 occasions, topping the bill an astonishing 21 times; who, within a hectic two months, was twice a winner against hardman Fritzie Zivic and also Henry Armstrong; who made bundles for his managers, not to mention Uncle Mike and the ticket touts along Broadway, and the restaurant owners and the barkeepers, the newsvendors and the programme sellers . . . everyone made a buck, but Beau never had his for long.

Beau Jack, who along with Montgomery attracted a crowd which purchased a staggering $35,864,000 worth of war bonds to see their fourth and final meeting in the Garden. That evening, the fighters received $1,500 each to cover their training expenses.

Sidney Walker was born in Augusta on April 1, 1921 – April Fool's Day – and in the years to follow, there were many who fooled and conned the boxer who became famous as Beau Jack. The city sharks dined well off the lightweight when he was a headliner, and they discarded him when the big purses were just a memory and he was through as a fighter.

But somehow Beau's innocence and integrity, his basic belief in goodness, shielded him from the bitterness and despair that might have haunted him when his boxing days were done and he was back shining shoes. The conmen may have robbed his loot, but they could not snatch his soul.

Young Sidney was reared by his grandmother, Evie Mixom, an extraordinary lady who lived until she was 112, and she it was who started calling the little boy Beau Jack – just why, she never disclosed. She also encouraged him – with the aid of a slipper – to fight back when his shoeshine pitch was in peril from rival youngsters who had an eye on his boot polish and his takings, and Beau discovered that he loved to fight and was good at it – good enough by the time he reached his teens to enlist for the notorious battle royals.

Battle royals were popular with the white sporting gentry throughout the southern states: four, five, sometimes six black youths were put into a ring blindfolded, and they slugged one another until only one remained upright. A sorry excuse for sport, but the betting was as ferocious as the action, and Beau earned his first fifty-dollar bill from a delighted and grateful gambler. In comparison, fighting one-on-one without the blinds was a picnic.

By now he was shining shoes at the swank Augusta Golf Club, home of the Masters, but his ambition was to head north and become a real pro boxer. Over a period of years he badgered the legendary golfer Bobby Jones about funding the venture, and eventually Jones succeeded in getting the members to stump up the required cash. The eighteen-year-old Beau set off north accompanied by a club steward, Bowman Milligan, who became his first manager, and settled in Holyoke, Massachusetts, then a thriving fight town.

Success did not come overnight. For a year he was confined to the gym, learning his trade, but on his debut on May 20, 1940, he could scrape only a draw against Frankie Allen. In fact, he won just twice in his first six starts before going on a roll that saw him lose only once more in his next 29 fights.

Beau was always in terrific condition. He could throw a sharp left, punch hard with both hands, and toss a crowd-pleasing bolo – an exaggerated uppercut that Kid Gavilan would later claim as his own. He had a stern taskmaster in trainer Sid Behr and his aces were superb fitness, stamina and aggression. With the possible exception of Rocky Marciano, no champ ever entered the ring better prepared than The Beau and his exhausting schedule demanded that he must be super-fit.

In his first twenty months as a pro he packed in 37 contests, inevitably outgrew Holyoke, and began building a reputation in New York. Aside from back-to-back losses to the clever Freddie Archer, his rise was spectacular – from the clubs like the Fort Hamilton Arena in Brooklyn to the big top on Eighth Avenue.

By now a well-connected Broadway character called Chick Wergeles had taken over as his principal manager, and a points win over Chester Rico planted Beau on the map. Just ten days later he beat the East Side's hotshot, Terry Young, and he clinched his spot as a leading lightweight contender when he cut up and stopped slippery Allie Stolz in seven rounds. He was 21, the toast of the Garden, and a title shot beckoned.

On the same day that Beau stopped Stolz, the reigning champion Sammy Angott announced his retirement, and his belt was up for grabs. Mike Jacobs wasted no time matching the boy from Georgia against the New Jersey hero Tippy Larkin for the vacant title, but only New York State gave its blessing. There is little doubt, however, that the match had valid claims: Larkin had won his last 23 fights against decent opposition; Beau Jack was unbeaten in his last dozen and improving all the time. Larkin never got started: Beau scored a knockdown in the first minute, and finished the job in the third thanks to a terrific right uppercut.

Beau Jack was the champ, perhaps only in the state of New York, but New York was the town that mattered. The 21-year-old could barely read or write, but at last he had money in his pocket and hordes of new friends to spend it on. The word spread quickly that Beau and his dough could be easily parted.

The lightweight scene was becoming even more complex. Angott, the former boss, had changed his mind about the easy life, explaining that recurring hand problems had finally been sorted out, and he resumed in March 1943, scoring a stunning upset over little Willie Pep, outpointing the featherweight champion who had previously gone undefeated in 63 bouts. And just seven months later the National Boxing Association – the rival organisation to New York State – recognised Angott as its champion following a points win over Slugger White in Hollywood.

Compared to the ludicrous title chaos of today, two champions in one division might appear relatively straightforward, but it was not until 1947 that the lightweights were unified. And in those intervening years no fighter was busier in the hectic 135lb scramble than the pride of Philadelphia, lean and mean Bob Montgomery.

Like Beau Jack, Montgomery was a southerner. Unlike Beau, there were no wealthy golfers to bankroll his boxing aspirations. Born in Sumter, South Carolina, on February 10, 1919, the fifteen-year-old Bob hitched north to Pennsylvania to join up with an elder brother, and not too long after that he found his way into a Philadelphia gym.

Back then Philly was a booming boxing city and its many gyms were crowded with talented unknowns, desperate for that big break. The sparring sessions were often as competitive as many main events, and the trainers who lorded over the action were as well known as many of the fighters. All over town, Joe Gramby was respected as one of the best.

Gramby had been a good featherweight in the 1920s when tutored by the great Jack Blackburn – widely acknowledged as one of the brainiest fighters and trainers of all time. Now Joe was passing on Blackburn's wisdom to a new generation and the teenage Montgomery was fortunate enough to become one of his pupils, the partnership lasting throughout The Bobcat's career, with Gramby also taking over the managerial role from Frankie Thomas in 1944.

He taught Montgomery the Blackburn basics of good balance allied to a serious straight left, but the youngster also possessed a relentless aggression, plus a streak of meanness that could only come from within. Bob was a natural.

Montgomery's amateur career was brief and unremarkable, and he may have had as many as ten semi-pro fights before he made his official debut as a nineteen-year-old, knocking out Young Johnny Buff in the second in Atlantic City on October 23,

1938. By the end of the following year he had earned sixth spot in Nat Fleischer's annual *Ring* ratings and had lost only once in 25 fights – on points to Tommy Spiegel.

He was given few easy gigs. In 1940 he dropped a decision to the reigning champion Lew Jenkins and also lost to Angott, whose style gave every fighter nightmares. He was still on that learning curve, remaining unbeaten through 1941, and gaining revenge over Jenkins. And although Angott (now the champion) beat him twice in 1942, Montgomery was now a well established attraction. When Jacobs booked him to challenge Beau Jack in the Garden on May 21, 1943, The Bobcat was a fresh 24-year-old who had lost just six of his 59 recorded fights.

Champion Beau, two years younger, had also been beaten six times – from 53 fights – and he was bidding to extend an impressive Garden sequence. Clearly Uncle Mike had planned his pension fund around The Beau.

On February 5, his lightweight champ outpointed Fritzie Zivic in a catch weight contest and the fight provided enough thrills to warrant a return on March 5, with a similar outcome. No rest for Beau, and on April 2 a crowd of 19,986 saw him beat a fading Henry Armstrong. An exceptionally demanding preparation for his title defence and more than enough to make him a heavy 3/1 favourite to beat Bob.

A packed Garden looked set for an early night when their hero set about Montgomery in the opening round, swarming all over the challenger and catching him with hard shots from both hands. The Bobcat survived the first, but there was no respite in the second and third as Beau maintained the furious pace and the almost non-stop bombardment. Montgomery was taking plenty but he never lost his poise and gradually found his rhythm. Two inches taller than the 5ft 6″ Jack, he started reaching the champ with his excellent left and, becoming more adventurous, enjoyed further success with dazzling combinations that halted Beau in his tracks.

The styles of the two fighters guaranteed thrills and the fans were going wild, but now their champion was being outboxed and outpunched, if never outgamed. When the final bell rang, Beau was still charging forward, but even his staunchest supporters were under no illusions, and the decision was unanimous. Beau was exhausted, both eyes swollen and practically shut, his lips bruised and bloodied. But, as ever, he had fought his heart out, and the fans paid him his due.

Of course there was a contract for a rematch. The first fifteen rounds had been hugely entertaining; there would be no problem shifting the tickets; and, more important, Jacobs desperately needed both Montgomery and Jack. Many of his headliners were away on war duties; the Detroit Olympia had secured episodes two and three of the Ray Robinson–Jake La Motta saga; in fact, Beau and The Bobcat would provide New York with its only two championship fights in 1943.

And yet Uncle Mike waited until November 19 before staging the return. Possibly this was a tacit acknowledgement from the great man that he had made far too much use of his golden goose form Georgia in the first half of the year.

Criticism never troubled Jacobs, and anyway he had the majority of the media dining at his table, but around Stillman's the gossip was that he had used up the best of Beau Jack. And when in October, following comfortable wins over Maxie Starr in Washington and Johnny Hutchinson in Philadelphia, Jack dropped a decision to smart Bobby Ruffin on his return to New York, the rumours seemed well-founded. In an incredible betting swing, this time all the money was for Montgomery, and on Friday, November 19, he went into the ring a prohibitive 4/1 on favourite.

The Philadelphia fighter had scored four wins since becoming champion and, although there had been slight concerns about his weight, The Bobcat had looked terrific in his final sparring sessions. The experts were almost unanimous in tipping the champion to retain his title.

Nobody wanted to risk a buck on Beau Jack, but there were still thousands who would pay to see him perform.

Despite the apparent predictability of the outcome, a crowd of 17,866 produced receipts of $96,873 for what they believed would be Beau's last stand. Instead they were lucky enough to witness his finest night. His trainer, Behr, was a terribly difficult man to please, forever grumping and grumbling for more effort from his fighter, but after this unforgettable night even sour Sid allowed a smile to spread across his face. Beau had been that special.

Without the aid of a computer, some ringside genius announced that Jack threw more than one hundred punches per round: the statistician may have been out by one or two jabs either way, but the frenzied fans kept neither a count nor their seats.

Right from the first bell Beau again went for broke, charging in behind a stinging left jab, following up with clubbing swings, never giving Montgomery a moment's peace. This was a rerun of their first meeting and once more Bob weathered the assault. Too educated a boxer to panic, he countered with blistering combinations, and there was pandemonium throughout the arena as the two stood centre ring swapping punches. In a sensational fifth, Beau was caught by a tremendous volley and looked as if he might go down, but, incredibly, he came storming back in the following round to regain control.

No argument, Montgomery was boxing brilliantly and was always a danger, but he just could not match his opponent's fantastic workrate. The big question was: could Beau Jack possibly maintain such a breakneck gallop for the full trip? He had run out of steam the last time, and in the champion's corner Joe Gramby was still calm, still convinced that Jack must burn himself out. The plan was for Bob to launch an all-out attack over the final three rounds. Gramby miscalculated by seconds.

By round fourteen Jack had punched himself to the point of exhaustion, and for the last six minutes Montgomery unloaded everything he had left. Bob also was tired and hurt, but in a riotous final round he had his challenger reeling all over the ring on the verge of a knockout, and on the brink of sparking off 17,000 coronaries. Beau was back to his old days of swinging blindfold, refusing to go down, and at the bell the fighters fell into an embrace to a tremendous reception. There could be only fractions separating them on the scorecards, but the votes all went to the challenger, and the Garden erupted.

The *New York Times* report the following morning summed up perfectly: '. . . one of the biggest upsets of modern times. Thought to be at the end of his tether, Beau Jack turned the tables in savage outbursts of fighting that had Bob Montgomery shaken and weary.'

The Bobcat was philosophical about the defeat. Years later, he would recall, 'I didn't feel bad when I lost. I was young and had a return contract to fight him again. I knew I would win it back.'

What he hadn't known was that before he would get Beau Jack back in the ring The Bobcat would squeeze in two fights that would make headlines across the country. In the first he displayed a cruel streak that shocked even his own cornermen; in the second he was flattened inside one round.

In January 1944 Philadelphia's leading promoter, Herman Taylor, matched Bob with another excellent lightweight, Trenton's Ike Williams. This was a natural attraction, spiced by the fighters' genuine dislike for one another – the result of a brutal beating that Williams had given Montgomery's close friend Johnny Hutchinson. The Bobcat vowed to make Ike pay the hard way.

Ike Williams would go on to become one of the finest 135lb champions of all time, but before 14,000 fans in the Convention Hall he was torn apart by the merciless Montgomery who softened him up with a sustained body assault before switching his attacks to the head. There were many who believed The Bobcat could have applied the finisher any time he liked, but Bob waited until the twelfth and final round – with the fans screaming for referee Ernie Resto to step in – before a crushing right catapulted Ike through the ropes and on to the ring apron, completely unconscious. Montgomery rushed to the other side of the ring to celebrate with his pal, Hutchinson; many at ringside feared that Williams would never be able to box again.

Montgomery had looked awesome and perhaps that was why Jacobs risked booking him into the Garden to face Al Davis just two weeks before he was due to box Beau Jack for the third time. Today, such a match would be deemed insane and just would not be allowed. But back then, if Uncle Mike wanted something done, then so be it: he had a date to fill. Brownsville's Bummy Davis threw a terrific left hook and sold blocks of tickets, which endeared him to Jacobs, but like the promoter, the experts forecast that he lacked the know how ever to land his pet punch on the classy Philadelphian. Wrong. Bummy came out firing, hit the jackpot with a perfect hook that Bob never even saw, and the action was all over in 63 seconds.

Today, such a stoppage would incur an automatic suspension, causing at the very least a postponement of the title fight. In the 1940s it would have required a platoon of Marines to mess with the plans of the Garden overlord: Jack–Montgomery III was still scheduled for March 3, and that Friday night a monster 19,066 paid $111,954 to see if The Bobcat was still hungover.

The customers would never tire of cheering on two such exciting competitors: they seemed incapable of producing a dull round, much less a poor fight, and the outcome was always so hard to predict. This time, Montgomery, because of the blowout against Davis, found himself the 9/5 outsider, but he was unfazed. Bob dismissed that result as no more than a fluke, and he was by no means gun-shy when he stepped out to face Beau. In fact, for the first time, he started faster than the Georgia boy, racing into an early lead and catching the champion with damaging left hooks and accurate rights. As always, Beau kept pressing forward, coming in low and scoring with both hands. But the Philadelphian never lost his rhythm.

For nine rounds Bob maintained a slight edge and, although every round was bitterly contested, Beau required something special. In round ten he ripped into Montgomery, catching him with clusters of shots that had The Bobcat in serious trouble. With the crowd screaming for more of the same, Beau became a punching demon in rounds eleven and twelve, doubling up Montgomery with mighty whacks to the body, bouncing his head back with the bolo, but his challenger refused even to take a count. Beau's frantic assault had made the fight very close to call but had also taken a massive effort. Somehow Montgomery regained his poise, once again found the range with his left and banged home hard rights; the champ kept swinging, but he was missing more now. Right to the final bell the old rivals gave it their all, but there was no doubt, Bob's punches were the sharper . . . the din was deafening. Referee Young Otto and judge Bill Healy returned identical cards, eight rounds to six with one even in favour of The Bobcat; judge Marty Monroe saw Jack as the winner 8–7. The pro-Beau crowd did not dispute the verdict: instead they acclaimed two great lightweights and another fantastic fight.

Beau was scheduled to join the army, and so, just fourteen days later, before the bruises and the aches had been forgotten, he was back in the Garden to outpoint Bummy Davis. And only two weeks after that the insatiable Jacobs packed the house yet again, with Beau this time beating the tough Mexican Juan Zurita. Compared to Uncle Mike, a drill sergeant was going to seem like a kindly counsellor to the rookie soldier.

Bob Montgomery and Beau Jack would clash one final time, on August 4 of that eventful 1944, when Jacobs decided to back the war effort. Montgomery's title was not at stake, and although they were boxing only for pride and expenses, Beau and The Bobcat produced an entertaining ten rounds with Jack being awarded a split decision. Their series had finished all square, which was fitting. Of more significance, the great rivals had raised the incredible sum of almost $36 million in the sale of war bonds.

Beau would remember that night in the Garden with tremendous pride. Montgomery, also due to join the army, would have mixed memories. Many years later, when his money had been spent, Bob approached the army for some form of assistance. No reply. He was more disappointed than bitter.

Bob earned well from title defences against Allie Stolz and Wesley Mouzon, and on August 4, 1947 he was paid a career-high $47,000 to face his old enemy, Ike Williams, now the NBA champion, in a unification match. As expected, the exchanges were savage, but in the sixth Williams administered a terrible beating and the fight was stopped. That sixth round ruined Montgomery and he fought only six more times, losing the lot. He quit in 1950 with an honourable record of 75 wins from 97 fights.

First Thomas, then Gramby had managed him well and ensured that he got a fair shake; nobody had ripped him off. He retired owning apartment houses and a pool room, but three divorces and a reckless gambling bug ate up the dough. For a time he earned a living as a beer salesman, then had a job counselling delinquents, but his proudest boast was that he put his son through university. He lived to the fine age of 79, dying on August 25, 1998.

Beau Jack would survive him by two years, dying on February 9, 2000, aged 78.

Following his battles with Montgomery, there were still big bucks to be made out of The Beau. In 1947 a crowd of 18,000 paid to see him box young Tony Janiro at the Garden, but the fight had a disappointing conclusion when Jack seriously injured his knee in the fourth and was forced to retire. Despite that setback, he was considered good enough to challenge undisputed champ Williams in Philadelphia the following year but, just like The Bobcat, he was stopped in six rounds.

No longer a contender, he remained popular – but not in New York. Now he was an attraction in Los Angeles, Montreal and Chicago, Boston, Providence, and even Hawaii. He saw little of the money he earned, and eventually wound up back down south where he had fought all those battle royals. On August 12, 1955 he boxed for the last time, losing in nine rounds to the faded former champion Williams in his hometown Augusta. Ike also announced his retirement that night.

Beau Jack won 83 of his 113 fights and won them the hard way. But his grasping connections, his army of tappers, and his naivety ensured there was no nest egg. And so he returned to the only other trade he knew – shining shoes.

Over the years Beau was often pictured at his stand in Miami's plush Fontainebleau Hotel and offered up as a cautionary example of what can happen to a fighter who squanders his cash. In fact, Beau knocked out a decent living at the Fontainebleau, and his days were cheered by a seemingly endless stream of visiting celebrities from the world of sport and show business who just wanted to shake his hand and stuff a few bucks into his pocket. He also kept fit, and trained young fighters at the old Fifth Street Gym where he was renowned as a hard taskmaster.

He was happy, and the jackals could not feed off that.

CHAPTER SIX

Willie Pep *v* Sandy Saddler

FRIDAY, FEBRUARY 11, 1949

Champions come and champions go and never with more rapidity than today, when there are truckloads of former title claimants who are remembered only in their local pub, bar, or *cantina*. And only if they have the price of their next glass. In this fast-forward world of ever-decreasing values, where massive hype and a compliant media can guarantee almost anyone their fifteen minutes of fame, they are boxing's examples of the anonymous celebrity.

Even a dedicated boxing buff might struggle to name the reigning XYZ super bantamweight champion, but query him – or her – about either of the Sugars, Robinson or Leonard, and be prepared to sit mute for at least forty minutes; just mention one of the Kids, Lewis, Berg, Chocolate, Gavilan, or either of the Rockys, Graziano and Marciano, and start unzipping the overnight bag.

More than in most other sports, the bygone champions of boxing are revered by their own, their exploits remembered with a special affection. There is now the renowned Hall Of Fame in Canastota, New York, where every year the heroes mix with their fans; in Britain, ex-boxers' associations flourish throughout the land. And whenever a gang gets together the arguments are sure to begin . . . who was merely great and who was truly legendary? And just how does a great grow into a legend? Fair question.

Gene Tunney is remembered with respect, but seldom warmth, as the guy who got lucky with a long count rather than as a brilliant technician who twice beat an icon, Jack Dempsey. Ezzard Charles, never forgiven for thrashing an ageing Joe Louis, is dismissed now for being dull and over-cautious. Joe Frazier, George Foreman and

Larry Holmes could never escape the giant shadow cast by Muhammad Ali. And what about Sandy Saddler, who three times halted Willie Pep, an undisputed genius on all cards? Most often Sandy is recalled just as a prime exponent of illegal tactics.

Now that really is a bad rap, totally undeserved, and hard to understand. And one that rankled with Saddler long after his fighting days were done.

In 1971, fifteen years after his last fight, he told Peter Heller, '. . . Pep and I would be at a fight in the Garden and they'll say, "One of the greatest featherweights, Willie Pep. Here's another retired champ, Sandy Saddler." That's why I don't care to get introduced in the ring. Instead of saying, "Sandy Saddler, the undefeated featherweight champion of the world," instead "Take it and like it. If you don't want it, leave it."'

A fine boxer's injured pride, and Saddler put it all down to prejudice. He continued, 'Pep and I are great friends. But one thing, though, he is white, and when you're white you're supposed to be right . . . It's just plain ol' prejudice.'

Just not so, Sandy. Ali and Sugar Ray Robinson top most lists as the best ever pound-for-pound performers; Louis, Jack Johnson and Henry Armstrong are other accepted members of the pantheon. Saddler? He had to settle for being merely great.

And most galling of all for the mild-mannered feather from Harlem must have been living with the reality that of his four savage encounters with Pep, the single fight that little Willie won was by far the standout, and the outcome that night had absolutely nothing to do with skin colour. On that February Friday in the Garden, Willie Pep guaranteed his place alongside the gods of boxing, after producing a unique display of breathtaking speed and ringcraft, coupled with an unquenchable fighting spirit and amazing courage.

Small wonder that Sandy found him such an impossible act to follow.

But, we must remember, Willie had always been a special talent, a wizard who could make the extraordinary appear mundane; who could demoralise an opponent with just a feint or a pirouette; who could flit in and out of range, inflicting all sorts of hurt and humiliation with his dazzling left and a jarring right. When he first bumped into Sandy Saddler in the ring, Willie Pep boasted the remarkable record of only one loss in 137 fights.

He was born Gugliemo Papaleo on September 19, 1922 in Middletown, Connecticut, the son of immigrant parents. Always small, he went to the gym to learn how to defend himself and before long there was not a sparmate who could lay a glove on him. By the time he was sixteen he was the flyweight champion of the state, but he had a gentleman arranging his fights who believed he had discovered Superman. This guy allowed the 105lb Willie to box a featherweight from Harlem's famous Salem Crescent Club called Ray Roberts. Roberts' real name was Walker Smith, and, of course, he became Sugar Ray Robinson. Conceding 20lb to a young Sugar Ray! Pep lost on points, but he could have been seriously hurt and his career wrecked before it had really got underway.

Willie would be far more fortunate with the men he chose to conduct his affairs when he turned professional in 1940. His manager was a shrewd and experienced gentleman from Florida called Lou Viscusi, and the partnership would endure for nineteen years. Viscusi, however, did not come cheap: their contract called for the manager to be paid one third, which was standard, but snug in the small print was a clause stating that Lou's cut would be bumped up to 50 per cent if Pep became champion.

After an unbeaten run of 55 fights, culminating with a fifteen-rounds decision over the power-punching Chalky Wright in the Garden on November 20, 1942, Willie was the 126lb champion. Viscusi had been made to wait just over two years before qualifying for his half share in Pep Enterprises. In his favour, Lou took care of all the expenses, frequently bailed out the fighter when he was short of cash, always presented Willie with an honest accounting and proved a true friend in a crisis. Pep never regretted his choice.

Nor had he any problems with Viscusi's trainer, Bill Gore, a tall, relaxed, scholarly sort who had a calming effect on the highly strung youngster. Gore's strength lay in his uncanny ability to analyse an opponent's style and instruct Willie on how best to showcase his magic. Bill was very low-key but Pep could never praise him enough, claiming that he would have been acknowledged as the best in the business had he been based in New York. He expressed his gratitude for the care that the trainer lavished upon him many times.

Willie told columnist and author Bill Heinz, 'Bill Gore told me, "The way you talk now, you're gonna talk when you quit." He wouldn't let me get hurt. Against Saddler, the third time [Pep's eye injury occurred in the fourth fight] my left eye was shut tight. Bill Gore said to the referee, "He can't continue." I said "Thank you.'"

Willie made his pro debut as a seventeen-year-old flyweight, outpointing James McGovern in a four-rounder in Hartford on July 3, 1940. The Will O' The Wisp was off and buzzing, and Viscusi kept him busy. Lou, however, was a patient match-maker, confining the teenager to the New England club circuit, giving him plenty of time to develop his strength. In fact, before he won the championship from Wright, Pep appeared in New York on only three occasions. He also had one brief stay out on the West Coast.

Believing there might be plenty of work for a little man in California, Willie was sent to Los Angeles where he was paid $50 to beat Billie Spencer in the Hollywood Legion Stadium – a meaningless win. Shaking hands with screen tough guy George Raft before the fight made more of an impression on the teenager. But he did gain valuable experience, plus a dollar a day wages, sparring with the fine future bantam champion Manuel Ortiz. Less than four years later he would be paid a healthy $20,000 after outpointing his old employer over ten rounds in Boston.

Sammy Angott, the awkwardly clever champion lightweight, inflicted Pep's first defeat, getting a tight verdict in a New York non-title fight on March 19, 1943, but there would be another amazing 73-fight streak before he would lose again. A skinny but menacing guy called Sandy Saddler was about to play a major role in Willie's life.

Joseph Benjamin Saddler, the son of West Indian parents, was born in Boston on June 23, 1926 but reared in New York's Harlem. As a schoolboy he enjoyed his visits to the local Police Athletic League gym where he developed into a very promising amateur, losing less than a handful of his fifty contests and that record was impressive enough to attract the attention of the influential Johnston brothers.

There were four of them: Jimmy, Ned, Charley and Bill. Jimmy was the main man, the Liverpool-born Boy Bandit, a smart and imaginative manager who also took control at the Garden between the eras of Rickard and Jacobs. The other three were disciples, and it was Bill Johnston who became Saddler's first manager.

By a quirk of fortune, Bill approached none other than Viscusi – then flying high as the manager of a world champion and flush from promoting successful shows throughout New England – to give Sandy his start, and so the seventeen-year-old was booked to face Earl Roys in Hartford on March 7, 1944. Viscusi was doing the big-city boys few favours as Roys was a top attraction in New England, but, to his immense credit, Saddler emerged a points winner after eight rounds. A tough debut, but at the ringside Pep, who had been champion for seventeen months, was not particularly impressed.

However, the fight had been entertaining and a rematch was agreed for two weeks later. Roys, however, could not get leave from the navy, and come fight night, young Sandy found himself matched with a substitute . . . no bum off the street, but a solid puncher called Jock Leslie who would progress to challenge Pep for the title. This was a total mismatch: at that stage, Leslie was in a completely different league, and a bemused and outclassed Saddler soaked up plenty before the referee took pity on him in round three. Again Willie Pep was a spectator, and after witnessing the slaughter he forgot all about the lanky novice from Harlem.

Bill Johnston's approach to managing fighters had been cavalier in the extreme, and before too long he switched sports and started handling wrestlers. Brother Charley took over the Saddler account.

Charley Johnston was an astute businessman who also added the marvellous light heavy Archie Moore to his string following the death of brother Jimmy. Charley let his fighters see the world, and before he won the title Sandy had boxed in Mexico, Venezuela and the West Indies, Cuba, Honolulu and Panama. Moore and Saddler became fast friends, but Archie always harboured an intense dislike for his manager; Saddler, on the other hand, seemed quite content with the way his career was shaping.

The year 1945 was particularly satisfying with Sandy remaining unbeaten through 24 contests, only seven lasting the distance. That was an exceptional stoppage ratio for a featherweight, especially one who stood 5ft 8½" and might have been expected to poke out a long left hand to carve out his wins. Instead, Saddler developed a terrific left hook to the body, often doubling up to the head with pulverising effect; his right was not too bad either. In 1947 he boxed two future lightweight champions, stopping Joe Brown in three rounds and drawing with Jimmy Carter and by the following year he had established himself as the outstanding contender for Pep's title. The bout was arranged for October 29 in the Garden.

Sandy was 22, in his fifth professional year, and had lost just six times in 93 starts. He was ready and his camp believed that Pep just might be vulnerable. Only the year before The Wisp had been called upon to perform one of his miracles.

On January 8, 1947 Pep was a passenger on a plane which overshot Newark Airport and crashed in woods in Middleville, New Jersey. There were five dead and Willie was lifted from the wreck suffering a broken back, a broken leg and numerous other less serious injuries. In hospital, with a cast on his body and another on his leg, the doctors were sure that he would never be able to fight again.

But just as he left opponents bewildered inside the ropes, the champ made chumps of the doctors and their gloomy predictions. Far ahead of schedule, he had the casts removed and almost immediately returned to the gym; to the astonishment of all the experts, both boxing and medical, he was back in serious action on June 17 in Hartford, outpointing a tough Puerto Rican called Victor Flores. Another five wins quickly followed and, amazingly, by August he was spry enough to stop Jock Leslie in a title defence.

There was an expensive downside to this tremendous achievement. Following the crash Willie had sued for $250,000 damages, but the insurance company claimed that he had proved against Leslie that he was, in fact, better than ever, and his suit was thrown out. He received a modest $15,000 compensation, the bulk of which was eaten up by hospital bills.

The ring was the only place where Pep was going to make money. Leading up to the Saddler defence he maintained his whirlwind pace, winning another fifteen, including a defence against Humberto Sierra. Meeting Saddler was going to be just another big paynight in the Garden; for Sandy, this was his big chance.

There were, however, no first-night nerves. Right from the opening bell Saddler was the boss, ignoring Willie's feints and banging home hard lefts which drew blood from the champ's nose. In his training camp Archie Moore had advised him to stay on top of Pep, denying him room, and Sandy followed his friend's instructions to the letter. In the third the champ twice took a count of nine, and in the fourth Willie was a champion no more as referee Ruby Goldstein shouted out the full count. The boxing world was stunned and then the gossips got busy.

Ugly stories surfaced that Pep had been a non-trier. At the weigh-in, New York State Athletic Commission chairman Eddie Eagan had warned both boxers, 'You are two honest athletes. We are holding you responsible to uphold the good name of boxing.'

Had Eagan been tipped off? Who knows? His words, however, were sufficient to unleash the conspiracy theorists, but neither the ringside writers nor the fans had spotted anything suspicious, and Eagan, satisfied that he had witnessed a straight fight, never called for a follow-up inquiry. Willie Pep was a mere human after all and had been the victim of a staggering upset – an upset that paled into insignificance only five days later when Harry Truman shocked the world by beating Republican Tom Dewey in the battle for the White House. The *Chicago Tribune*, convinced of a Dewey landslide, jumped the gun with an edition announcing him as president. No sports editor had shown such blind faith in Pep.

There would be no comeback for Dewey, but Willie did not have to wait too long for a second crack at Saddler. The Garden rematch was set for February 11, 1949. Under the terms of the initial contract, Viscusi and Pep would again collect the bulk of the money, but Sandy would still enjoy his best paynight.

Fight fever gripped New York, but two days before the showdown the headlines were all about actor Robert Mitchum being sentenced to two months' jail in Los Angeles following a marijuana bust. Come the day of the fight, however, Pep and Saddler were again dominating the front pages, and the city's bars and hotels were overflowing. More than 8,000 fans arrived from Connecticut, and the touts were in wonderland as the crowds jostled along Eighth Avenue searching for that priceless ticket.

Eventually, 19,097 squeezed into the arena, and paying a top price of $10, the crowd returned receipts of $87,563 – a record for featherweights. Pep was also looking to break new ground: no 126lb champion had ever regained the title.

Despite that ominous statistic, and despite the fact that Sandy had been such an overwhelming winner the first time, the betting exchanges were extremely lively. Following the lunchtime weigh-in (Pep right on the limit; Saddler 2lb lighter) the odds fluctuated all afternoon as serious sums were lumped on both fighters. But for the flood of money from the loyal New Englanders, the champion would have been a clear favourite, but at the first bell, Willie was only a fractional outsider at 6/5.

Pep never started faster . . . perhaps no boxer ever started faster. In the opening round The Wisp sped around the ring, flashing in and out, never allowing Saddler the opportunity to toss the grenades that had caused such havoc three months earlier. *The Ring*'s Nat Fleischer counted 37 left jabs that landed without reply, and when Sandy did get in close Pep promptly grabbed him, earning a warning from referee Eddie Joseph for wrestling. There was another warning for Willie in the third, this time for heeling (rubbing his palm across the opponent's face) and he continued to frustrate the champ on the inside and dazzle him at long range.

Saddler was the guy with the reputation for flaunting the rules. True, he might on occasion tramp on an opponent's foot, or take a tug at a bicep, or perhaps follow through with a forearm, but in his entire career he was disqualified only once. Pep never lost on a foul, but he was no choirboy either and was fully schooled in the rough stuff . . . whatever it took.

The Wisp was going to need all his expertise and experience. In the fourth Saddler at last got his range and ripped home savage, strength-sapping belts to the body, and in the fifth a hard right opened a cut under Pep's left eye. But the challenger was still up on his toes, still moving and hitting with blistering speed, still piling up the points, still making Sandy look silly.

By the ninth the Harlem fighter was trailing badly on the cards, but he was far from discouraged and his chilling power could swing the fight in a second. That crucial second appeared to have arrived in the ninth when he swatted the mosquito with a vicious right to the head, followed by another hard right and a sickening left hook that made Willie's legs perform a different dance. Again in the tenth the Saddler backers were on their feet as Sandy launched a combination of fierce shots to the head, followed by a withering body attack that had the little man desperately hanging on. Neither Saddler nor referee Joseph could prise him loose until

Willie had recovered, and then once more, The Wisp was off, jabbing and running. The Garden was going wild.

Pep always marked up easily and by now his face was a mess: blood flowed from cuts above and below both eyes, but he was in wonderful shape, and his legs were back obeying orders. For the next three rounds he called upon all the skills acquired over the years, and once again he was the master, catching the ever-stalking Saddler with a textbook display of punching, roughing up the so-called dirty champion when they wrestled inside, dancing out of reach when he required a breather. He was very tired, but so too was Sandy.

The champ may have been flagging but he was still a menace. In round fourteen he charged forward furiously, but just could not pin down the elusive Pep long enough to cause lasting damage. At times Willie was running for his life, then he would dart in with his own stinging replies, but just before the bell, he danced into an explosive left hook that jarred every bone. Saddler, however, had no time left to follow up. Could he get lucky in the final three minutes?

As the bell signalled the start of the last round, the 19,000 in the Garden rose to acclaim two great fighting men, and they never sat down again as Willie and Sandy produced the most marvellous finale.

Saddler had to go for the knockout. For the first two minutes he battered Pep around the ring; the exhausted challenger, mouth open and bloody, was now boxing on automatic, but he was punching back, and when the champ missed with a wild right and fell into the ropes, Willie still had the strength to grab him from behind and cling on despite the referee's best efforts to pry him loose. He was running down the clock, killing off the seconds, but incredibly, in the final minute he bounced back into the attack, hurting Saddler with a bewildering two-fisted assault that brought the house down.

Even such seasoned observers as Nat Fleischer were stumped for superlatives. *The Ring* chief described it as, 'The greatest exhibition Willie Pep has ever put forth as champion or contender . . .'. His colleague, Jersey Jones, later to become the manager of Nigerian hero Dick Tiger, added, 'What Pep may miss in brawn is more than equalised by his stout fighting heart and one of the keenest brains in the ring.' Writing long after the event, Bill Heinz recalled, '. . . the second Saddler fight in the Garden was the greatest boxing exhibition I ever saw.'

Heinz had watched an awful lot of boxing.

The decision, of course, was unanimous. Referee Joseph scored 10–5 in rounds, judge Jack O'Sullivan returned 9–6, and judge Frank Forbes differed only marginally at 9–5–1. All for Willie Pep, the champion once again. The Saddler faction offered no arguments and immediately started talking about a third match; commission doctor Vincent Nardiello closed Willie's cuts with eleven stitches before the champ got around to thinking about his future.

Viscusi was in no hurry to accommodate the Saddler camp: there were much easier ways to earn a good buck. Following a three-month break to allow the cuts to heal and his body to recuperate, the indefatigable Pep racked up another fifteen wins, including championship defences against Eddie Compo, Charley Riley and Ray Famechon – all good fighters but nowhere near Willie's class. Saddler, back working just a month after the Garden thriller, won the vacant junior lightweight belt in a bout against Cuban stylist Orlando Zulueta, and added another 23 victories to his tally before he again trapped The Wisp.

On September 8, 1950, a crowd of 38,781 paid $262,150 to see the boys again, this time in the Yankee Stadium. Pep was collecting a career-best $93,000, Saddler a more modest $31,000, and, at 8/5, the champion was the outsider. In their first fight, Sandy had demonstrated his dynamite punching; in the second, Willie had displayed his ring artistry. This third clash saw both feathers bring out their brilliant best . . . but also a repertoire of dirty tricks that would have sent the Marquess of Queensberry into a swoon.

Saddler claimed that Pep initiated the rough stuff, stabbing a thumb into his eye in the first round, and that he was unable to see properly until the third, when he poleaxed the champion for a nine count, thanks to his deadly left hook. But Willie survived, and in the next three rounds he was superb, outboxing and outpunching Sandy, but also spinning him off balance as well as heeling him when the opportunity arose.

Saddler, naturally, replied in kind. In the seventh he hurt Willie with two cruel rights to the kidneys and, as ever, Pep grabbed tight to earn a respite. But this time, as referee Goldstein tried to haul the fighters apart, Sandy took a firm grip on Willie's left arm and wrenched hard. Pep's face contorted with pain, but he made it to the bell.

Consternation in his corner, and when the bell rang to signal round eight, Willie remained on his stool, head lowered, his arm dangling loose. He claimed his shoulder had been dislocated. 'He beat me with a double arm lock', moaned the once-more ex-champion. An unrepentant Saddler countered, 'I thought a punch to the kidney did it. But if they say I twisted his arm, okay I twisted it.'

The subsequent X-ray showed only a slight swelling, but on Dr Nardiello's recommendation Pep was sidelined for two months. Until the unsatisfactory finish, the fight had been developing into another classic and a fourth battle made sense. Big mistake.

A year later, on September 26, 1951 in New York's Polo Grounds, the pair met for the final time in what sadly turned into one of the dirtiest fights ever, a wild, foul-filled travesty of boxing, and an indelible stain on the records of two outstanding performers.

Saddler enjoyed early success, cutting Pep's right eye and scoring the one clean knockdown in the second. After that it was no holds barred and referee Ray Miller proved a helpless bystander. The fighters thumbed, heeled and butted; they applied chokeholds, tripped one another, and wrestled around the ring. In the sixth both tumbled to the canvas and Pep tried to knee Saddler in the throat; in the following round they fell again, this time taking Miller with them. The fight had degenerated into a farce which was brought to a conclusion when Pep – handicapped by a grotesquely swollen right eye – failed to come out for the tenth.

The New York State Athletic Commission was outraged. Saddler was suspended indefinitely (he lost to Paddy De Marco in New York less than three months later) and Pep was banned for life (he was reinstated after twenty months). The new commission chairman, Robert Christenberry, had been seen to do his duty.

After Pep, Saddler became regarded as an extremely able champion rather than the great featherweight that he truly was. An enforced absence on army duty did not help his cause; neither did the frequent trips overseas to Caracas, Paris, Tokyo and Manila. He would drop a decision now and then, but only against leading lightweights. He was still much too good for his 126lb challengers and comfortably defended his title against Red Top Davis and Flash Elorde. He was only thirty and could have expected to earn well for a few more years, but on July 27, 1956 he sustained serious eye injuries when riding in a taxi which was involved in a crash. The end of a fine career, and he retired the undefeated champion with a proud record of only sixteen defeats in 162 fights, scoring an incredible 103 knockouts.

A non-drinker and non-smoker, Sandy became the athletic director at New York's National Maritime Union and also worked with fighters at Gleason's gym. In the 1970s he returned to the spotlight when, along with his friend Archie Moore, he helped train heavyweight champion George Foreman. Separated from his wife, his later years were spent alone, and his failing health made him a vulnerable target for neighbourhood muggers until his old boxing pals rallied round and arranged for his stay in a Bronx nursing home. He died on September 18, 2001, aged 75.

The Wisp fought another 76 times after Sandy. He lost his New York licence for good in 1954, following a shock two-rounds knockout against Lulu Perez in the Garden. His old acquaintance Vincent Nardiello decided that Willie's reflexes were gone, and over the next few years Pep delighted in proving the good doctor wrong. In 1958 he was still sharp enough to outspeed the reigning champion Hogan Bassey for eight rounds before getting caught in the ninth.

He quit the ring for five years, but then surprised the sporting world by returning in 1965 as a 42-year-old curiosity, at first intending to box only exhibitions but winding up in serious contests. The money was handy, but Willie had missed the buzz, and the opponents that agent George Shepard lined up were no Sandy Saddlers. He won nine straight before Calvin Woodland convinced him that this was a game for younger men. The obscure Calvin was only his eleventh loss in 242 professional appearances. Quite remarkable.

Willie Pep was an active pro during the reigns of eight heavyweight champions and outside the ropes he was equally busy but not nearly so successful. There was a succession of costly failed marriages; bad investments and regular visits to the racetrack also proved expensive. He ran a couple of nightclubs, worked as a brewery rep and even a tax collector. Willie was always on the hop, and refereed fights as far afield as Brazil and Australia; he was also in great demand as an after-dinner speaker. But as this is being written, the years have finally caught up with The Wisp, and he is confined to a nursing home.

Londoner Dennie Mancini, a veteran manager and cornerman, has been Pep's friend for thirty years. He insists that Willie must be included in the list of the top ten fighters of all time. And who can argue?

For Mancini, Willie's crowning achievement came with his unbelievable recovery from the plane crash to be able to defend his title in the same year. For others, Pep's peak arrived the night he predicted to a journalist that he would win the third round against Jackie Graves without actually landing a punch – and then did just that. But a one-time victim, Kid Campeche, spoke for all the boxers who had to share a ring with The Will O' The Wisp when he said, 'Fighting Willie Pep was like trying to stamp out a grass fire.'

And Campeche was just partially explaining the legend that is now Willie Pep. Sandy Saddler? Alas, just a great, great featherweight.

True Grit

No boxer who successfully negotiates the journey from his introductory visit to the gym to that first long walk into the arena lacks courage.

Many of the bravest battles take place in the mind and true grit does not only mean the willingness to accept punishment and come back for more. Perhaps that is the easiest way for courage to come to the fore.

Far more difficult to shrug off a painful and humiliating loss and plan revenge in the return . . . equally hard to ignore the advice to find a day job after a set-back or two . . . extremely traumatic to box in a foreign land, often the victim of a dirty-tricks campaign.

Bottle, moxie, *cojones*: Call it what you will. The Garden has witnessed all forms of valour.

CHAPTER SEVEN

Harry Greb *v* Gene Tunney

TUESDAY, MAY 23, 1922

The Roaring Twenties . . . and in the States, prohibition, bootlegging, loud toe-tapping jazz and sexy silent-screen idols. No matter that in Italy Benito Mussolini's Fascists were flexing their muscles, or that in Ireland civil strife was rampant, New York was a city hellbent on showing the world how to have a good time.

Despite the ban on booze, an estimated 32,000 speakeasies, scattered throughout the five boroughs, were conducting frantic business, and in response an increasingly harried administration ordered a crackdown on the carrying of hip flasks! New Yorkers, however, have never taken kindly to being told what they must do, and many of the 13,000 who flocked to the ornate Garden on Madison Square to see local boy Gene Tunney face The Pittsburgh Windmill, Harry Greb, were 'loaded' in the back pocket. Just for the hell of it.

These were fabulous times for boxing. True, Dempsey's appeal had outgrown the Garden, and in 1922 he was concentrating on a movie career in California. But there were so many other wonderful attractions like Benny Leonard and Jack Britton and Ted Kid Lewis, Johnny Dundee and Mickey Walker. And no fighter epitomised that merry, madcap era better than the extraordinary Harry Greb.

Harry trained on champagne and calmed any pre-fight nerves by enjoying the company of an accommodating blonde or brunette in the dressing room – or so we are led to believe. He brawled on the streets, intimidated referees in the ring, and subjected his opponents to a brand of assault and battery that made nonsense of the Queensberry Rules. Difficult to see how he could have kept his licence today, and yet the records tell us that he was disqualified just once in 299 professional outings.

His amazing schedule saw him hop overnight from one city to the next, yet when he challenged Tunney for the American light heavyweight championship, Greb was only starting to make a name for himself in New York. He was, however, marketing himself perfectly as the archetypal fast-living hellraiser, so admired in the boisterous Jazz Age.

Nobody tried to market Gene Tunney: he was far too serious, much too focused to lend himself to the usual promotional hype. Already his fellow New Yorkers accepted him as an extremely able if somewhat predictable light heavy; his workmates in the gym were wary around him, uncomfortable in conversation; the newspaper mob was cool but had not yet ganged up against him; and not even his staunchest supporter, promoter Tex Rickard, knew anything of his burning ambition. The fight crew would have laughed, but Gene was already charting the path that would lead to Jack Dempsey and the heavyweight championship of the world.

James Joseph Tunney was born on May 25, 1897 at Perry Street in Greenwich Village, the second oldest of a family of seven born to John Joseph Tunney, a native New Yorker, and Mary Lydon Tunney, who hailed from County Mayo in Ireland. The young James became known as Gene, thanks to a younger brother who had difficulty pronouncing 'Jim'. Soon the entire family was referring to him as Gene, and the name spread and stuck.

The elder Tunney worked as a longshoreman and brought home just about enough to keep his family afloat, but money was tight. By the time he was twelve young Gene, a bright student at St Veronica's Grammar, was doubling as a butcher's boy, adding a valued $2.50 to the pot.

The youngster moved on to the De La Salle Academy, run by the Christian Brothers who charged the not-inconsiderable sum of $45 a year in fees. Tunney, however, was intent on earning rather than learning, and though the Brothers offered to continue his education free of charge, at the age of fifteen, he started work as an office boy for the Ocean Steamship Company. After teaching himself typing, he moved up the rungs to become chief mail-order clerk, collecting a very handy $25 a week. Already he was showing the steely determination that was to serve him so well throughout his life.

He had also discovered boxing, becoming a keen student at a Village gym where he impressed the regulars to such an extent that opponents were drafted in to test him. Few did, and for the cash-conscious teenager turning professional was only a matter of time. He maintained his job, and in July 1915 survived a tough introduction, beating Bobby Dawson at the Sharkey Athletic Club. He was on his way, though not exactly at rocket pace, but early manager Billy Roche kept him busy in the small clubs until he enlisted in the marines in 1918.

His short spell in uniform did plenty for his career. In France he gained precious experience and publicity when winning the American Expeditionary Forces light heavyweight championship, battling through twenty eliminators before beating Ted Jamison, a former national amateur champion, in the final. Ringside dignitaries included Prince Albert of Belgium, and the old warriors General Pershing and Marshal Foch. Their presence pleased Gene as much as winning the title.

Back in the States, and now managed by Frank Bagley, he scored fifteen knockouts in his twenty contests through 1920 and 1921, but perhaps the most significant was a seven-rounds stoppage over Soldier Jones in Jersey City. That was the day when Tunney convinced himself that he could win the heavyweight title.

The date was July 2, 1921, and an 80,000 crowd flooded into Rickard's specially constructed arena at Boyle's Thirty Acres to see Dempsey defend his championship against the French idol Georges Carpentier. This was boxing's first million-dollar gate – receipts soared to $1,789,238 – and Tunney–Jones featured on the undercard. Their match did not provide too much excitement, and the fans, buzzing with anticipation for the main event, paid little heed as Tunney ground down the Soldier. But Gene was also eager to catch a first look at the Manassa Mauler up close, and after disposing of Jones he remained in a ringside corner to put the champ under the microscope. Of course, the much more powerful Dempsey easily stopped the game Frenchman, but Tunney spotted one straight right from Carpentier that, for a second, dazed Jack. That single punch persuaded Gene that The Mauler was vulnerable and that one day he could beat the great Dempsey.

Rickard, however, entertained no such wild dreams. He regarded the young New Yorker as a future contender for Carpentier's light heavyweight title and, now billed as The

Fighting Marine (Dempsey was still reviled as a draft dodger), Tunney drew a big crowd to the Garden to watch him stop a fair fighter called Eddie O'Hare. Encouraged by the big turn-out, Tex matched him with the punched-out Battling Levinsky and announced that the bout would be for the American championship. Nobody was surprised when Tunney hammered out a twelve rounds decision, and the promoter did not even stump up a belt for the winner. But he was more convinced than ever that his light heavy could take Carpentier's crown.

As a further stepping stone he offered Gene and manager Bagley a May payday in the Garden against Greb, now a battle-hardened, ten-year campaigner who, curiously enough, had fought only a handful of times in New York and was becoming impatient to get a shot at a championship, even one with just an American tag. Doc Bagley respected the Pittsburgh boxer's extraordinary record, and had been impressed when Greb made a recent and rare Garden appearance to unanimously outpoint clever Tommy Gibbons – a future Dempsey challenger. Still, he was convinced that Harry's flailing style would be tailormade for the much bigger, heavier and more skilful Tunney.

At that time, Doc Bagley's team worked at Billy Grupp's gym at 116th Street and Eighth Avenue, an establishment frequented by most of the leading New York fighters. But Grupp preached anti-Semitism when he hit the bottle, as he often did, and many of his most prominent clients were Jewish. And when the lightweight hero Benny Leonard persuaded the Jewish faction to train elsewhere, Bagley and Tunney joined the general exodus. First stop was Marshall Stillman's small gym in Harlem, which was run by a gentleman called Lou Ingber who knew or cared little about boxing. Ingber, however, quickly realising the potential of having so many of the world's top fighters training at his joint, soon leased a far larger building on Eighth Avenue and, along the way, changed his name to Lou Stillman.

Tunney would never become a favourite with the Stillman regulars, but Bagley, a stooped, gaunt figure, was liked all round and recognised as a smart and conscientious manager and a terrific cornerman. Nobody questioned his judgement when he accepted Greb as an opponent – the guy was four inches shorter, at least 14lb lighter, and not much of a puncher. Everyone was aware that he was a ruthless ruffian, but Tunney was a big boy and could look after himself. Rickard, Bagley and Tunney were unanimous that his name would look good on Gene's record.

The Doc's forte was his brilliant work during those vital sixty seconds between rounds, and one of his pupils was a very young Ray Arcel who was proud just to carry the bucket and swing the towel. Talking to author Ronald K Fried, Arcel fondly recalled Bagley's unorthodox expertise when dealing with cuts. 'If the fella got a cut he'd take a piece of chewing tobacco out of his mouth and press it against the cut. I didn't know whether it was the pressure applied or whether it was the tobacco juice or whatever it was, but he was successful in stopping the cuts.'

Disgusting, and the only time Arcel tried to copy the maestro he swallowed a large chunk of tobacco, was violently sick and collapsed in the corner. The Doc would be forced to use up plenty of baccy when Greb got to grips with Tunney.

The man from Pittsburgh was a fighting freak, a natural middleweight who regularly tackled light heavyweights, and if the price was right was prepared to concede lumps of weight to good-class heavies. He was only three years older than the new American champion, but he had somehow managed to pack in an astounding 226 pro fights. And in those fights he had collected every illegal dodge ever known, and invented a few of his own.

Of Irish-German stock, Edward Henry Greb was born on June 6, 1894, the son of Pius and Annie. He had a strict upbringing and neither parent approved when, as a teenager, he started boxing around the local clubs; in fact, they totally rejected their son's chosen profession and never once saw him fight. They passed up plenty of opportunities.

The teenager had the last fight of his brief amateur career in May 1913, and before the end of the month he made his professional bow in Pittsburgh's Exposition Park, receiving the newspaper vote after a six-rounds no-decision against Frank Kirkwood. The Windmill had started turning and at a whirlwind rate. In the ring he was a relentless, non-stop bully; out of it he must have spent most of his time catching trains, bouncing from one venue to the next.

His diary for 1919 can only be described as astonishing. He boxed no fewer than 45 times – a grand total of 456 exhausting rounds – and not against bums or fairground fighters but against many of the best around – guys like a still-fresh Battling Levinsky,

Bill Brennan and Billy Miske (who would both challenge
Dempsey the following year), and future light heavy champion
Mike McTigue, and Mike Gibbons and the Zulu Kid . . . all
serious practitioners.

Almost all of those fights wound up as no-decisions, but
according to the most thorough examination of his record,
compiled by James E Cashman, Greb was awarded the newspaper
vote on every occasion. The newsboys liked to write that Harry
shunned training, could never be found in the gym. The truth was
that he was never out of condition; he was fighting so often there
was little need to punch bags in the gym.

Nothing seemed to derail this express. On August 29, 1921
the newspapers voted against him after ten rounds with Kid
Norfolk who enjoyed a 17½lb weight advantage. Of far more
importance, Greb sustained a detached retina following a
retaliatory Norfolk thumb to his right eye, which was useless for
the rest of his life. And yet just one week later he was back in the
ring, beating up Chuck Wiggins and taking a bite at Chuck's nose
for good measure.

Today, the tale of the eye seems hard to credit. How could a half-
blind fighter, even a great fighter, hold his own with such famous
names as Tunney and Tommy Loughran, Johnny Wilson, Jimmy
Slattery and Tiger Flowers? How did they not catch on? How could
Greb have passed even the most cursory medical examination? It all
sounds like so much malarkey from a newspaper corps which, in the
1920s, regularly played fast and loose with the facts, only . . . After
Harry's untimely death his personal physician, Dr Carl S
McGivern, confirmed that indeed the fighter had been blind in the
right eye following the Norfolk fight, and that he had recommended
having the eye removed. Greb had refused. The doc had no good
reason to spin such a story.

Greb's longtime manager Red Mason must have been in on the
secret, but the headstrong Harry seldom listened to advice that did
not suit, and actually, Mason was more of a booking agent, finding
the next date for his fighter. After Norfolk, Red arranged thirteen
bouts in the eight months before the match with Tunney. Greb
emerged on top in all of them, looking particularly good when he
pounded out the win over Gibbons in a sell-out Garden.

That was the start of Harry's charge towards a title. He could
still scale middleweight, but light heavy would do just as well, and

aside from Gene's American crown, the match was widely regarded as a final eliminator for Carpentier's championship. The Pittsburgh fighter was so confident of success that he had his manager try to bypass Rickard and open negotiations with the French camp while still preparing for Tunney. The ploy came to nothing, but the public shared his confidence, and on May 23 Harry was a hot favourite.

All of which meant nothing to the cool and collected Tunney who was sure he possessed the right tools, and who was totally unmoved by repeated warnings about Greb's bag of dirty tricks.

Just how rough was Harry Greb? Over the years, the stories of Harry's misdemeanours, his all-round thuggery inside the ropes, have taken on a life of their own. But the old maestro Arcel, who always tried to stick to the facts, was in no doubt that, 'Greb was great, but as great as he was, that's how dirty he was – all of the dirty tricks of the game.' And back then, the murky repertoire included biting, gouging, choking, back-handing, hitting low, using the laces, and even kicking. Apparently most referees were there only to make up the numbers, and Greb's only redeeming feature was that he did not squeal when an opponent repaid him in kind.

Forty seconds was all that it took for Gene Tunney to discover that he was sharing the ring with a wild man. Greb rushed straight from his corner at the opening bell, and at the first opportunity banged his head hard into Gene's nose. Tunney was badly shaken, his nose was broken in two places, and the first blood started to pump. He tried to regroup, tried to remember his boxing and his excellent straight left, but the smaller man swarmed all over him, launching an avalanche of punches from all angles. Greb was no heavy hitter, but his shots ripped and tore, and before the end of the round he had opened a deep gash over The Marine's left eye.

Returning to his corner, Tunney was already in a shocking state. Doc Bagley set to work with his chewing tobacco. The smart move would have been to retire right then on the stool, claiming the badly broken nose and the horribly cut eye were far too serious for Gene to continue. Few would have argued.

But Tunney had no thoughts of quitting, either early or late, and round after round as his nightmare continued he implored referee Kid McPartland not to intervene. And Bagley? He was ordered to keep quiet and do the best he could with the cuts.

There was more than one now. In the third, a ferocious Greb sliced open Gene's right eye and more blood spurted forth. At ringside, James R Fair wrote, 'The gore was so thick on Greb's gloves that he had to step back and hold them out so the referee could wipe them off with a towel.'

These were the only times that Harry took a backward step all night. But the one-eyed Windmill did not have to look far for his opponent. Because of the blood, Tunney was having trouble seeing his tormentor, and his burst nose was causing severe breathing problems, but still he stood his ground. He kept throwing his textbook left, kept trying for a quick finish with his right, and his sheer bravery might have discouraged a lesser man.

But this was Harry Greb. Doc Bagley would have required cement rather than tobacco to close the cuts, but somehow he managed to clean up his fighter for the start of every round. Within seconds, however, Greb would undo all his work, grabbing Tunney behind the head with one hand and bludgeoning him with the other. The crowd howled in protest, but McPartland warned him only once, and Harry looked as if he might take a swing at the blood-stained referee. He boasted phenomenal stamina and there was no way he would get tired – or tire of using Tunney for target practice.

'He cares nothing at all for the rules and regulations,' declared *The New York Sun*. 'He has two active hands that fly around in all sorts of weird motions, but the top of his head is his most dangerous weapon. If the rules of boxing were strictly enforced, Greb wouldn't last a round without being disqualified.'

Under today's conditions Greb certainly would have been thrown out early, or the slaughter would have been halted long before halfway on medical grounds. There were cries from the ringside for McPartland to step in, but the majority of the Garden crowd had been seduced by Gene's heroism: in the last blood-splattered rounds they were willing him to defy the villain for the full trip, and a tremendous roar greeted the final bell, almost as if the local boy had won. But the hoisting of Greb's arm was a mere formality.

Swathed in stained towels, Tunney's legs managed to carry him through the applauding fans to the mournful quiet of his dressing room, where he collapsed from exhaustion and loss of blood. Estimates measured the loss in quarts rather than pints.

Many who filed out of the old Garden, hip flasks and emotions drained, were convinced that they had seen the last of the boy from Greenwich Village. A game, talented kid, sure, but no way could he recover from that awful battering. Tunney's parents, always supportive, but never at ease with his chosen profession, now wanted him to retire.

Years later, Tunney remembered, 'I was so busted up I couldn't go home for a couple of weeks after the fight. I didn't want them to see me looking like that.'

He did not, however, go into hiding. On the second day after the massacre, he somehow found the strength to match his will, and despite looking like the survivor of a plane wreck, he turned up at the athletic commission offices – not to protest about Greb's foul tactics or the lenient referee, but to lodge a $2,500 bond to secure a return fight. Writer Grantland Rice was a witness at the commission office and described Gene as looking like the victim of a razor assault.

After declaring his intentions, Tunney headed off for the quiet of the countryside where he rested in bed for a week, allowing his wounds to heal, pondering over where he had gone wrong. No self-pity, no self-doubt. Despite the pain-filled humiliation, he was still certain that he could make it all the way to the very top. And, we must remember, Gene Tunney was no self-deluding mug.

He possessed a fortitude granted to only a precious few. Just over six weeks later, his cuts healed, his nose fixed, he returned to the ring, boxing a no-decision with Fay Keiser in Rockaway, New York. And eight fights later – on February 23, 1923 – he was back in the Garden, back in nightmare alley, with the same merciless mugger weighing him up from the opposite corner.

Greb's American championship was growing in importance. Three weeks earlier in the Garden he had scored a unanimous decision, defending against the highly regarded Philadelphia stylist, Tommy Loughran, and a challenge to Carpentier was put on hold when the Frenchman opted for a cosy defence in Paris, facing an eccentric from Senegal whose ring name was Battling Siki. Bad career move for Georges, but by that time most Americans were convinced that the best 175lb fighters were to be found at home.

Since the first fight Tunney had made a significant change in personnel. Bagley and his baccy had been replaced by a new manager, Billy Gibson, an extremely astute character who also took care of Benny Leonard. Gibson fired the opening shots in the lead-up to the return with a letter to *The New York Journal*: 'It is a matter of public knowledge that Greb is a flagrantly foul boxer. I am requesting the state athletic commission to take special note.'

An outraged Red Mason protested that Gibson was attempting to influence the officials. As if! Commission chairman William Muldoon, an authoritarian old buffer, strangely enough found nothing wrong with Greb's past ring antics, and guaranteed Mason that he would get a fair shake. Rickard did not require these exchanges to fill his house: the Garden was a sell-out days before fight night. A big support arrived in town from Pittsburgh with money to wager but Tunney was not friendless in the betting, and at the ringside the odds favoured Greb, but only at 8/5 on.

Before the action got underway, Harry was up to his tricks, trying to score some points over not only Tunney but also referee Patsy Haley, regarded at that time as the top ref in the state. As, centre ring, Haley tried to issue the customary instructions, warnings, and pleas for fair play, the champion argued about what he could do and what he could not do, several times manhandling Tunney as he allegedly sought clarification. The crowd booed, Tunney remained unruffled.

As ever, The Windmill started fast, swarming into the attack and Gene countered with hard rights to the body. This was a new tactic suggested by Benny Leonard when the pair trained together in camp at Red Bank, New Jersey, and it proved a masterstroke. By the end of the fifth, Greb's left side was red and angry, and when he did get in close, he discovered that Gene had found some tricks of his own. Harry maintained the furious gallop, but Tunney had learned so much from their first meeting, and by the twelfth, Greb was scrapping desperately and fouling more openly than ever.

Eventually, a frustrated Haley halted the action to remonstrate with the Pittsburgh fighter who, instead of looking suitably chastened, shaped to take a swing at the ref as he angrily protested his innocence.

The fight was still on a knife-edge, and in round thirteen it was Tunney's turn to draw a warning for some choice work inside, but The Marine still had plenty of ammunition, and in the penultimate round, he launched the fiercest attack of the fight, rocking Harry with terrific rights to both head and body. Harry's ribs had taken a pounding all evening, now Tunney was testing his chin. Another great right landed flush, almost dropping Greb, but as the crowd screamed for the payoff the Pittsburgh battler kept swinging, and somehow remained upright to the bell.

But he was spent and had to stand up under another battering for almost the entire three minutes of the last. That final rally made Gene the victor on two cards, and the majority of the fans and the newspapers agreed with the verdict. Not Red Mason, who naturally screamed robbery.

The merit of Tunney's win, the courage required even to face Greb a second time, cannot be overstated. Yet he celebrated the win calmly, as if it were no more than he always expected, and he was prepared to give Harry as many chances as he wished to put matters beyond argument. Before the end of the year, they met again in the Garden, and this time the decision was unanimous; the following year they boxed a no-decision in Cleveland, and in 1925 in St Paul Gene broke two of Harry's ribs when readily getting the better of another no-decision. That was the convincer, and they went their separate ways.

Tunney was going only one way – up in weight, and up in ambition. Dempsey was now in his sights, and at last Rickard believed he could make a credible opponent. Even the fact that the champ was banned in New York – for failure to defend against Harry Wills – did not deter Tex.

On September 23, 1926 Rickard took the fight to the Sesquicentennial Stadium in Philadelphia, attracting a crowd of 120,000 who forked out $1,895,733 to see Gene clearly outpoint The Mauler. A Tunney right almost did for Jack in the opening round, and only grit kept the woefully rusty legend on his feet for the full ten. Just as he had planned, the boy from Greenwich Village was the heavyweight champ, but overnight he turned into a public enemy.

Dempsey had always been the bad guy, the so-called draft dodger who was booed into the ring and roasted by the press. Now the newspapers changed tack, and a huge wave of sympathy for the ex-champ swept the land. Tunney? He was the snooty social climber who hobnobbed with highbrows like Hemingway and George Bernard Shaw.

So unfair, but just a month after his triumph the fans let him know how they felt. Attending a promotion in the Garden, both

Dempsey and Tunney were introduced in the ring: Jack received a boisterous ovation; Gene was barracked and heckled by his fellow New Yorkers. An embarrassed and angry Dempsey told the press, 'That was an outrage! I felt just as badly as Gene did.' Tunney stayed silent.

But that inexplicable and disgraceful reception most likely prompted him to earn as much as he could in the fastest possible time and then quit the business. He had only two more fights, but, boy, were they earners!

Rickard upped his ringside prices to $40 for the return, and this time the gate in Soldier's Field, Chicago, zoomed to an astronomical $2,658,660. On September 22, 1927 Tunney retained his title on points, but not before he survived the infamous long count in the seventh.

Dempsey dropped Gene with a two-fisted flurry, but he was slow going to a neutral corner; referee Dave Barry played it by the book and four seconds had elapsed before he picked up the count. Could Tunney have risen before ten? Catch the film and make up your own mind. What is certain is that Gene recovered brilliantly to pound Dempsey throughout the last three rounds, and was a decisive winner.

Controversy over the count caused Tunney's stock to plummet below zero, but he consoled himself with a cheque from Rickard for $990,000 – more than a year's wages plus bonuses for the then world's highest-paid executive, movie mogul Louis B Mayer. The following year, he made his farewell appearance, when on July 26, 1928 he beat up the outclassed New Zealander, Tom Heeney, in eleven rounds. This time his fee was $525,000 and Rickard dropped a bundle on the promotion. Sadly Tex never got the opportunity to recoup, dying six months later in Florida.

Gene now had other ambitions. The newspapers had got wind of his romance with Polly Lauder, a wealthy socialite and the grandniece of steel magnate Andrew Carnegie, but Tunney was too nimble for them and took off to Europe where he met the Prince of Wales in London and Eamon De Valera in Dublin before heading for Italy where he planned to get married. The world's press massed in Rome for the big event, and on October 3, 1928 the couple were wed, but not before a near riot when Gene barred all photographers and reporters from the bash. The newlyweds remained in Italy for a year until the fuss died down, then they settled in Connecticut where they raised three boys and a daughter – son John becoming a US senator.

Wealthy and successful in business, Tunney lived to be 81, dying on November 7, 1978. He could be seen ringside for the special fights, followed the sport quite closely, and over the years his fellow New Yorkers finally forgave him for beating Dempsey. No more than he deserved.

Wild-man Harry Greb did not enjoy similar good fortune. Between the second and third matches with Tunney, he scaled down to middleweight and won the world title on August 31, 1923, outpointing Johnny Wilson. There is no doubt that he was at his best at 160lb, and he made six successful defences, the most memorable being a unanimous decision over the great welter champ Mickey Walker before 50,000 fans in the Polo Grounds.

That was the fight made even more memorable when the participants met up later in a nightclub, enjoyed a few bottles of champagne together, then started arguing over who fouled who earlier on. The debate was taken outside, and Walker always claimed that he came out on top in the street fight. Just another typical Greb story, and Harry provided the Broadway hacks with plenty. But Nat Fleischer, for one, insisted that the tales of Harry's drinking and womanising were often greatly exaggerated to get his name in the papers, and masked a deadly serious pro. Perhaps.

Greb's eye problems grew worse. The sight in his left eye deteriorated, and in February 1926 he lost his championship on a split decision to Tiger Flowers. On August 19, 1926 The Pittsburgh Windmill fought his last fight, again dropping a split verdict to Flowers in the Garden.

Two weeks after attending the first Tunney–Dempsey clash in Philadelphia, Harry was injured quite badly in a car crash. Shortly after, on October 22, 1926, he underwent an operation on his nose in Atlantic City, but went into cardiac arrest and suffered a cerebral haemorrhage. He was 32.

New champion Gene Tunney was the chief pallbearer at his funeral. After 299 pro bouts, this was the only time that an opponent carried Harry Greb.

CHAPTER EIGHT

Dick Tiger *v* Joey Giardello

THURSDAY, OCTOBER 21, 1965

At first glance, a streetwise Brooklyn-born tough guy and a proud Nigerian tribesman would make the most unlikely soulmates. But Carmine Orlando Tilelli, who – so the story goes – borrowed Joey Giardello's birth certificate in order to become an under-age soldier, and Richard Ihetu, who was unveiled to Lagos fight fans as Dick Tiger, were blood brothers, united by a remarkable self-belief that saw them shrug off life's heaviest punches and keep coming back for more.

That they both won world championships says as much for their incredible tenacity as their undoubted talent, and there must have been countless occasions when the best-intentioned advice was to quit and find a real job. Very early on, Tiger's career barely beat the count after a nightmare start to his English campaign during a cold, wet and miserable Liverpool winter; and Giardello was a battle-scarred veteran in his sixteenth professional year when, finally, he won the world title.

How appropriate that Joey should win his belt from Tiger; just as fitting that the Nigerian should gain revenge in the rematch. Over the years, these two middleweights had earned one another's respect, battling for survival in a red-hot 160lb division, made even more cut-throat by the insatiable demands of the television networks who, every week, expected yet another ring classic to satisfy the fans and the sponsors.

Tiger and Giardello were old acquaintances long before they first boxed for the championship. Four years earlier, in 1959, they had fought twice, Tiger winning in Chicago, Giardello getting the vote in Cleveland just over a month later. That is how it was back then: a defeat did not signal banishment from the airwaves just as long as the fight had been entertaining, and Joey and Tiger seldom failed to deliver. But there were few easy gigs, and for the most part the opposition was equally motivated and almost as talented.

There were so many rivals, common to both of them. Tough guys like Rory Calhoun and Holly Mims, smart operators like Wilf Greaves, Henry Hank and Spider Webb, and champions and future champions like Terry Downes and Gene Fullmer. And the form lines were impossible to chart. Giardello might outpoint Calhoun who would go on to beat and draw with Tiger. But the Nigerian had beaten up Terry Downes who, in turn, handled Joey quite comfortably. Different styles . . . different nights . . . different moods . . . different fights. No risk of the television dough drying up as long as the defeats did not become a habit and the fans remained happy.

But Giardello, in particular, was anything but happy. True, he was never short of work, but he could not get near the important purses and was even further away from a title shot. When Joey turned professional, Joe Louis still reigned as heavyweight champion; when, after 106 bouts, he finally found himself in the ring with NBA boss Gene Fullmer, Floyd Patterson was about to become the first heavyweight to win back the championship. Giardello had been made to serve his time.

After fifteen bitter, foul-filled rounds in Bozeman, Utah, the fight was called a draw, and Fullmer was still the champ. A furious and frustrated challenger might well have retired in disgust. But Joey was never a quitter.

Carmine Tilelli was born on July 16, 1930 in the Bedford-Stuyvesant neighbourhood of Brooklyn, but when he was only months old the family moved to a more upmarket address in Flatbush. Young Carmine enjoyed a stable upbringing, but he was a headstrong kid, frequently seeking out street battles and always ready to accept a dare. Perhaps that was why he found himself in the army at the ripe old age of fifteen. Urged on by a pal, he used the birth certificate of one Joey Giardello and enlisted – a move that would lead him circuitously to a lifetime in boxing.

The new Joey G soon discovered that being a member of the boxing squad at Fort Bragg, North Carolina, brought many perks. The boxers were treated to the best food, were excused regular duties to work out in the gym, and if they actually won a fight, then a three-day pass was of far more use than a cheap cup or a plaque. Joey earned plenty of passes as his natural aggression, allied to a quick grasp of the basics, made him a standout, and when he completed his army stint in 1948 he did not even sample the amateurs before turning professional.

He was now based in Philadelphia, and on October 2, 1948 he made his debut, stopping Johnny Noel in two rounds in Trenton, New Jersey. And going into the 1950s he extended his unbeaten sequence to eighteen before dropping an eight-rounder to Joe DiMartino in New Haven. He was on his way, but the enthusiastic teenager could never have dreamed that his trip would turn into a marathon. Especially as he was supposed to have the blessing of the mob.

Back then, however, it would have been far quicker to name the leading fighters who had absolutely no ties to organised crime. The bad guys seemed to be everywhere and their word was law. Some great champions like Graziano and Marciano were linked indirectly to mobsters throughout their careers yet somehow ducked the negative publicity. Others, like Giardello, were labelled mob fighters from the start and could never quite escape the stigma.

The International Boxing Club and its figurehead president, James Norris, were portrayed as boxing's major players in the 1950s. Multi-millionaire Norris had the contract to promote in the Garden, and as his family owned the Chicago Stadium, the St Louis Arena, the Detroit Olympia, and other prime venues across the country, he had excellent outlets to showcase boxing. Unfortunately, and very naively, he chose Frankie Carbo as a running mate. Bad, bad choice.

Paul John Carbo, a product of New York's tough East Side; a hoodlum implicated in several high-profile murders; eventually a prominent member of the Lucchese crime family; and the underworld's ambassador to the world of boxing. How he ever got close to a blueblood like Norris will forever remain a mystery, but the man they called Mr Gray never spurned an opportunity.

Back in the 1930s Carbo was introduced into the fight business by another racketeer, Gabe Genovese, who happened to manage the middleweight champion Babe Risko. Carbo was given a share of Risko's contract, and not long after he was making himself busy acquiring shares in many other contracts. Carbo preferred the friendly approach but he found the threat of a gun or a lead pipe equally persuasive. He controlled an increasing team of managers who, in turn, controlled the fighters, and though he tried to remain in the shadows, everybody knew the guy who decided who should fight in Norris's arenas.

Carbo's power was immense, but eventually all bad things must come to an end and in the late 1950s the law caught up with him and he was handed a 25-year sentence for trying to extort with force a share of the purses of welterweight champion Don Jordan. Around the same time the IBC failed to survive an investigation, being forced to disband because it was judged to be exercising a monopoly.

But when Giardello first crept into Nat Fleischer's *Ring* ratings in 1952, no two men wielded more influence in boxing than the millionaire and the mafioso. Fleischer must have been a ringside witness to much of the chicanery – the *Ring*'s offices were actually in the Garden building – but he never really took on the mob, seldom named names, preferring to paint the rosy picture.

Dan Parker had no such qualms. For years, the big, burly *New York Daily Mirror* columnist carried on a crusade against Carbo and his cohorts, and his frequent exposés did much to bring down the IBC. Over the years Parker built an impressive network of informants, all willing to grass on the bad guys, and he regularly featured in his articles such worthies as Hymie Wallman, Blinky Palermo and, on several occasions, a Philadelphia pal of Blinky's, a gentleman called Tony Ferrante. At that time Tony happened to manage a promising young middleweight called Joey Giardello.

Just how much clout had Ferrante? Not too much, in comparison to his friend, the notorious Palermo. In a 1971 interview with author Peter Heller, Joey recalled his September 1953 bout with Johnny Saxton, who would go on to win the welterweight championship the following year. 'Saxton, that was another phoney-baloney. That night I was robbed in my hometown, Philadelphia, because of Blinky Palermo. He bought the fight. One official gave it seven rounds even! I know I didn't lose it. I couldn't understand how that many rounds were even.'

But Giardello was getting close. In 1952 he twice outboxed the brilliant New York welter Billy Graham, and the result of their second fight – on December 19 – created a tremendous furore, which spilled over to the front pages and guaranteed both fighters priceless publicity.

Everybody agreed that the fight had been very close, Giardello getting a majority decision thanks to the votes of the referee and one judge. Shortly afterwards, however, the New York commissioners, Christenberry and Powell – without any authority – changed the card of judge Joe Agnello and declared Graham the winner. The Giardello team went ballistic and the dispute travelled as far as the New York Supreme Court who ruled that the commissioners were out of order. A big victory for Giardello, and by 1954 he was established as the leading contender for Bobo Olson's middleweight championship.

The 24-year-old was ready, manager Ferrante had okayed the contracts, and then Joey's world fell apart. Once more, he was on the front pages, and this time, all the publicity was horrendous.

Giardello had never been a saint, but he was wild and impetuous rather than wicked, and until 1954 he had no criminal record. His case was bizarre, senseless and provided the tabloids with some great headlines. Giardello had been injured in a car smash, and his career was temporarily on hold as he hobbled around on crutches. Out with some South Philly friends one evening, he became part of a dispute with a petrol-pump attendant who claimed that the fighter belted him with his crutch. A high-profile case, eventually a guilty verdict, and Joey was given a sentence of from six to eighteen months. He wound up serving four-and-a-half months in the grim Holmesburg Prison on the outskirts of Philadelphia, and would be missing from the ring for eleven months.

Aside from the traumatic effect on his wife Rosalie and his family, there was further trouble. While Giardello was inside, Ferrante lost his manager's licence for consorting with the wrong people, and Carmine Graziano took over. Giardello could easily have become a forgotten fighter, but thanks to his connections he was quickly back on television, back mixing it with the guys who barred his way to the title.

There were, however, worrying signs that he was slowing up, perhaps losing some of the spark that had once burned so brightly. The crisis came when he lost three important fights in a row – to quality middleweights, Joey Giambra, Spider Webb, and Tiger Jones – and then, to end his 1959 campaign, he shared the honours after two exciting and bruising encounters with the former Mr Ihetu, not long arrived in the States, and finding life quite hard.

The Mormon tough guy Gene Fullmer now held the title, and his connections were looking for a well-paid but relatively cosy defence on home ground. Manager Marv Jensen figured that Giardello would be the ideal opponent: thanks to television Joey was a familiar face, even in Utah, and having lost four of his last eight fights he was showing definite signs of wear. The fight was arranged for Bozeman on April 20, 1960, and the 29-year-old visitor was friendless in the betting.

Fullmer, a rugged, awkward practitioner with limitless stamina, was often as dangerous with his head or his elbows as he was with his fists. In the early rounds, despite frequent warnings from referee Harry Kessler, he dished out the full treatment, catching his challenger with a lowered head, following through with a forearm, getting lucky with an elbow. Fullmer was not a bad fellow: that was just the way he fought.

Joey, of course, was no angel, and he soon tired of being banged about. He replied in style, and dropping his head, he beat Fullmer to the butt, opening a gash on his forehead and from then on, the fight degenerated into an ugly brawl. The official verdict was a draw – clearly a moral victory for Giardello in Bozeman – but neither Joey nor his sizeable cheering section who had travelled from Philly were interested in moral victories.

The Philadelphia fans took out their frustration on the locals. Their favourite fighter fretted that he had blown his big chance and might never get another opportunity to become a champion; and for a spell, he seemed resigned to the idea. Giardello was outpointed in London by a future title-holder, Terry Downes; was outpointed again in Cologne by a former victim, Peter Mueller; was outpointed for the third time in a row by the fast-dancing Ralph Dupas in New Orleans. He was earning fair money and giving good value, but in the trade he was fast becoming known as a stepping stone, a decent name that could still mean something on a challenger's record.

He was by no means a lost cause, but he was not getting any younger and he always appeared to be just one or two fights away from that elusive title chance. Things began to look up: from 1961 to 1963 Joey got his act together, started winning more than he lost, and scored over leading middles like Wilf Greaves, Henry Hank and Jesse Smith. From somewhere, he had regained his enthusiasm, was training with his old zip, and that title fight was becoming a possibility – if he could beat Sugar Ray Robinson. Giardello had no doubts.

His old rival from Nigeria was now the proud holder of not only an MBE but also the middleweight belt, having placed Fullmer on his mantelpiece following three tough encounters. The ancient Sugar Ray was convinced that he still had the brain and the legs to beat Tiger, but the deal was that first he must beat Giardello. Joey's heavy connections were at last flexing their muscles, and Robinson was backed into a corner. Over the years, he had several times blanked a match with Giardello, mainly because of Joey's cute style, but this time he had no choice. On June 24, 1963, in his home base of Philadelphia, the 32-year-old gained huge satisfaction in winning a ten-rounds decision over the legend.

Tiger confirmed that he was glad to accommodate Giardello. The Nigerian recognised much of his own career in Joey's stop-start slog to the top, and believed him to be a worthy contender. That was how Tiger's mind worked. Of course, his management team was equally eager to defend against the Philadelphia veteran, but for less altruistic reasons. They figured that the challenger was a tired old man – even though he was actually eleven months younger than the champ! But Joey had been to war 123 times when they met in Atlantic City; Tiger's 63 pro appearances made him appear fresh in comparison

Giardello did not dwell on the reasons, only that he was being given a shot, and he handed all the credit to Dick. Like so many other fighters and trainers and managers who were lucky enough to cross this Tiger's path, Joey has only fond memories of the Nigerian.

A member of the Ibo tribe, Richard Ihetu was born on August 14, 1929 in Amaigbo, in the Orlu district of Nigeria. After school he worked as a farmhand, then as a caretaker, and he grew to a wide-shouldered and powerful 5ft 8″ with a liking for most sports. He began boxing as an amateur, but progress was not particularly fast, and he was a mature 23-year-old when he made his professional debut in October 1952, stopping Simon Eme in two rounds in Lagos.

The fashion in Nigeria was for the fighters to adopt colourful ring names, and so Richard Ihetu became known as Dick Tiger. And in the early 1950s, when Giardello was tackling such headliners as Harold Green, Gil Turner and Ernie Durando,

Tiger was learning the business against such notables as Easy Dynamite and the Koko Kid, Mighty Joe, Black Power, and Superhuman Power. In 1954 he won the national middleweight title, beating Tommy West, and he started thinking about a move to England where the wages would be better.

A huge gamble. Tiger was already married to Abigail, and would eventually father seven children, but his countryman, little Hogan Bassey, was doing well in Britain, and a Lagos-based English salesman called Jack Farnsworth was convinced that the middleweight could be equally successful. Farnsworth, who founded the Nigerian boxing commission, arranged for Tiger to train with Peter Banasko in Liverpool, and Tony Vairo, a leading light on the then bustling Mersey boxing scene, became his manager.

But The Tiger had arrived during a cold, wet English winter, and he had forgotten to bring a coat! The food was strange, the locals difficult to understand, he missed his wife, and his crude ring style had few admirers. Victories over Black Power, or even Superhuman Power, had not prepared him for the more technically aware English boxers.

He was in trouble, and he lost his first four fights, all on points against workmanlike opposition. The best that could be said for him was that he was brave and willing. How tempting it must have been to grab the first boat back to Abigail and his friends! But as the weather improved so did his form. He started winning some bouts, including confidence-boosting victories over Alan Dean and Jimmy Lynas who had beaten him early on. But his big break came in May 1957 when a brash young matchmaker called Mickey Duff made an uncharacteristic blunder, and booked Tiger to box the highly regarded Terry Downes at London's atmospheric Shoreditch Town Hall.

Duff went on to become one of the most powerful figures in British boxing, and Downes did not do too badly either. But that night, they seriously underestimated the Nigerian, who dropped Terry three times, closed his eyes and opened a cut across the bridge of his nose, forcing a stoppage at the end of round six. Tiger got paid just £60, but now he was a name and not just an opponent.

Working in a paint factory to augment his ring earnings, the Nigerian sent home as much as he could afford to Abigail, and following the win over Downes the purses started to improve; in fact they almost became decent after he stopped Pat McAteer to win the British Empire championship in March 1958. But neither in nor out of the ring was life easy, and the dangerous American imports, Spider Webb and Randy Sandy, both outpointed him, though he would gain speedy revenge over Sandy. Another dramatic career switch was on the cards.

Despite the fact that he was a 29-year-old, there was a small but loyal band of supporters who were convinced that Tiger could go to America and win the middleweight championship. The latest trainer, Maurice Foran, had refined his style, but he would not learn the art of body punching properly until he reached the States; Merseyside bookmaker Harry Ormesher was another fan, always there to provide financial backing when required; Hogan Bassey was a constant source of inspiration, especially after he became world featherweight champion in 1957; and, of course, there was Abigail.

Mrs Ihetu made a rare ringside appearance when Tiger lost to Sandy in Liverpool, and she may have been the one to convince her husband that he could just as well send home dollars from the US as pounds from England. After the second Sandy bout, Tiger never boxed again in Britain.

Kid Bassey recommended an American manager, the veteran Jersey Jones, who for a lifetime had boxed, then trained and managed, and also wrote about his sport. Jones was one of the good guys, as was his trainer, Jimmy August, who was respected coast to coast for his calm work in the corner. Tiger had excellent back-up, but once again he was slow in acclimatising.

He made his American debut in the Garden on June 5, 1959, but could only scrape a draw with Rory Calhoun who beat him in the rematch; he won, then lost to Giardello; and in 1960 in Edmonton he lost, then regained his Empire title in two good earners against Canadian Wilf Greaves. He was gathering an enthusiastic television following, and even at his advanced age he was still improving, still learning new moves under Jones and August. But he needed some major scalps, and after defeating Greaves he finally delivered, beating leading contenders like Spider Webb and Hank Casey, Billy Pickett, Henry Hank and Florentino Fernandez. He was on a roll and was now the foremost challenger for Fullmer's title.

The hardcase champ had fought them all, from Sugar Ray to Basilio to Giardello, and although he had soaked up plenty along the way, he was still considered to be in prime condition following an unbeaten 1961 when he earned top dollar defending against Robinson, Fernandez and the ill-fated Benny Paret. But on October 23, 1962, at Candlestick Park in San Francisco, age and a mean machine called Dick Tiger caught up with him, and after fifteen rounds the Nigerian was a convincing winner.

Fullmer did far better in the Las Vegas return – a hectic encounter which saw both men battered and bloodied – and only a late Tiger rally earned him a draw. A very close call, but seven months later, fighting before his own people in the Liberty Stadium in Ibadan, an inspired Tiger set the record straight, hammering Fullmer so severely that the Mormon's corner withdrew their man at the end of the seventh.

Fullmer never fought again, but an extraordinary ovation from 35,000 Nigerians helped ease the pain. A triumphant Tiger received an even greater reception, and now he felt free to give Joey Giardello the okay to step forward and take his best shot.

On December 7, 1963, in the Convention Hall in Atlantic City, Tiger and Giardello, old foes yet old friends, met for the third time. The 3/1 odds against Joey suggested that the champion was only doing an old pal a favour, only providing one last decent payday before the curtain came down. A focused Giardello did not worry about the odds.

He had waited too long, had been kidded and conned too many times to slip up now. This fight was not about betting or even about money, but about achieving the impossible dream. And not so impossible. Back in 1959 in Cleveland he had worked out a way to beat this guy, and the fans were forgetting that he was actually younger than the champ! He had done his work in the gym and on the roads, and now all he needed was for his 33-year-old legs to behave themselves through a fast fifteen rounds. Joey did not plan to loiter too long in any one spot.

From the opening bell the challenger was on his toes, jabbing and moving, circling, jabbing again, timing his counters, seldom letting Tiger get close enough to land his sapping body shots, grabbing him tight when the African did succeed in reaching the danger zone. From the Philadelphia angle, Giardello was fighting the perfect fight, using all the right moves to frustrate a champion who had never been too nimble, and avoiding any wild exchanges that might land him in trouble. But Tiger supporters could only see a robbery in progress, as the artful dodger thieved the points and ran away from an increasingly incensed champion.

This was not how a man was supposed to become a champion. Joey had been given his big break because Tiger had respected him, but he refused to stand and fight like a true contender. Round after round, Giardello hit and moved, feinted, kidded, held when he had to. His legs never threatened to betray him.

At the final bell, the Philadelphia fans hoisted their hero aloft when the solitary judge, referee Paul Cavalier, deciding that crime did pay, voted 8–5–2 in favour of Joey. Tiger was disgusted, but at least he could console himself with the prospect of a return. Giardello was in wonderland.

He told Peter Heller, '. . . that was the greatest moment. I don't think I'll ever feel like that. You can't explain it. It isn't that I was fighting three years and I won the title. This was a long time coming.'

Joey was determined to repay Tiger and give him his shot, but his connections decided that there would be more money and less risk defending against Rubin Carter, the much-hyped Hurricane. They were correct on both counts: despite the claims in Carter's movie that he was robbed against Giardello, the official scores suggest a different script – 72–66, 71–66, 70–67, all for Joey. And to keep up the pressure for a return, Tiger also took on Carter and beat him. After that, Giardello insisted that the Nigerian must be next in line.

Thursday, October 21, 1965 was an extra-special date for Giardello. Not only was he making a second defence of his 160lb belt, but he was celebrating a long-awaited return to the Garden. Not long after his spell in the pokey, Giardello stopped boxing in New York, apparently because his managers could not acquire a licence. His last appearance had been spectacularly brief: a one-round knockout over Tony Baldoni in July 1956; now, nine years later, he was back in the Garden, but he anticipated a long night this time.

Giardello's preparation had been poor. Between fights he had always enjoyed the good life, often allowing his weight to soar to a soft and sloppy 185lb, but as he grew older he found shedding the excess extremely difficult. Preparing for Tiger, his reducing turned into torture, and in the countdown days he was on a starvation diet to make 160lb.

A noisy crowd of 17,064 piled into the Garden to welcome Joey home and to say hello once again to The Tiger, who was as popular in the big top as any hard-punching hero from the East Side. The betting market was volatile, unsure which of the old men had more left in the tank, but they did not have to wait long for the answer.

The Nigerian usually started at a snail's pace, but not this time. He came out fast, banging with both hands to head and body, crowding a surprised Giardello back on to the ropes. The champion tried to grab, tried to stall, but Tiger was too strong and referee Johnny Lo Bianco kept busy breaking the fighters. Which was bad news for Joey: he was going to get no rest inside.

Two years had passed since their last fight, but for Giardello it must have seemed like a lifetime. The split-second timing which had driven Tiger mad in Atlantic City had deserted him; his jabs fell short; he was easy to find with hooks; and, most serious of all, there was lead in the legs that had performed so well when he took the title.

But if he could dance no more, he could still fight – like a champion. In the fifth he tossed three great lefts which hurt the African and temporarily halted his charge. And in the seventh, after being swamped by a Tiger attack, he battled back bravely, scoring with vicious hooks that might have swung the balance against a weaker opponent. Joey was good enough and game enough to win some rounds; but he was no longer spry enough or strong enough to win the fight.

The last three rounds were simply a tribute to his tenacity. 'If my corner so much as made a remark about quitting, I'd have fired them all on the spot,' he said later. 'I'm no Liston: I never thought of quitting. They'd have to carry me out of the ring before I'd quit.'

The fans were delighted he had lasted the distance and had not been badly hurt. And the official scores – 9–5–1, 8–6–1, 10–5 – were far from embarrassing.

During the next two years, Giardello tip-toed into retirement, boxing four more times, losing twice, but signing off with a points win over Jack Rodgers in Philadelphia on November 6, 1967. He finished with a career record of 100 victories from 133 fights against the very best over two decades. With money in the bank, he settled surprisingly well into civilian life. Based in Cherry Hill, New Jersey, he and Rosalie brought up four sons, and dedicated much of their time and energy to raising funds for the local St John of God's school for retarded children. Not bad for the so-called streetwise tough guy.

For Dick Tiger, however, some of the greatest and grimmest battles still lay ahead. Though he lost his 160lb title to Emile Griffith in his first defence, the old man continued to confound in the ring. On December 16, 1966, aged 37, he finally stepped up to light heavy, and caused a major upset when he outfought, outboxed and took the championship from Jose Torres in the Garden. Their rematch was much closer, but the amazing Nigerian was still champion when he agreed to a defence against the intimidating Bob Foster in May 1968.

Foster was nine years younger, seven inches taller, and had a considerable reach advantage. He was also a ferocious puncher, and though he experienced some rocky moments early on, a right uppercut-left hook combination poleaxed the African in round four. The Tiger's champion days were finally over, but now he was fighting battles on all fronts.

Back home, there was increasing civil unrest, sparking off several massacres. On May 30, 1967 the Ibo leader, Colonel Odumegwu Ojukwu, announced the secession of the Eastern Region of Nigeria and proclaimed its independence as the Republic of Biafra. Tiger was an Ibo, now he was a Biafran, and he was going to pay dearly.

His properties – paid for by all those hard battles in Liverpool and London and fight clubs throughout the States – were confiscated, but he still managed to finance a transport plane packed with food and medicine for his starving Biafrans. Though he was now 40, he continued to box, believing that his purses might make a difference back home. That he was able to concentrate on training was quite remarkable; that he was still able to beat men like Nino Benvenuti was almost beyond belief.

After losing his title to Foster, Tiger fought four times, winning three before being outpointed by his old rival Griffith in the Garden on July 15, 1970. There was now no reason to box on, because earlier in the year – in January – Colonel Ojukwu had announced the Biafran surrender. All Tiger wanted to do was return home and help his family and friends survive the terrible hardships. But the Nigerian authorities would not allow him back into the country.

He found work as a security guard in New York, but a pain in his side which he had first noticed before the second Griffith fight began to get worse, and he was diagnosed as suffering from advanced liver cancer. There was no hope of a cure.

The Nigerian government now changed its mind, and in 1971 Tiger was allowed to return home to live out his final days with his family. Visitors from all over the country made the pilgrimage to pay tribute to the great man . . . but only for six months. Richard Ihetu died on December 14, 1971, aged 42.

Joey Giardello once said that he would have to be carried out of the ring before he would quit. Dick Tiger never felt the need to express similar sentiments.

CHAPTER NINE

Ken Buchanan
v Ismael Laguna

MONDAY, SEPTEMBER 13, 1971

In a sport which all too often exposes a sleazy underbelly, offering a soft target for its battalions of relentless detractors, the International Boxing Hall Of Fame has been welcomed as one of the brighter ideas helping the business to combat its tawdry image. No doubt that was not the founders' original intention, but every June for the past thirteen years the village of Canastota in New York state has hosted a three-day gala where former greats and fans from all over the world mingle in a grand celebration of their sport, and the wonderful vibes generated have proved priceless PR for boxing around the globe.

For some of the fighters the gathering brings an opportunity to embrace and reminisce with old rivals; for others the buzz comes from being recognised once again, being in demand for autographs and pictures. And, as we shall see, an invitation to Canastota totally reshaped the life of at least one former world champion.

Situated 20 miles east of Syracuse, Canastota, with a population of around 5,000, might seem an unlikely setting for a shrine to world boxing, but the village claims a proud heritage, dating right back to the days of the bareknuckles when it was a bustling stop-off for the barges on the Erie Canal. Canastota can also boast of two former world champions, the lionhearted welter and middleweight great, Carmen Basilio, and his nephew Billy Backus who also won the 147lb belt. And it was to pay tribute to those local heroes that the concept was first born.

In 1982 two residents, Joe Bonaventura and Farrell Miller, decided that something should be done to commemorate the deeds of Basilio and Backus. They raised $30,000 from local businesses to construct a building to showcase memorabilia from the careers of the champs. The structure, with its tall picture windows and overhanging roof, was dedicated in 1984, and was to prove the springboard for a much more ambitious project.

Now known as Boxing Hall Of Fame Inc, with another local fight buff, Edward Brophy, as executive director, the group set about building a museum to honour the sport worldwide, and thanks to state grants, generous local backing, guarantees from collectors to supply memorabilia, and a great deal of hard work, the dream became a reality. Most important, there would also be a Hall Of Fame in which boxing's legendary names would be recognised and remembered for all time.

The Hall is divided into four categories: Modern; Old-Timer; Pioneer; Non-Participant, and is annually updated by a carefully selected panel of boxing experts, historians and writers from all over the world.

In June 2000 Ken Buchanan from Scotland was inducted; the following year came the turn of Panama's Ismael Laguna to join the chosen few. Thirty years earlier those two fine lightweights, in the bedlam that was Madison Square Garden, had punched one another to the point of total exhaustion. Their efforts had not been forgotten.

For Buchanan in particular, the long trip to Canastota was a crowning reward for a lifetime of battling the odds. He had been a true champion, thrilling ringsiders not only in the Garden, where he appeared six times, but in cities all over the world . . . a great draw everywhere, bar his home country. He had been forced to travel abroad to earn his living and win his titles. In the year 2000 he returned to the States to reinvent himself.

Kenny Buchanan was born on June 28, 1945 and raised on a working class council estate on the outskirts of Edinburgh. He never knew the desperate poverty of the young Roberto Duran or countless other future champions but, like everyone in the neighbourhood, the Buchanans had to be careful with their cash. They were, however, a close-knit family – father Tommy, mother Cathy, and a younger brother, Alan, who would also box pro. A stable home life, but on the streets and at school the young Ken was a terror, forever in punch-ups. Sooner or later, he was sure to discover boxing.

It was sooner, much sooner. When he was eight, a visit to the cinema with his father to see a movie called *The Joe Louis Story* made an extraordinary impression on the little boy, and for the next few days he badgered his dad to take him to a boxing club. Because of Ken's age, Buchanan Sr had reservations, but eventually he relented and the pair went along to the Sparta Club, one of the top outfits in Edinburgh.

There are many youngsters who flirt with the notion of a boxing career . . . the glamour, the money. But most are quickly disillusioned by the hard graft and discipline, or are waylaid in their teens by more attractive pursuits. Not Buchanan. From his first day at the Sparta, the tiny tot lived and breathed boxing.

He served his apprenticeship as a carpenter, but by then, his classic left hand had made him one of the foremost amateurs in Scotland. At seventeen, he was boxing in the highly competitive European championships in Moscow; two years later he was the ABA featherweight champion and also a bronze medallist at the Europeans, held in East Berlin. There was never any question but that Buchanan would turn professional, and now the family decided the time was right.

There were plenty of offers. Former British featherweight champion Bobby Neill was the front-runner to become his manager. Neill also hailed from Edinburgh, and now based in London, he had the connections to move a young fighter. But he wanted to alter Buchanan's style, which many in the trade reckoned too upright and amateur for the more rigorous professional game, and an affronted Buchanan decided to shop elsewhere. Already he was showing the tough, independent streak that would serve him so well in the ring, but create much friction outside the ropes.

Eventually, he signed with Eddie Thomas, a one-time British, Empire, and European welterweight champion, who counted the brilliant American, Billy Graham, among his victims. The bluff Welshman was enjoying great success managing the featherweight wizard, Howard Winstone, and having Winstone as a gym mate was the major persuader. But there was one serious drawback in joining up with Thomas: Eddie was at loggerheads with the team who called the shots in London – Mickey Duff, Harry Levene,

Mike Barrett and Jarvis Astaire – and bigtime exposure was always going to be difficult. In fact, all but impossible.

Buchanan made his debut on September 20, 1965, stopping Brian Tonks at the National Sporting Club, whose headquarters were at the plush Café Royal in Piccadilly. Some culture shock for the youngster. The NSC members enforced a strict dress code, remained silent during the rounds, and wined, dined, and puffed on large cigars while the boxers slugged it out in the ring. In reality, private club boxing belongs to another age, but Ken was to get to know the curious atmosphere all too well.

Sporting Club wages were basic and the media coverage sketchy, as the bouts did not take place until late, after the members had eaten their fill. People in the business were aware of the Edinburgh lightweight's unbeaten progress, but to sports fans at large he remained a secret.

Occasionally, Buchanan would be given an opportunity on a public promotion, like on the August Saturday in 1966 when he outpointed tough Ivan Whiter at London's vast Earl's Court. But even then he drew scant attention, because topping the bill that night was none other than Muhammad Ali, defending his heavyweight title against an outclassed Brian London. And even after he stopped Maurice Cullen in eleven rounds to become the British lightweight champion on February 19, 1968, his polished performance caused scarcely a ripple.

Buchanan was a champion, but after extending his unbeaten sequence to 33, he found himself still appearing before the winers and the diners. He was disgusted: so disillusioned with Thomas's inability to secure him worthwhile purses that he wrote to the Board Of Control, asking to be released from his contract, at the same time sending back his Lonsdale Belt. Desperate measures, but it is extremely unlikely that Ken could have walked away from boxing for good. He was, however, now married to Carol, and his earnings were well below the young couple's expectations. Thomas feared that Tommy Buchanan, who worked in the corner, planned to manage his son, and the rift grew wider.

A family tragedy reunited the boxer and his manager. In October 1969 Cathy Buchanan died, an all-too-young 51, and her distraught son shook hands with Thomas at the funeral. They would never be best mates, but they resolved to work together to win a world championship.

The first step was a shot at the vacant European title against the Spaniard, Miguel Velasquez, in Madrid: the beginning of Ken's travels, and also his first defeat. The decision after a hard fifteen rounds may have been of the hometown variety but the confusion over Buchanan's weight certainly did not help. In his auto-biography, the boxer blamed the blunder on a test weigh-in on a faulty set of scales – supplied by Eddie.

A defeat, but far from a disaster, and three winning fights later Ken received a call from London promoter Jack Solomons, offering him a September world title shot in Puerto Rico against the classy two-time champion, Ismael Laguna. Buchanan was ecstatic, unworried about fighting far from home and going in a big outsider.

Solomons no longer wielded the massive power that he had enjoyed from the early 1940s through to the mid 1960s, having been squeezed out gradually by his younger rivals. But he had developed an interest in Buchanan's career, had been one of the loudest protesters in Madrid after the controversial Velasquez verdict, and still retained impressive international contacts.

One of those old pals was a veteran American operator called Bill Daly, an affable gentleman, equally at his ease with the leading New York columnists or the city's top mob representatives, all the way up to Frank Carbo. His relationship with Solomons stretched back over twenty years to the time when the pair made a bundle from two fights in London between the heavyweights Bruce Woodcock and Lee Savold, and as late as 1963 Daly's world lightweight champion, Carlos Ortiz, won a ten-rounder against Maurice Cullen on a Solomons promotion at Wembley.

Now Daly, thanks to his association with Ortiz, was a major player in Puerto Rico with a particular interest in the lightweight division. Ortiz had lost his title to Laguna in Panama City in April 1965, but had regained the belt seven months later on home territory in San Juan. Laguna had lost the decider in New York in 1967, but now Carlos was retired and Ismael was once again the champ after stopping Mando Ramos in Los Angeles.

Daly had first call on the champion's services, and the word from Solomons to Buchanan was that the Panamanians were looking for an easy defence. Perhaps. More likely, the crafty old-timers were doing one another a favour, and were going to earn a few bucks, no matter who won.

Certainly Solomons would have been aware that the odds would be heavily stacked against the Scot in the sizzling heat of San Juan, but he knew also that Buchanan's grim determination guaranteed that he would be a severe test for any fighter, even a world champion. And as for Laguna wanting an easy defence? That is every champion's ambition, and having three stoppage wins – including two title victories – in the first half of 1970, he appeared to be hitting a peak. Blindingly fast and smart, the champion looked a class above his top-ten rivals and in no need of a fall guy.

Two years older than his challenger, Ismael shared the same birthday, being born on June 28, 1943 in the fishing village of Santa Isabel in the province of Colon. His father, Generosa, worked for the Colon police department and also served a spell as the village mayor, but with ten children to feed the budget was tight, and the youngster's contribution from shining shoes and selling papers was appreciated. Laguna left school at fifteen to work in a slaughterhouse and hated every minute, but by then his prowess as a street battler had led him to Kresch's gym. His mother, Modesta, was strongly against him becoming a boxer – she and Ismael's twin brother Carlos never saw him box. They were outvoted, however, by the rest of the clan who became enthusiastic fans.

The gym proprietor, a wealthy Pole called Isaac Kresch, spotted something special in the boy, and singled him out for intensive coaching from his trainer Ramon Dosman. He was eventually deemed ready for action, and after a brief amateur stint, during which he won the national bantamweight title, the seventeen-year-old turned professional, halting Al Morgan inside two rounds in Colon on January 8, 1961. Progress was rapid, and Laguna ran up a sequence of 27 wins, becoming the Panamanian featherweight champion before he suffered his first loss – a disputed points decision against Antonio Herrera in Colombia.

Three months later, back in Panama, he stopped Herrera in seven rounds, and then he hit the road, boxing twice in France, and also in Brazil, before being booked for his most important test yet in Mexico. Before 10,000 fans in the Tijuana bullring he dropped a close decision to Vicente Saldivar in what was regarded as a final eliminator for the featherweight championship. The excellent Saldivar took the title from Sugar Ramos in his next fight, and the twenty-year-old Laguna, still filling out, moved up to lightweight.

Like Buchanan losing to Velasquez, the Saldivar defeat was hardly a catastrophe, and inside a year – on April 10, 1965 – Laguna was given his first shot at champion Ortiz, in the Anoche Stadium in Panama City. Having impressed in racking up four successful defences, Ortiz took the job lightly, and a brilliant Laguna outboxed and outsped him. Referee Jersey Joe Walcott scored 143–132, Panama's Ramon Moynes returned 149–137, but the American, Ben Greene, somehow made the fight a draw, 145 apiece.

Ortiz remembered, 'He looked like a young, skinny kid. I thought it would be a walkover. Then the fight began and I couldn't see him he was so fast. Jabbing him, even grabbing him, was difficult. What made it worse was the place was so hot.'

Laguna was champion for only seven months before the inevitable return. Daly and Ortiz played the hosts in the Hiram Bithorn Stadium in San Juan, and this time the roles were reversed, Carlos punching out a comprehensive victory. Even the Panamanian judge voted for the Puerto Rican. Ismael had to wait almost two years for another shot, while Ortiz earned well from four defences, but before an 18,000 crowd in New York's Shea Stadium the slick champion again proved far too smart, scoring a unanimous and lopsided decision. No doubt about it, Carlos had Laguna's number.

For two years Ismael was forced to mark time. Daly still hovered on the periphery of his career, but by now the main man on the management team was a wealthy New York estate broker, Cain Young, who had become known in boxing after his association with light heavyweight champ Jose Torres from Puerto Rico. Young and Ismael enjoyed a solid relationship, and the lightweight was kept busy, appearing mostly in the States, but travelling twice to France and once to Ecuador to boost his earnings. In Quito he was judged a loser against Eugenio Espinoza, but he gained immediate revenge, and was once again accepted as the leading contender for the title, now in the grip of a spectacular puncher from California called Mando Ramos.

On March 3, 1970, at the Sports Arena in Los Angeles, Laguna produced all his sharp-shooting skills to slice up Ramos, who was rescued by his corner before the start of the tenth. Laguna was a champion once more, and a stoppage defence against Guts Ishimatsu from Japan only increased his confidence for the September showdown with Buchanan.

Boxing's bureaucrats did their best to ruin the occasion. The World Boxing Council no longer recognised the 27-year-old from Santa Isabel as champion, after he failed to honour a contract, and now Laguna had only the backing of the World Boxing Association. Bad news for Ismael, but worse for Buchanan. The British Board of Control was affiliated to the WBC, and refused to sanction the fight as being for the championship. And so Ken entered the ring on September 26, 1970 without the blessing of his home authority.

Buchanan had more pressing matters on his mind: the searing 100-plus degrees heat of San Juan; the prospect of travelling fifteen rounds; and a vastly more experienced opponent who was a 5/2 on favourite to retain his title.

The Scot shook up not only the Panamanian, but the entire boxing world. Even old Jack Solomons, who dug up a parasol from somewhere to shade Ken from the scorching afternoon sun between rounds, could scarcely believe what was unfolding before him. Buchanan survived Laguna's anticipated blistering early assault and, relying on his ramrod left, he was trading on at least equal terms by midway. The challenger was cut around the left eye and marked up, but he stood his ground in the fierce exchanges and refused to wilt. Amazingly, in the final three gut-sapping rounds he was the stronger, and at the welcome last bell the gladiators collapsed into one another's arms.

All down to the judges, and after a few nail-biting moments, the 25-year-old from Edinburgh was the new lightweight champion of the world. The scoring reflected how close a contest it had been: 145–144 twice for Buchanan; 145–144 once for Laguna. There would have to be a rerun.

But not before Kenny started making some money. Only his immediate family turned up at Edinburgh airport when he returned in triumph, and he received a far warmer welcome when, in December, he made his debut in Madison Square Garden, delighting New Yorkers with a dazzling display of boxing to outpoint the Canadian welter, Donato Paduano, in ten rounds. Again, he shared a bill with Ali, who knocked out tough Oscar Bonavena, but he was not overshadowed this time.

Next stop was a February gig in Los Angeles, a tough defence against the Laguna victim, Mando Ramos, and the WBC announced that they would grant recognition to the winner; the British Board of Control followed suit. At last they were acknowledging their own man. Three days before the action in the Sports Arena, Ramos injured his groin and he was replaced by a local hardcase, Ruben Navarro, who gave it his best shot, but was eventually outpointed by wide margins.

This time the welcome home party was huge: an open-top bus parade through the streets of Edinburgh; cheering crowds; a civic reception. At last, the Scottish capital realised that it could boast a genuine sporting superstar.

But the tensions had resurfaced between the champion and manager Thomas, principally over Eddie's percentage from the Navarro purse. Their contract had only months to run and Eddie's position looked extremely dodgy, especially when Ken accepted a non-title date for the so-called opposition, stopping Carlos Hernandez on a Harry Levene promotion at Wembley. Buchanan was now running the show, but Thomas still had a massive role to play in his continued success.

The champion had enjoyed a wonderful year, but there was unfinished business with Laguna. In comparison to the Scot, Ismael had maintained a very low profile. He had been very depressed after losing his title, fretting that he had let down his countrymen; had looked lacklustre when outpointing Lloyd Marshall and Chango Carmona; and hit an all-time low, losing to the obscure Eddie Linder in Miami. He claimed he was ill for that one, but the rumours persisted that he was a shot fighter, and all the smart money was going on Buchanan.

Monday, September 13, 1971 was a carnival night in a packed, noisy, but good-natured Garden. The Panamanians were out in force, not only to root for their hero but also to capture a brief look at another lightweight from the homeland, a wide-shouldered young man called Roberto Duran who took care of the unfortunate Benny Huertas inside a round. But the skirl of the bagpipes echoing around the arena signalled that Buchanan was not without friends. And the New Yorkers? Remembering Ken's virtuoso display against Paduano, the veterans around the ringside were anticipating another classic exhibition from the new Benny Leonard, the latest Jimmy McLarnin.

They were to see a lot more than they expected. Laguna was right on the lightweight limit at 135lb, Buchanan a trim 1½lb lighter, and from the opening bell the pace was fast, the exchanges brisk. Referee Jimmy Devlin twice checked the Scot for punches that strayed low, and both men found success with solid right hands, but this time around Ismael seemed to be more fighter than boxer.

He had early rewards. By round three a large and ugly swelling had developed under Buchanan's often vulnerable left eye, and Laguna was pot-shotting to make it worse. He was using all his know how, and in the fourth was warned for kidney punches, but he also landed with a hard left hook. Although the Scot scored with a fierce right before the bell, Ken's left eye was a hideous mess as he returned to his stool.

Crisis time in the corner, but Thomas, the old hand, kept his cool. He removed a razor blade from his bag of tricks and with the sure hand of a surgeon he opened a slit in the grotesque lump. The blood started to trickle, relieving the pressure on the swelling. Buchanan could see again with both eyes – just about – and any waning confidence was restored. No question, Eddie had already earned his cut this time!

But this was hard going. The two left-hand experts were now down off their toes, banging away furiously in a bitter battle of wills; twice in the fifth Devlin had to warn the Panama fighter for fouls, but in the sixth Buchanan drew huge applause, making Laguna miss, and hurting him with his full repertoire of left jabs and hooks and thumping rights to both head and body. By far his best round, but now there was a cut along his left eyebrow to accompany the swollen sore beneath it.

Laguna had chosen to brawl rather than box; because of the eye Buchanan had been forced into revamping his tactics, and he was adapting brilliantly.

Laguna was still pressing forward, still trying to force the Scot on to the back foot, but this was a thankless task. In the eighth Ismael managed to trap Buchanan in a corner, but Ken slipped and ducked his punches, expertly turned him, and then banged the challenger with both hands. This was boxing worthy of a Garden headliner, and the fans rose to him. Laguna was still throwing good shots, but despite the worsening eye the champion was scoring the cleaner blows, and more of them. His incredible workrate was matched only by his dour, inbred determination to buck the odds, and in a wildly exciting round eleven he drove the Panamanian back. For the first time Laguna returned to his corner with head bowed.

Buchanan backers had only the battered and bleeding eye to worry about now. More than once, referee Devlin stared long and hard at the damage, and at the end of the twelfth, for the first time, the commission doctor, Ed Campbell, stepped up on the ring apron for a closer inspection. But that only served to spur on Ken, and in round fourteen he electrified the crowd with an all-out assault, capped by a great left hook which sent Laguna halfway through the ropes, stunned, and on the verge of a knockout.

Nobody was going to stop Buchanan now – not Dr Campbell, nor Jimmy Devlin, nor a brave but exhausted challenger who was still trying to trade blows in the final three minutes, but who was inexorably inched back by the non-stop Scot. The tremendous din almost drowned the bell, and a jaunty champion wrapped an arm around Laguna and escorted him back to his stool.

Only warped judging could sabotage him now, but announcer Johnny Addie had no bad news. Judge Tony Castellano: 8–6–1 for Buchanan; referee Devlin: 9–6 for Buchanan – the final score was lost in the huge roar of approval that rocked the Garden as Ken hugged his father. That last card was the widest score of all: 10–5 for the champ, and quite an accurate reflection of the Scot's superiority.

Ken Buchanan was the toast of New York. The 26-year-old, who had been equally praised and damned for his Corinthian abilities, had proved that he was as brave as any battler in the trenches: as rugged as a Basilio, as ruthlessly unyielding as a Marciano. And Ismael Laguna? At 28, the elegant, gifted and extremely plucky pride of Panama had fought his last fight.

For some time wild rumours had been afloat about his health, and it is a fact that on several occasions Ismael attributed defeats to 'being sick'. But he would never expand. The writer James Dusgate, a specialist on Central American boxing and boxers, interviewed Laguna on several occasions, years after he had retired, and revealed that the lightweight had long suffered from sickle-cell anaemia, a hereditary blood disease which is apparently prevalent in his birthplace, Santa Isabel.

But such a claim should not cloud Buchanan's achievement. Before their first meeting Laguna had been in devastating form, stopping Ramos and Ishimatsu in title bouts. Going into the return, he was in the eleventh year of a demanding career which finished with only nine defeats (he was never stopped) in 75 contests, and of course, he had to cope mentally with that shock loss in San Juan. Probably 30 rounds with Buchanan was the convincer that the magic had gone.

He and Duran remain idols in their homeland, and though his health is reportedly not great, he looked smart and happy at his induction ceremony in Canastota in 2001. Financially, he is in good shape, living in a comfortable house in an upmarket section of Panama City.

In Canastota, he offered the definitive explanation for his abrupt retirement in an interview with Jack Hirsch for *Boxing News*: 'I lost all motivation after Buchanan. I felt terrible that I'd let the Panamanian people down. I was sick when we boxed at the Garden, but still should have won. It was close, but I have no complaints about the decision.'

Few great fighters can be truly gracious in defeat, but Laguna never has had anything but good words for Buchanan, conceding that the Scot might not have reached his peak when they first met. His countryman, Duran, was even more effusive, telling Hugh McIlvanney that Ken was the best lightweight that he ever faced – a compliment that did nothing to erase the intense loathing for the great Roberto that festered within the Edinburgh boxer for all too many years after he had quit the ring.

Bad enough that The Hands Of Stone took his treasured world championship; worse that the final blow was delivered below the belt, and after the bell; and worst of all, the fact that Duran never honoured the promise of a return.

The pair met on June 26, 1972 – two days before Ken's 27th birthday – in another big night in the Garden. Buchanan's old buddies from the WBC had stripped him of their version of the championship for failure to defend against the Spaniard, Pedro Carrasco, but he still retained WBA backing, and a $100,000 purse helped him forget about the loss. In retrospect this does not seem an over-generous wage to face a future four-weight champion and a true ring legend. But back in 1972 Duran was just an ambitious 21-year-old with a string of knockouts in an unbeaten sequence of 28 wins: a dangerous challenger, but no superman.

Roberto was fast, smart and clinically rough, and most neutrals
had him ahead after twelve rounds; Buchanan, however, still
swears he was bang in the fight and actually had Duran in trouble
in the thirteenth. Maybe. But he was against the ropes when the
bell rang, prompting the challenger to fire the late, low one. Still
frames show referee Johnny Lo Bianco, with both arms trying to
restrain Duran as his glove buries into Buchanan's groin.

Ken dropped, his face contorted, clearly in agony, and both sets
of seconds jumped into the ring. The divorce from Thomas had
become absolute, and American Gil Clancy was sharing the
principal corner duties with Tommy Buchanan but they could
have done with back-up from a New York attorney. Lo Bianco
denied seeing the crippling blow, and ignored pleas for the Scot to
be allowed out for round fourteen. Far from the referee's finest
hour, but the raging controversy could have been put to sleep had
a return match been speedily arranged.

It never happened. Over the next six years Roberto successfully
defended his title twelve times against the deserving and the well-
connected, and only Edwin Viruet survived the full trip. He wiped
out the 135lb division . . . all but Buchanan. Manager Carlos
Eleta promised, then reneged, and always found another excuse.
Given his future accomplishments, it seems unthinkable that
Duran himself was running scared, but the bottom line remains
that Ken never got that merited second chance – the only black
mark on the Panamanian's otherwise glorious lightweight reign.

Buchanan was still in demand, still a top-class performer,
earning well in the Garden and Miami and Toronto and
throughout Europe. But it required a thirteen-fight unbeaten run,
dating back to Duran, before the WBC okayed him to fight for
their version of the title. Typically, he had to travel to Tokyo to
get the chance and, just as typically, Ken still believes he did just
enough to become champion once again. But the record books
show us that Guts Ishimatsu won a fifteen-rounds decision on
February 27, 1975. Five months later, after a successful European
title defence against Giancarlo Usai in Cagliari, Buchanan
announced his retirement.

He had money in the bank, owned a hotel, and now he had time
to spend with Carol and the kids, Mark and Karen . . . and he also
had all those memories of fabulous nights in the Garden and San
Juan, and even the sporting clubs.

Sadly, the good life was short-lived. There was a divorce from Carol; he was forced to sell the hotel; and in 1979 he returned to the ring in Denmark, outpointing Benny Benitez on his 34th birthday. All told, he boxed nine times, losing five; there were even two bouts on the unlicensed circuit before the comeback petered out and he passed ignominiously from the sport he had graced for so long. He was no longer a celebrity, just another struggling old pro trying to earn a living and if his name did appear in the papers the stories were usually negative. Though not quite out, Ken was taking a count.

He was not saved by the bell, but by a call telling him that in June 2000 he would be inducted into the Hall Of Fame. The news had a remarkable effect on him, almost as profound as the day when, as an eight-year-old, he saw the movie about Joe Louis and decided to become a fighter. He stopped drinking and started preparing for the trip as he would for a big fight.

Now all the media coverage was positive, the pictures happy. In full Highland regalia he set off for Canastota and received a royal welcome. He mixed with many of boxing's greatest names, regarded as an equal; once again there was a queue for auto-graphs; he received his Hall Of Fame ring and saw his plaque hung in the museum alongside the other legends. At long last he was being given the respect that he craved.

And that respect filtered back to Britain. Further awards followed and he was in demand to speak at functions and appear at ringsides. There was a documentary film, and a new generation of Scots learned about a local hero. He even met up with his old enemy Duran, and they embraced.

There are few fairytale endings in boxing, but Ken Buchanan is living one of them. Long may it last.

Those Damn Judges!

Scoring a fight is a most subjective exercise, as much so for the three judges, perched in prime ringside positions, as for the fan at home with his can of beer. A preference for a particular style; a liking for aggression over pure boxing; a taste for head shots rather than good work to the body. Interpretations of the action can vary wildly.

Britain, of course, still soldiers on with the referee as the sole arbiter, unless a world or European title is at stake, when the governing body appoints its own officials. Most countries, however, reckon the ref has enough on his plate without keeping score. But both systems still produce howlers.

And there are still all too many hometown decisions and incompetent, even corrupt judges, and the fans just have to scream and bear it. But sometimes the furore refuses to die down and the arguments rage on.

CHAPTER TEN

Joe Louis *v* Jersey Joe Walcott

FRIDAY, DECEMBER 5, 1947

Only the night before, a new kid had taken Broadway by storm. Marlon Brando had electrified the opening-night crowd for Tennessee Williams' play *A Streetcar Named Desire* and the papers were going crazy. But along Eighth Avenue and up in Harlem, Brando's brutish Stanley Kowalski created scarcely a ripple: bums like this Stanley hung around Stillman's all the time, and anyway, this was Friday, and The Bomber was fighting at the Garden. No contest.

No matter that not much of a contest was expected at the Garden either. This was Joe Louis, and a Louis fight was as much a social celebration as a sporting event, and who cared that old Jersey Joe Walcott was on offer as high as 20/1 to become the new heavyweight champion of the world? Or that the bout had been considered such a mis-match that it had first been touted around as an exhibition contest? Only Tommy Farr and Arturo Godoy had lasted the title distance with Joe, and be it one round, five or ten, The Brown Bomber was always worth the ticket money.

On Joe's last New York appearance Tami Mauriello had been blasted out inside one round, but there had certainly been no shortage of thrills. That fight had taken place fifteen months earlier and the great man had been missing for far too long, but that had not been the champion's fault. He had expected, in fact, urgently required, a major outdoor defence in one of the ballparks. Though the public was yet to learn about Joe's financial woes, he was already deep in hock to the tax authorities and he needed a big purse to keep them at bay. But for a variety of reasons the vital summer date never materialised.

In 1946 Mike Jacobs suffered a cerebral haemorrhage, and although he remained the titular head of the Twentieth Century Sporting Club – the organisation which ran boxing in the Garden – his cousin, Sol Strauss, was now the main man. Right away, lawyer Strauss realised he had inherited at least one severe headache: Louis did not have a logical contender for his title, and the immediate post-war crop of heavies was less than inspiring.

Ezzard Charles was still campaigning as a light heavy, and fighters like Elmer Ray, Curtis Sheppard and Lee Q Murray, Gus Lesnevich and Joey Maxim were all capable enough but lacked the charisma to sell outdoors. There was one possibility: Strauss and his back-up team, matchmakers Nat Rogers and Lew Burston, had been impressed by a big bruiser from Pennsylvania called Joe Baksi who back in April had demolished another fringe contender, the British champion, Bruce Woodcock. Baksi was big, could hit, possessed a sound chin, and he was white. Lucrative championship fights had been made with much less.

But Baksi was, to put it mildly, a headstrong character. Despite Rogers and Burston constantly upping their offer, Baksi got greedy and insisted on first taking an apparently easy July booking in Stockholm against the local hero, Olle Tandberg. And though the verdict was of the hometown variety, the record books tell us that he lost. Nobody could hope to sell Baksi for a ballpark title fight after that.

The months raced past, Louis was left without his outdoor date, and even a viable 1947 winter earner was causing problems. Since knocking out Mauriello, Joe had kept himself in reasonable shape and in spending money – The Bomber spent bigtime! – boxing exhibitions in Honolulu and Mexico, but while waiting for Baksi to make up his mind he had suspended his tours and had not been seen in the ring since going through the motions with his old rival, Godoy, in Mexico City back in February.

And so, to cover Christmas expenses, another exhibition was arranged, a ten-rounder against his former sparring partner, Joe Walcott, who could always use a dollar. The New York State Athletic Commission, however, would not play ball, insisting that any bout scheduled for more than six rounds must be recognised as being for the title. Overnight, the match had been given a gigantic upgrade, but Joe Walcott was still Joe Walcott – not that

Louis' legions cared. At long last they would see their hero back in action and on familiar canvas.

The champion had scant regard for Jersey Joe or his talent, believing him undeserving of a title shot. But for the veteran from Camden, this was the answer to his most desperate prayers. Old Joe read his Bible and believed in miracles: finding himself challenging The Bomber for the heavyweight championship was indeed a wonder.

To say that Walcott had survived hard times is an understatement. Until 1945, when an extremely influential operator called Felix Bocchicchio took an interest in what could loosely be called his career, Joe was always scrapping just to feed his wife and children, battling, and several times failing, to stay above the poverty line. He had known no other life since the day he was born Arnold Raymond Cream on January 31, 1914 in a New Jersey town called Merchantville, a few miles from Camden.

His West Indian father worked at anything he could find to feed a wife and ten children, but there was never nearly enough money, and the Creams often went hungry. When Arnold was fourteen his father died (mother Edna's youngest was just two months old) but he left the teenager a legacy: a love of boxing. His dad had often regaled him with stories of the great black fighters like Jeff Clarke, an uncle who was a phenomenal performer known as The Joplin Ghost. And there were also many tales about The Barbados Demon, the pint-sized welterweight marvel called Joe Walcott. Young Arnold became fascinated by Walcott's story. He was determined to adopt his name some day and make a fortune in the ring.

At the age of sixteen he headed for Philadelphia to learn his trade, but there were no money trees in Philly and precious few opportunities to fight. Most record books agree that he made his professional debut on September 9, 1930, knocking out Cowboy Wallace in one round in Vineland, New Jersey, but in those dark Depression days there were hundreds of youngsters looking to earn a buck from a fight, and openings were few. Arnold, however, was fortunate enough to catch the eye of a great teacher, a former exceptional lightweight called Jack Blackburn.

Blackburn was a legend: another great black fighter denied his chance because of his colour; a scientific master who regularly beat up far heavier men; an intimidating character with a razor

scar stretching from his left ear to his mouth and a history of
violence that included a five-year stretch for manslaughter; and a
terror when drinking, which was often. But a genius when
coaching young hopefuls.

He believed the youngster, still a middleweight and now calling
himself Jersey Joe Walcott, possessed the proper tools to progress
a long way, but fate decreed that Jack would never complete the
kid's education. Instead, he accepted an offer he could not refuse
and wound up handling another rising young star, an amateur
sensation called Joe Barrow, who, of course, would become The
Brown Bomber.

John Roxborough, a black Detroit businessman whose mild
appearance belied his profession of numbers entrepreneur, first
approached Blackburn at the Arcadia gym on Philadelphia's
Cherry Street: his mission was to hire Jack to train Louis for the
pro ranks. The old fighter was cool, convinced that because of
Jack Johnson's chaotic rule, no black would ever get another crack
at the heavyweight title, but Roxborough was persistent. A second
meeting was scheduled, this time at Trafton's gym in Chicago,
where Blackburn renewed acquaintances with Roxborough's
partner, a tough, streetwise club owner, numbers operator and
undertaker called Julian Black. He also saw Louis for the first
time, and though not especially impressed, decided that $34-a-
week wages were too good to turn down.

Part of the deal was for Jersey Joe to accompany Blackburn to
Chicago to continue his education, but the youngster contracted
typhoid and was out of the ring for more than a year. By the time
he was fully recovered Blackburn was totally committed to Louis,
and Walcott again had to start from scratch.

Would Louis have attained the same level of greatness without
his trainer's considerable input? How much better a fighter would
Walcott have become had he completed his schooling with Jack?
What might have materialised had the two Joes become stable-
mates? Fun to speculate. But one thing is certain: had he been
bankrolled by Roxborough and Black, Jersey Joe would never
have experienced the desperate, humiliating days that lay ahead.

In 1933, the year before he fell ill and parted from Blackburn,
Walcott married Lydia, a Merchantville girl whom he had known
since childhood. A year later, while Louis was getting off the
mark, knocking out Jack Kracken inside a round and running up

a spectacular sequence of wins, Arnold, the first of the six Walcott children, was born. And Jersey Joe, still recuperating, was forced to go on relief, receiving a weekly welfare handout of just $9.50.

He accepted any job he could find, sometimes for a week, often for just a day. He worked as a stevedore, manned garbage and ice trucks, toiled on a road gang, and sweated in a Camden soup factory. A fight purse was a bonus, and always an insult. Walcott became prey for larcenous managers who invariably gave him a fast count, and for promoters requiring a late replacement. In January 1936 in Camden he took on tough Al Ettore on two days' notice, and was well ahead until exhaustion set in and he was stopped in the eighth. Just months later Ettore lasted five rounds with a peak Louis in Philadelphia.

Insiders were well aware of Walcott's capabilities, but they also knew that he seldom had time to train properly and that regular eating was a luxury. Joe was the archetypal hungry fighter.

When given some notice, he had talent enough to stop Elmer Ray and outpoint Curtis Sheppard, but all too often he relied on the last-minute call-up. He had done absolutely no training when in February 1940 he faced lumbering Abe Simon, who would go on to challenge Louis twice for the title. Just like the Ettore fight, Walcott gave Abe a boxing lesson for five rounds before he ran out of steam and was halted in the sixth. The record books, however, do not include excuses or explanations.

Jersey Joe was often disgusted and disillusioned, and frequently told his wife that he was quitting. After Simon, he boxed only once in 1941, stopping somebody called Columbus Grant on a rare excursion to Memphis. When he returned home he informed Lydia that he was finished for good. America was about to enter the war and there would be plenty of work for everyone. The 27-year-old no longer needed the fight business which had done him so few favours.

And that would have been the last heard of heavyweight Jersey Joe but for a small, dark-eyed man named Felix Bocchicchio, who conducted his many business interests from the Camden Athletic Corporation, a modest structure at 221 Market Street, just across the road from the soup factory where Walcott had been glad to earn a buck. Now Joe was earning $90 a week working in the shipyards, and although in 1944 he did accept two easy fights in Batesville, NJ, in his mind, he was an ex-fighter.

Bocchicchio had other ideas. He had made his money through running booze and gambling, and he owned the local pro football team, the Camden Bears. Now he was going to promote fights, with the help of his friend, a manager called Joe Webster, the proprietor of a restaurant just a few doors from Felix's club. The pair had seen Walcott and reckoned that he just might still have a chance, considering the dearth of outstanding heavies.

Walcott took a deal of persuading. Now he had a degree of security, but he still had an itch for the sport and, more important, he knew and trusted Webster. His new sponsors did not seem to care that he was a 30-year-old, and they convinced him that he would be well looked after and given a fair shake financially. Once again Jersey Joe hit the comeback trail.

Webster and Bocchicchio were true to their word. They made sure that Joe had decent training quarters and always ate well; and if, like any other guy with six kids, he was sometimes short of a few bucks, they took care of him. The Walcotts had never had it so good, and despite a points hiccup against Johnny Allen in the new partnership's second outing, Jersey Joe had never fought so well. Victories over the unpredictable Baksi, Steve Dudas, Lee Q Murray and Curtis Sheppard wound up a fantastic 1945, and now he was a rated heavy.

The following year he caused a major upset, outpointing Jimmy Bivins in Cleveland, before impressing with wins over Lee Oma and Tommy Gomez in the Garden. He was a headliner now, living in a nice house, driving a new car, often pictured with his well-dressed family. Even points reverses against Joey Maxim and Elmer Ray could not wipe the smile from his broad face.

He twice beat Maxim in 1947 rematches, and also put Ray in his place, yet few in the trade took his title claims seriously. But Bocchicchio, Webster, trainer Dan Florio and a hardcore band of Camden supporters were confident that on his best night the jinking, feinting, hard-hitting Jersey Joe could give any heavyweight nightmares. Louis, however, lost no sleep.

There was very little that ever troubled The Bomber, except for money. He always needed his next payday, and had forever been in hock to Uncle Mike Jacobs, who encouraged his borrowing, but religiously took the debt off the top of the next purse. Louis reckoned that he was entitled to enjoy himself because he too had known hard times, and had been as poor as Jersey Joe. Maybe, even poorer.

The newspaper guys seldom mentioned that any more.

Joseph Louis Barrow arrived on May 13, 1914 in Lafayette, a hamlet in Chambers County, Alabama. He was the seventh of eight children born to Munro Barrow, a sharecropper, and Lillie Reese. Munro barely scraped a living and eventually the struggle took its toll; he was committed to an asylum, from which, time and again, he would escape and return home. But after a period of years, Lillie was informed that he was dead, and she met and married a widower, Pat Brooks, who had a large family of his own. Before long, the united Barrow and Brooks clans made the trek north to Detroit, Pat finding work in a car plant. Only many years later did Lillie discover that the information about Munro had been wrong, and that, in fact, he had lived another twenty years.

Life was hard in the Detroit ghetto, but the children never went hungry. Somehow Lillie found the money to enrol Joe for violin lessons, but he proved a reluctant pupil, preferring the excitement of the Brewster Center gym where he started learning the basics of boxing. He shaped up well, and when he applied for his amateur card he gave only his first two names, hoping that his mother would not find out that he had taken up fighting. And so Joe Louis was born.

His career almost came to a swift conclusion after just one fight. For his ring debut he was matched recklessly against a 1932 Olympian named Johnny Miler. Floored seven times, he was stopped in the second, and quite badly marked up. A disgraceful mismatch, but after a lengthy time-out for self-assessment, Joe returned to the Brewster Center, and soon he was the hottest ticket in town. Winner of 50 of his 54 amateur contests, 43 by knockout, Louis won the 1934 National AAU light heavyweight title, and the offers to turn professional flooded in.

Enter Roxborough and Black, followed by Blackburn, and finally by Mike Jacobs, the essential white man, who could open doors leading to the championship that would have remained tightly shut to the black trio. They made a formidable team. While Blackburn worked on the prospect's balance and left jab, the other three – ever mindful of the race-hatred stirred up by the only black heavyweight champion, Jack Johnson – worked on a code of conduct for Louis, primarily designed not to offend whites.

Louis was warned never to have his picture taken alone with a white woman; told never to enter a nightclub alone; reminded to keep a solemn expression before the cameras, and never to gloat over a fallen opponent. There were many more instructions, ludicrous in today's world, but deadly serious and smart back then, when blacks, even great black sportsmen, were shunted to the back of the bus. Deadpan Joe obeyed the rules, and personal details of his life and loves remained a tightly guarded secret for his entire career.

Not that the media were too intrusive. Jacobs was a generous host, and the journalists had a genuine star to write about. The Bomber just kept delivering: a spectacular New York debut, hammering the former champion, Primo Carnera, in six rounds; a million-dollar gate when he disposed of another old champ, Max Baer, in four; Louis seemed unstoppable.

But on June 19, 1936, the German, Max Schmeling, yet another ex-title-holder, proved that Joe was only a human and just as vulnerable to a hard right as any other fighter who continually dropped his left. Max won in the twelfth, but the Louis express was derailed only temporarily and on June 22, 1937 he beat up brave Jimmy Braddock in Chicago, winning the title in round eight. Black America celebrated joyfully; the whites, remembering Schmeling, reserved judgement.

But on June 22, 1938 at Yankee Stadium The Bomber united the nation when he knocked out Schmeling in the first round of their return. This fight had been hyped as a showdown between the superhero of Hitler's Master Race and the champion of the free world. In Washington and especially in Berlin the propaganda experts pulled out all the stops during the countdown. All total bunkum, of course, but it heightened the pressure on Louis, already hellbent on revenge, and helped swell the crowd to a massive 70,043, bringing in receipts of $1,015,012.

The fight lasted just two minutes and four seconds, but the fans were treated to an awesome display of precision punching. Afterwards, Schmeling was stretchered off to hospital. Joe Louis was the toast of the nation, and would remain so for the rest of his life.

His service years, which did little for his career or his ever-fluctuating bank balance, strengthened his position as America's favourite sportsman. He defended his title twice in 1942 against

Buddy Baer and Abe Simon and donated his purses to the army and navy relief funds – a well-intentioned but badly handled gesture that would spark off his troubles with the taxman. He boxed exhibitions for the troops overseas, boosted morale, made speeches – most memorably one in the Garden where he concluded, '. . . we will win, because God's on our side'. When he was discharged, he was awarded the Legion of Merit medal, 'for exceptional meritorious conduct'.

Joe Louis, it appeared, could do no wrong. But by 1947 he had tired of the training grind, and found it so hard to motivate himself. In 1946 he had remarried Marva Trotter, whom he had first wed on the morning of the Max Baer fight, and now his thoughts were on retirement. After he had taken care of Walcott, he would make the announcement.

The Bomber and Jersey Joe had crossed paths before. Back in 1936 Walcott had been hired as a sparring partner for Louis before the first Schmeling fight. According to the challenger, he had twice floored The Bomber wearing 16oz gloves and was promptly fired from the Pompton Lakes camp. The Louis team replied that Jersey Joe had simply quit on his second day, after a particularly painful session. The sportswriters at least had an angle, but in truth none was needed to shift the tickets. On the night, 18,194 fans packed the arena, paying $216,477 – then a record Garden gate.

Walcott was more than a stone lighter than the 211lb champion, who had actually dried out in the final few days' training, hoping to make his body look svelte. But Louis could never again be the trim 200lb destroyer who had so majestically disposed of 23 challengers. A bald patch shone under the lights and his face was fleshy, but this was still The Bomber, and his Garden fans prepared for the early explosion. Sure enough, there were first round fireworks, but it was the champ who was dumped on the canvas.

The jigging, feinting, clowning, irritating Jersey Joe had suckered Louis on to a hard right hand, and the champion had fallen for it. Louis was at his most dangerous when hurt but, up at two, he could only cover up as the challenger scored with both hands, and before the round's end The Bomber was staggered by another great right. The noise was deafening and now many of the cheers were for the Camden underdog.

By the opening of round two Louis had regained his composure, but Walcott was a terribly elusive opponent, and the champ always had problems against runners. Jersey Joe was outboxing him, landing with sneak punches, but finally in round three the Louis jab began to bang home and the crowd responded, confident that a crunching right would follow up at any time.

Wrong again. Walcott could not miss with his right which was fast and accurate. In round four he again dropped Louis after cleverly feinting him into position. On his hands and knees, the champion took a count of seven, and he was still dazed when he regained his feet, referee Ruby Goldstein having to wrestle him free as he clung close to Walcott. But strangely, the challenger did not go in for the finisher, as if wary of a counter-attack, and by the time the bell rang the champ's head had cleared.

Jersey Joe was enjoying himself but he was taking no chances, and the fans were not impressed as he bobbed and weaved out of range, several times going walkabout. In rounds five through seven he danced and clowned and kidded, and was even warned by Goldstein for a blatant backhander, but he was doing little scoring. But neither was Louis, who stoically shuffled forward, looking to land his hard shots, but not finding much success. Who won those rounds? A matter of interpretation, but there was no disputing that the left side of Louis' face was now sore and badly swollen. And in round eight his left eye started to swell alarmingly after yet another Walcott right found the target.

Between rounds, a large icepack was pressed hard against the champion's eye, while trainer Mannie Seamon, who had taken over on the death of Blackburn in 1942, poured advice into his ear. Louis had to cut off the ring, close down Walcott, like he had done so memorably against Billy Conn. But this guy was even trickier than Billy.

Round nine, and Walcott started fast, firing two good rights, but Louis set him back on his heels with some vintage jabs, and followed with a terrific right that jarred the challenger. Walcott was cut over the right eye and badly hurt and the crowd rose screaming as The Bomber got serious with both hands. A game Jersey tried to stand and trade, but just before the bell a vicious short right almost toppled him. A big, big round for Louis, and the fans knew it.

During his training, Walcott obviously had only eaten the best and ran for long hours on the roads, for there was no sign of a sudden collapse like those that had cost him against Ettore and Simon. He recovered quickly, and danced through the tenth, repaid a solid Louis right with an equally hurtful left hook in the eleventh, and in the twelfth picked off the champ, whose left eye was all but closed and his lip badly swollen. By round thirteen the old boy from Camden was so upbeat that he tried to get lucky with a haymaker right, missed, and fell to the canvas. He rose smiling, and he had plenty to smile about.

There were grins too in the corner from Joe Webster and Dan Florio who told him that he had only to avoid trouble for six minutes and the championship was his. Jersey Joe obeyed his cornermen, but perhaps too well.

Louis kept pressing forward, kept trying to unload the payoff, and Walcott skipped backwards, then shifted sideways, then turned southpaw, and finally went into full retreat as the seconds ticked away and the crowd booed and whistled. The champ just could not land a telling punch, and at the final bell he turned away in disgust, trying to duck through the ropes before the result was announced. His handlers hauled him back.

Later, The Bomber claimed that he had just been disappointed by a poor display; the other slant was that he was expecting the worst. But now, all ears were on announcer Harry Balogh. Judge Frank Forbes, 8–6–1 Louis. Loud boos for the champ. Referee Ruby Goldstein, 7–6–2 Walcott. Loud cheers for the challenger. Judge Marty Monroe, 9–6 Louis, and a great angry rumble swelled up in the Garden. For the first time in his life Joe Louis walked to his dressing room amid a storm of catcalls and abuse, and in the centre of the ring Florio raised Walcott's arm. Bocchicchio was having fits, and a stunned Jersey Joe fought back the tears.

In the champ's dressing room, a reporter – alluding to a pre-fight statement from Louis – yelled, 'Was Walcott a second-rate fighter tonight?' Joe tapped his chest and replied, 'No. I was.' But he was still adamant that he had won. A desperately disappointed Walcott declared, 'I thought I won big. Louis' punches never hurt me. My corner told me I was ahead and to coast the last round.'

Walcott supporters included 22 out of 33 journalists polled at ringside. One scored a draw. Leading British boxing writer Peter Wilson swore that he had just witnessed a robbery in the Garden.

But Louis' voters included the respected Red Smith, and Nat Fleischer, who reckoned that the champion had done just enough – or more pointedly, that the challenger had just not done enough.

Walcott's safety-first tactics in the final two rounds had backfired, but he could console himself with the thought of a well-paid return. There was no way that The Bomber could retire on such a sour note, and the rematch was arranged for the following June in Yankee Stadium, where the champion's magic attracted a 40,000 crowd, despite the fact that the fight was twice put back a day because of rain.

Louis had always been dynamite the second time around, but now he looked old and ponderous, and in the third he was again floored by a left-right combination from Walcott, who was ahead on two judges' cards going into the eleventh. That was when Jersey Joe got down off his toes, elected to swap punches, and discovered reality. The Bomber may have slowed up, but he still packed tremendous firepower, and after a wild exchange referee Frankie Fullam tolled the full count over Walcott with four seconds of the round remaining.

Louis had finished a dreary contest in champion style, his fans were cheering once again, and in his dressing room he announced over the radio that he was retiring from the ring. With Louis gone, Walcott could still achieve his impossible dream.

The heavyweight league was in a sorry state: the challengers were either too old or too ordinary, apart from the dangerous light heavy, Ezzard Charles, who had been tempted to move up among the big boys, and a Walcott–Charles fight-off for the vacant title made sense – at least to the National Boxing Association. The powerful New York commission, favouring an elimination tournament, stalled on granting recognition.

On June 22, 1949 Jersey Joe got his third shot at the championship in Chicago's Comiskey Park, and again he blew his chance, dropping a unanimous decision to Charles after a lousy fight. But Joe was earning too much money to retire, and he guaranteed himself another niche in boxing folklore when he stopped Harold Johnson in three rounds in Philadelphia. Fourteen years earlier he had knocked out Johnson's father, Phil, also in the third, and also in Philly. At the close of 1950, however, after losing a hard-fought ten-rounder to a young Rex Layne in the Garden, the years appeared finally to have caught up with Walcott.

Bocchicchio did not think that way. The wily Felix had powerful allies in the business who could deliver big favours: the Layne loss was conveniently forgotten, and the following March Joe was back challenging Charles in the Detroit Olympia. Down in the ninth, he lost another unanimous decision. Incredibly, this still did not signal the end of Walcott's title aspirations.

Four months later the amazing 37-year-old was handed a fifth shot at the championship, and in Pittsburgh's Forbes Field he upset the odds and shocked the boxing world, thanks to a devastating left hook that knocked out Charles in the seventh round. The old man had finally reached his goal, and overnight his pension plans were coming up roses. He survived a first defence – again against Charles – and then came his most glorious night, albeit a losing one, in Philadelphia's Municipal Stadium.

Unbeaten Rocky Marciano was his opponent. For twelve rounds Jersey Joe boxed and punched like a sprightly youngster: he floored Rocky in the first, cut him up badly, took some tremendous belts without flinching, and was ahead until Marciano delivered one of the best right hands ever thrown in round thirteen. All over, and just a pity that there was a return clause.

On May 15, 1953 in the Chicago Stadium Joe fought his last fight – if one could describe it as a fight. Marciano caught him in the first with a left hook and a right uppercut, and though Walcott seemed alert to referee Frank Sikora's count, he failed to rise in time. A sad finale, but that night he left with the bulk of the money and a career record of 53 wins from 72 bouts was far from a fair reflection of his ability.

And he did live happily ever after. He enjoyed making personal appearances and often worked as a referee; became a town sheriff in Camden; was appointed chairman of the New Jersey State Athletic Commission; and was made director of special projects for New Jersey governor, Brendan Byrne. He died age eighty on February 25, 1994, and was correctly described by the great trainer Eddie Futch as, 'One of the finest technicians in heavyweight boxing history.'

Joe Louis, of course, would earn far more glowing eulogies, and was buried with full military honours at Arlington National Cemetery. But in his later life he would never find the contentment that Walcott enjoyed. In 1949, though they remained great friends, there was a second divorce from Marva, and the following year persistent demands from the IRS forced him to make a comeback. Very sad.

On September 27, 1950 only 13,562 turned up at Yankee Stadium to watch him challenge Charles for his old title. He was 36 but looked years older as he suffered a bad beating from a reluctant Ezzard for the full fifteen rounds, yet he still could not afford to retire.

The Bomber remained far too heavy-handed for the likes of Freddie Beshore, Omelio Agramonte and Lee Savold, but he was not fooling himself, and it came as a relief when a young and ambitious Marciano brought down the curtain on a marvellous career with a brutal eight-round knockout in the Garden on October 26, 1951. At least he bowed out against a great future champion rather than some palooka. Only Schmeling, Charles and Rocky ever beat him – fellow champions.

A legend like Louis could stop fighting, but he could never retire: he would always be regarded as the champ, and acted accordingly. Joe may have been pampered and irresponsible, totally hopeless with money, and intent only on living the life of a champion but he was also kind, gentle and humorous and generous beyond belief. Even in his darkest hours, and then in his final wheelchair days, he never lost that extraordinary aura of greatness. He died on April 12, 1981 in Las Vegas, aged 67.

Because of the unique dignity that he brought to a very rough sport, boxing, and especially all black boxers, will forever be in his debt. But, of course, The Brown Bomber never bothered to reclaim markers.

CHAPTER ELEVEN

Kid Gavilan *v* Billy Graham

WEDNESDAY, AUGUST 29, 1951

One of the most diabolical decisions ever rendered came that night in the Garden when the announcer, Johnny Addie, raised the arm of welterweight champion Kid Gavilan after fifteen enthralling rounds against the pride of the East Side, Irish Billy Graham . . . or so we are led to believe. Sure enough, the verdict did spark off spectacular fist fights and flying chairs as the Graham fans vented their rage and disbelief, and the following morning an indignant press was all but unanimous that Billy had been the rightful winner, dubbing him The Uncrowned Champion, a name that stuck. But diabolical?

Embellishments on the result grew more far-fetched with every retelling: Jesse James had been the referee, Butch Cassidy and The Sundance Kid the judges, and, incredibly, 33 years after the event, the New York State Athletic Commission announced an inquiry into the decision, promising to reverse it if any wrong-doing could be substantiated. Surprise, surprise: the commissioners came up empty.

The controversy had been revived thanks to Teddy Brenner, a busy and respected matchmaker and promoter around post-war New York, who rose as high as the presidency of Madison Square Garden Boxing Inc. for five years in the 1970s. Brenner had published his memoirs, the rather cynically titled *Only The Ring Was Square*, which included an intriguing explanation for the Gavilan–Graham carve-up.

The source of Brenner's revelations was Irving Cohen, a lifelong buddy, who was Graham's manager. The villains were our old friend Frankie Carbo and Arthur Schwartz, unlucky enough to be one of the judges on the infamous night. According to Cohen – according to Brenner – he received a summons to meet the gangster a few days before the fight at the Forrest Hotel, a boxing hangout near the Garden. Carbo got right to the point, 'You want your boy should be the champ? You give me twenty per cent of him and you get the title.'

Cohen gamely explained that there was already a co-manager, Jack Reilly, and there was no room for another partner. He was advised to talk to Graham who wanted nothing to do with Carbo, and when Cohen returned with the bad news, Carbo said, 'Does the kid know he ain't going to win?'

'He knows,' Irving said.

'He's got a lot to learn about life,' Carbo said.

So that was the explanation. Frank Carbo had administered the fix, and Billy Graham had no chance from the first bell. Of course! Always had to have been something like that. But Cohen – according to Brenner – had more to spill. We quote verbatim from Brenner and *Only The Ring Was Square.*

What else I remember is what Irving Cohen told me about Artie Schwartz, the judge who had a lopsided card in favour of Gavilan. Many years later, as Schwartz lay dying in a New York hospital, he sent a message to Irving to come and see him. When Irving went into the hospital room, he wished Schwartz well which was like Irving. He was the softest, kindest man I ever knew. Irving said Schwartz looked up at him from the bed and said, 'You know, Irving, I got to get this off my mind because you are a very decent fellow. When I voted for Gavilan against Graham I had to do it. I want you to know this. The boys ordered me to do it. I couldn't help myself and it's bothered me ever since. I'm sorry, Irving, for what I did to you and Graham.'

When Irving told me the story later, he said, 'Poor guy. I know what he meant. The boys order you to do something, you do it, if you want to live. At least Schwartz got it off his chest. He died in peace, I hope.'

Threats of extreme violence and a deathbed confession from the crooked judge: hard to top that . . . When the book came out, there were vociferous denials from Schwartz's aggrieved relatives who pointed out that Arthur had died of a heart attack on a New York railroad platform. No hospital bed, no final words of remorse to Cohen.

And what about Irving, the softest, kindest man Brenner ever knew? True, he was very well liked in the business, and writers frequently commented on how polite he was; how he and his wife were the proprietors of a lingerie shop; and how he spoke so quietly, and looked so innocent with his round, baby-blue eyes. But Cohen was familiar with both sides of the street: his most famous fighter was Rocky Graziano, and The Rock's managerial arrangements included a percentage for a choirboy called Eddie Coco, who had served serious time for an assortment of grisly misdeeds, and who was a close Carbo associate.

Irving knew the score, but somehow he was never branded as yet another lackey of boxing's overlord. Even the *New York Daily Mirror*'s relentless crusader, Dan Parker, never tried to turn the heat up under the lingerie salesman.

Anyway. Why would Carbo have waited until just a few days before the fight before trying to put the squeeze on Cohen? At that time, the man of many names boasted of having total control of the light, welter and middleweight titles, and though that may have been an egotistical overstatement, there was no doubt that a great number of contenders had to come into line before they were granted a championship shot. More than likely that before Billy Graham ever signed a contract to box champion Gavilan, all the details which could not be included, even in the small print, had been hammered out to everyone's satisfaction.

Boxing, however, always has thrived on tasty gossip and the knowing wink, plus a curious acceptance, even an admiration for the fast shuffle and the dodgy deal. Definitely Runyonesque. And so Teddy Brenner's melodramatic tale, right up there with the best of the old B-movie scripts, is widely regarded as kosher, and the Gavilan–Graham howler will forever be tarnished as a victory for the mob.

But there is a much less sensational scenario: one that absolves all three officials of corruption, but insists that they were put on the spot by two ringwise, cunning performers of widely contrasting styles, both of whom having a lengthy history of being involved in close and controversial decisions. And it is seldom mentioned that just the year before, Graham and Gavilan had met twice in non-title bouts, winning one apiece, and both were majority verdicts.

Gavilan was notorious for fooling the judges, thanks to his sudden and electrifying flurries of punches which were breath-taking to behold. He often coasted for almost half the three minutes, but with these spectacular outbursts he became a master at thieving rounds. Nor was Graham too straightforward to assess. He was a skilled all-round mechanic, but much of his work concentrated on body-sapping assaults, a strategy that is still regularly overlooked by many judges. In his 126-bout career Billy drew nine times, and of his fifteen defeats, nine came by a split vote. A far from easy man to appraise.

There were few straightforward rounds for the officials, and certainly none in which either fighter enjoyed a wide advantage or was on the brink of going down. Throughout their careers, Graham and Gavilan never failed to last the distance; in fact Billy never took a count, and The Kid, aside from being memorably upended by Carmen Basilio, may have been dropped just another two or three times in his marathon 143 appearances.

In the end the officials opted for flash over finesse, and they were wrong: they flunked their duties, but this was far from the worst decision ever announced in the Garden. What gave impetus to the ensuing uproar was not so much the injustice or the bundles of losing bets, but the nagging fear that Graham might never come so close again. This should have been his night, the night when all his blue-collar industry and technical expertise finally paid off with the title. On the East Side, Irish Billy could do no wrong: he was a local hero, but now an uncrowned champion.

William Walter Graham was born on September 9, 1922, the second oldest of four boys, but his East Side upbringing was miles removed from that of a young Graziano, running wild through the squalid backstreets. Billy's father ran a saloon at the corner of Second Avenue and 36th Street; his mother, from County Limerick, owned property in New Jersey. The Grahams did all right.

Billy liked to fight, and when he was ten his father took him to the local Catholic Youth Club where he was taught the rudiments, before moving on to the Madison Square Boys' Club. As a twelve-year-old weighing 95lb he beat another brilliant little puncher called Walker Smith, the future Sugar Ray, in a Police Athletic League competition in Greenwich Village.

Young Graham was that good, but in 1936 his progress came to an abrupt halt when he was denied entry into the prestigious Golden Gloves, the benchmark for all New York amateurs. The medical supervisor informed the youngster that he had a 'heart murmur' and the story was the same for the next four years, Billy applying, the Gloves' doctors declining and in the neighbourhood, his annual knockback became something of a joke, but the Grahams were not laughing. Eventually a heart specialist diagnosed that he had an irregular heartbeat, nothing to worry about, and nothing to prevent him from boxing.

Billy, however, was no longer interested in the Golden Gloves. Encouraged by a neighbourhood friend and adviser, a Cuban with the unlikely name of Jack Reilly, Graham successfully applied for a professional licence. Reilly – who much later in life would earn a law degree and wound up a judge – introduced him to Irving Cohen, then coaching young fighters in Bensonhurst, but already making inroads into the big league. The trio formed a career-long partnership.

On April 14, 1941 Connie Savoie lasted less than a round on Billy's professional introduction, and the skinny featherweight would remain unbeaten in his first 58 starts. Cohen was a cautious matchmaker, restricting the youngster to four- and six-round contests, developing him as an attraction in Elizabeth, New Jersey, then booking him into the New York clubs like the Coney Island Velodrome, the Broadway Arena, the Ridgewood Grove, and then the St Nicholas Arena, the longtime proving ground for future Garden headliners.

Graham was absent throughout 1943, serving in the Coast Guard, but by 1945 he was well-known around town as a very smart lightweight: brilliant left hand, dazzling footwork, a terrific in-fighter (Marciano nominated him as the best he ever saw fighting on the inside) with a sturdy chin. He did lack a concussive punch – only 26 quick wins throughout his career – but Cohen reckoned he was ready for an upgrade, and matched him with another hot prospect, tough Tony Pellone from Greenwich Village. The date was September 11, 1945 and this was Billy's first ten-round test, and also his first defeat, hotly disputed, of course.

Pellone would be awarded another debatable decision the following year, and the clever Tippy Larkin knew too much for Graham, but by the end of 1948 these were his only losses in

84 fights. He was growing into a welter, an established crowd-pleaser with a big following, but competition in the 147lb division was ferocious.

Ray Robinson was the champion, a marvellous superstar and way out on his own, despite the quality opposition. Gavilan was beginning to make his move, and there were other fine welters such as Johnny Bratton and Charlie Fusari, Bernard Docusen, Lester Felton and George Costner, all queuing up to stake a claim. Graham would have to be patient.

Billy had been a full-time fighter from the start. For three months he had been employed as a teenage stock clerk in a Manhattan department store, and that would be his only taste of packed lunches and nine-to-five until he quit the ring. But in October 1948, in the rectory of St Patrick's Cathedral, he married Lorraine, a girl he had met just the previous year. Boxing became a far more serious business, and he required regular fights.

There were nine outings in 1949, more than enough to ensure a pleasant home life, but he dropped important verdicts to Eddie Thomas (bitterly disputed, naturally!) on a well-paid visit to London, and, more significantly, to future lightweight king, the brawling Paddy De Marco in the Garden. The De Marco loss was a serious set-back for an aspiring welterweight contender, but the following year Graham got back on track. He exchanged those two split decisions with Gavilan, finally put one over on Pellone, beat a dangerous outsider, Phil Burton, and with Robinson about to invade the middleweights, Billy was right back in the shake-up.

Gavilan beat him to the punch. In fairness, the hugely popular Cuban had been the busier, and had consistently fought against a higher standard than Graham. He had given Sugar Ray two hard fights, one of them for the title, and in the usual mad scramble to find Robinson's successor, he emerged as clear favourite.

Bratton was already recognised as champion by the NBA, following a win over Fusari in Chicago; the European candidate, Charles Humez, simplified matters by moving up to middleweight. New York was prepared to acknowledge Bratton against Gavilan, provided Graham was given first crack at the winner; and so on May 18, 1951 The Cuban Hawk became the undisputed champion, handing the hard-hitting but brittle-chinned Bratton a severe beating over fifteen rounds.

Kid Gavilan . . . the silky smooth operator with the flashing smile and the scything bolo punch . . . the rhumba-crazy toast of the New York nightclubs . . . the hero of a generation of television fans who saw him on their screens no fewer than 34 times . . . one of the most colourful and best-loved fighters ever to hit New York.

The Kid came up the hard way. He was born Gerardo Mauras on January 6, 1926, in Berrocal in the province of Camaguey, but as an infant he became Gerardo Gonzalez after his father took off and his mother married a railroad worker of that name. There followed the all too familiar story of poverty, shared by so many future fighters, and by the age of twelve young Gerardo had left school and was swinging a machete on a sugar cane plantation, developing his strength, and his spectacular bolo, according to later press handouts.

Around the same time as he quit his classes, the youngster discovered boxing when a training school opened up in Camaguey. The coach, a man named Armando Valdo, spotting his enthusiasm and natural ability, soon singled him out for special attention. By the time Gerardo was sixteen, Valdo reckoned he was ready for the pros and sent him to Havana with an introduction to a café owner called Fernando Balido, who had extensive contacts in the world of boxing.

Balido's establishment was called El Gavilan (The Sparrowhawk) and the manager, deciding there were already too many boxers called Gonzalez, renamed him Kid Gavilan, and set him loose on the pros on June 5, 1943, when he outpointed Antonio Diaz over four rounds. He was a sixteen-year-old bantam.

In contrast to Graham, the Kid was quickly upped to gruelling ten-round bouts. He soon gathered an enthusiastic following in Havana, then a busy fight centre, and won the Cuban lightweight title in 1945, stopping José Pedroso in four rounds. That win earned him a three-fight visit to Mexico, where he suffered his first loss – speedily avenged in Havana – against Carlos Malacara. His rate of progress was impressive, and by the time he was twenty he had all but outgrown the local talent, and also the lightweight division. Next stop the States.

Balido lacked the influence to move a fighter successfully in America, but he was friendly with a countryman who was more than able, and so Angel Lopez joined the management team. Lopez was the proprietor of the popular Chateau Madrid nightclub in New York, and had been connected to many Cuban fighters, including Kid Chocolate, the sensational featherweight of the 1930s. Angel knew all the right faces, had played host to Carbo at the Chateau, and got busy.

Gavilan's New York debut was a relatively low-key affair, stopping Johnny Ryan in five rounds on All Saints Day 1946, but he was put to the test a month later, when booked into the St Nicholas Arena to face a good-class welter named Johnny Williams. The Cuban won the decision, and the fight was so entertaining that a return was arranged for two weeks later – in the Garden.

Back then, many decent fighters toiled for years before being granted an opportunity to box in the famous arena. The Kid, thanks to his powerful backers, arrived in record time, and once again he outpointed Williams.

He returned to Cuba for five fights, and then his American campaign began in earnest in August 1947, Gavilan soon discovering that he must earn and learn the hard way.

On his march towards the title, nobody was rated too tough or too tricky for the Kid, and inevitably there were defeats. A brainy boxer called Doug Ratford beat him twice, but at that time many top men would not entertain Ratford. And although Gavilan would exact satisfactory revenge, the great lightweight champion Ike Williams also proved much too good first time around. There were hints in the columns that the Cuban playboy was doing his roadwork in the nightclubs, and there was no denying that he loved the bright lights and the beautiful girls. But even after his career was over, the old champion still protested that he never cheated on his training and that back then he was still learning his trade.

There could be no better teacher than Ray Robinson, and after a 25-round crash course with the Sugarman Gavilan finally earned his degree. Their title fight was hard-fought and close, and he later paid tribute to the great man, saying that Ray had landed more good punches in their two fights than all his other opponents combined up until then.

On his run-up to Bratton he won eight straight, beating ranked rivals like Graham, Joe Miceli, Paddy Young and Gene Hairston (who enjoyed a great career despite being a deaf-mute), but the Garden championship fight proved to be a dreadful anticlimax. Early on, the Chicago fighter suffered a broken jaw (the third of

The talk of New York! Built on Madison Square, the ornate second Garden designed by architect Stanford White.

(Bettmann/Corbis)

[Inset]
The thrill of the circus...
a regular Garden treat.

(Bettmann/Corbis)

Jimmy Walker (top left), the man who legalised boxing in New York with (clockwise) the men who staged the Garden fights: Tex Rickard, James Norris and Mike Jacobs.

(All Bettmann/Corbis apart from top right: author's collection)

Before the bloodshed: Harry Greb (left), referee Kid McPartland and Gene Tunney. (Above) Tunney attends Greb's funeral. Arthur Donovan (below) counts over Benny Leonard during the McLarnin bout.

(Above left and right: author's collection; below: Bettmann/Corbis)

Billy Fox has Jake La Motta in dire trouble – at least that's how it looks!
(Bettmann/Corbis)

Let's be Frank. Mobsters Carbo (left) aided by lieutenant Palermo called the shots for far too long. (Bettmann/Corbis)

(Opposite) You lookin' at me? Jake La Motta, no longer a raging bull.

(Michael Brennan/Corbis)

Gotcha! Sandy Saddler puts the squeeze on Willie Pep. (Bettmann)

No quarter – Kid Gavilan (left) and Billy Graham slug it out. (Bettmann)

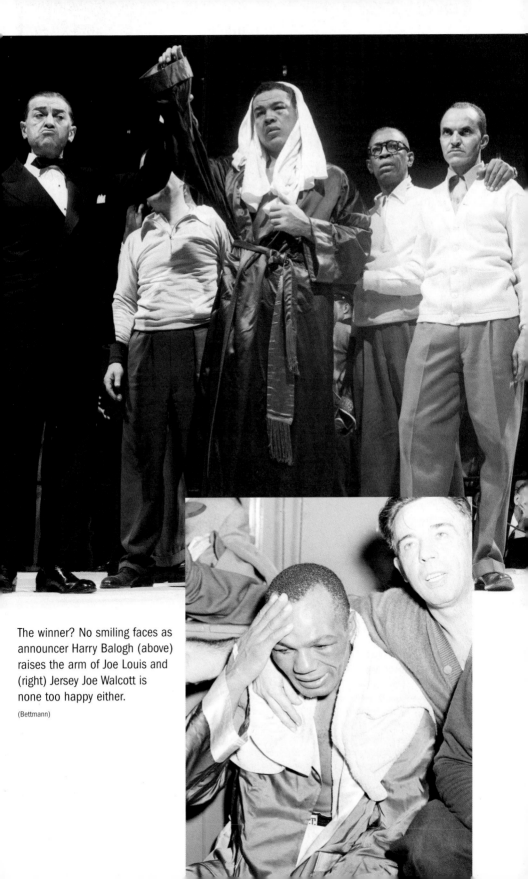

The winner? No smiling faces as announcer Harry Balogh (above) raises the arm of Joe Louis and (right) Jersey Joe Walcott is none too happy either.

(Bettmann)

The great and the ghastly. Joe Frazier drops Muhammad Ali during their epic encounter. Below: Riots kick off after Andrew Golota is disqualified against Riddick Bowe. (Above: Bettmann; below: Michael Brennan/Corbis)

his career) and then a double fracture of his right hand. His corner should have retired him. Instead, for fifteen rounds he was a soft target for the Kid, who enjoyed himself. Billy Graham would be a different proposition.

No hard sell was required for this showdown. The aficionados appreciated the considerable strengths of both boxers; even Gavilan's television supporters felt this one was worth the price of a ticket.

The East Siders were out in force to cheer home Billy, but despite their heavy betting action, Gavilan remained the solid 7/5 favourite. They were, however, in high humour, good-naturedly jeering a noisy but badly outnumbered Cuban faction who heralded their arrival by parading the national flag. Party time, and more than 18,000 were packed into the Garden when referee Mark Conn motioned the boxers to centre ring for the meaningless final instructions.

The bell for round one, and right away Graham slipped into gear, tossing trademark left hands. Early days, and some fell well short. A few connected, but high on the Kid's forehead or on a shoulder; a casual Gavilan expertly evaded others with minimum head movement as he gracefully glided around the ring, every now and then landing a searching shot of his own, finding his range. After their previous twenty rounds together, the boys had few surprises for one another, and the first three minutes were little more than reconnaissance.

But the champion was much more businesslike in the second. He ducked inside Graham's leads and banged home two hard left hooks that raised a welt under Billy's right eye. For good measure, he tried with the bolo, as much for the gallery as the eyes of the judges, but the challenger remained unflurried, as one might expect from a 100-fight pro, though his timing was off by those vital fractions. In comparison to the elegant Kid, the New Yorker seemed pedestrian.

There could be no question that Gavilan was definitely the boss through the first third of the fight. He was the better mover, although Graham, too, showed smart footwork; his spectacular bunches of punches were not just for show but were effective and hurtful; and when he did decide on a breather, he found it surprisingly easy to tie up Graham inside, denying him punching room.

The Kid was boxing intelligently, forever changing the tempo of his dance: one minute a sedate waltz, the next a furious jitterbug. But he failed to hassle Billy or persuade him to alter his gameplan, and the fighter's calm spread to his corner, where Cohen and Whitey Bimstein remained unperturbed. Their boy was getting ever sharper, and the other bum? He was just showboating.

And there was no doubt that by the seventh Graham was coming on strong. He looked to be boxing at the same controlled pace, but now Irish Billy was beating the Cuban to the punch, for the first time upsetting his rhythm, following up with accurate looping rights that sent the spray flying off Gavilan's head and the fans into a frenzy. This was more like the real Billy Graham, and now there was no hiding place inside for the Kid, as his challenger beat him up around the body.

Gavilan had by no means wilted, and he still looked sensational when unleashing those blistering combinations, always clocking his grandstand play for the last half minute, as if awakened by an alarm inside his head. But this was now as much a battle of wills as skills, and Graham seemed to be in the greatest shape of his life. Trudging back to his corner at the end of the tenth, the champ looked not only weary, but also downcast that he had so far failed to break Billy's spirit.

He had dictated a fast pace, and now his legs were sending out warning signals; increasingly, he was forced to stand and trade inside, and, as Marciano said, that was Graham territory. Up close, Billy was remorseless: short rights to the head, sickening left hooks to the ribcage, uppercuts that jolted back the Kid's head, and all delivered with textbook accuracy. Gavilan had survived the trenches before, and he grimly battled back, but his was a desperate rearguard action as his early lead was inexorably clawed back.

No longer did he try to entertain with the bolo: the situation was much too serious for that. Approaching the final bell, Billy was performing like an old master, and Gavilan, chin on chest, could only swing, as much in hope as expectation. As referee Conn sent them back to their corners, the cauldron that was the Garden rose to acclaim two fine competitors and a marvellous fight. Gavilan was exhausted and looked concerned; Graham was still sprightly, and with the air of a guy awaiting good news.

Irving and Whitey jubilantly embraced their fighter. If they knew that robbery was just a few seconds away, all three should have been nominated for Oscars. The noise level dropped to an excited buzz, as the scorecards were handed to Johnny Addie.

At that time in New York the officials used both round-by-round scoring and supplemental points scoring. If an official scored a fight level on rounds, then the points came into play. The points were awarded on a scale of one to four per round. A lot of maths for a mere boxing match, but time to go over to announcer Addie.

Conn and judge Frank Forbes both scored seven rounds apiece with one round level. Conn made Gavilan the winner by 10–7 in points, but Forbes gave his supplement to Graham by 11–10. Arthur Schwartz did not require to tot up his points: he scored a decisive 9–6 in rounds for the winner and still champion Kid Gavilan.

The crowd bayed their disbelief and then their outrage, and then all over the arena fighting broke out; ducking flying bottles and chairs, the cops hustled the officials off to the safety of the dressing rooms. Midring, the tears flowed as Graham and Cohen stood shellshocked. Crocodile tears? According to Brenner, they had been aware of the outcome for several days.

The Kid's early ascendancy was forgotten by many, and the middle rounds had been a minefield, both fighters having their big moments, but there is no doubt that the late rounds belonged to the challenger, and he won them more convincingly than Gavilan had taken the opening stages. That should have earned him the title, but although Schwartz's card was definitely over-generous to the champion, that does not mean that he had buckled under gangster pressure; only that he had fallen for the Cuban's eye-catching assaults and failed properly to reward Graham's less-obvious industry.

The indignation in the newspapers did not last long. Far more column inches were devoted to yet another Graham fight the following year, when, as already recounted, Joey Giardello had to go all the way to the Supreme Court to get justice after two New York commissioners had a brainstorm and altered a judge's card.

And what is often conveniently forgotten when discussing the robbery in the Garden is the fact that Graham had to wait only just over a year for an opportunity to set the record straight against

Gavilan. For a boxer whose connections had allegedly refused to play ball with the powerbrokers, Billy was not suffering too much.

The fight took place on October 5, 1952, a rare home appearance for the champion in Havana, and a 35,000-crowd watched their local hero win easily. For the only time in their four-fight series, Graham never posed a threat, and for the first time the decision was wide and unanimous.

Graham was now thirty and there were signs that he was on the slide. But like everything with Billy, the slide was gradual, graceful, and never without its moments. In 1953 there were good wins against Art Aragon, Giardello and Paddy Young, and there were two hard battles against Carmen Basilio in Syracuse – the first going to Carmen, the second declared a draw.

By now he was fighting only for the wages. He lost his last four, bowing out against the youthful Chico Vejar, an occasion made memorable thanks to A J Liebling's brilliant account of Billy's last fight in *The Sweet Science*. Liebling was a great admirer of the welter's class and style, both in and out of the ring, as was W C Heinz, another fine writer who put much that was Billy Graham into the character of Eddie Brown, the middleweight hero of his fine novel, *The Professional*.

Explaining his admiration for Irish Billy, Heinz wrote in 1982, 'A diminishing number, who still remember him, think of him as "The Uncrowned Champ", but I will always remember him as the professional, the honest workman who, more than the champions with their great gifts, represented the rest of us.'

Liebling's verdict? 'He was as good as a fighter can be without being a hell of a fighter.'

After boxing, Billy finally took the plunge and found himself regular employment, adapting as readily to his job as a rep for a distillery as he had done to facing up to a southpaw in the ring. He stayed with the same firm for more than 25 years, raised a family of four, and retired with Lorraine to a comfortable life in West Islip, Long Island. He died there on January 22, 1992 aged 69, after a lengthy battle with cancer.

As one might expect, Kid Gavilan's life was much more of a roller coaster ride. There were fabulous nights in the ring when he produced all his skills: outfighting Gil Turner before 39,000 fans in Philadelphia; outclassing Chuck Davey in Chicago. The southpaw former college boy had outstripped the Kid in the television ratings, but a supreme Gavilan kept bouncing him off the canvas until even the viewers got the message.

And, being Gavilan, there would be other nights when the fans screamed for justice. He scraped home by a majority vote against Bobby Dykes in Miami – the first mixed-colour bout held in Florida – and he had to get off the deck to beat Basilio in Syracuse, yet another split decision, and one more night when the law had to shield the referee from the wrath of the locals.

There were, however, other occasions when the Cuban was the victim: in London against Peter Waterman, in Paris against Germinal Ballarin, and, most notoriously of all, in Philadelphia on October 20, 1954 when he lost his title to Johnny Saxton.

All that day, rumours of underworld skulduggery were far louder than any surrounding Billy Graham's night in the Garden. Saxton was managed by the diminutive Blinky Palermo, Carbo's running mate, and the word was out that the Kid would need a knockout to win. Neither fighter looked capable of firing a decent shot, much less scoring a stoppage, and the charade was best summed up by the disgusted Pennsylvania Commission chairman, Frank Wiener, who told the new champion, 'I congratulate you on your luck . . . If Gavilan had made any kind of fight, you wouldn't have won. You disappointed me, and he was worse.'

Murky politics decreed that Gavilan was denied the opportunity to atone, but he soldiered on for another four years, until in June 1958 he announced his retirement after being outpointed by Yama Bahama in Miami Beach. He had won 107 of his 143 fights against the best, drawn six and was outpointed 30 times. More diligent researchers can discover just how many split decisions he figured in.

The Cuban Hawk grossed well over a million dollars during his sixteen-year career, but how much filtered down to the fighter is anyone's guess. The dough that he did see never lasted long: expensive cars and even more expensive women; three wives, luxury apartments, tax complications. Five years after his last fight the Kid was broke.

By then he was back living in Cuba, but when Fidel Castro came to power in 1959 life was all downhill for the one-time hero of the people. His property was confiscated, and then the authorities took away his passport. He had surprised many by becoming a Jehovah's Witness in America, and in Havana he would often wander the streets, making speeches, handing out literature, and frequently wound up in jail.

His sight was failing because of cataracts, and at last the Cuban Sports Ministry showed some compassion, granting him a $200-a-month pension and finding him somewhere to live. His plight became known to old friends in America who lobbied for his return to the States and on September 16, 1968, he was finally allowed to fly back to his second home. Benefit dinners and appeals took care of the expenses for the cataract operations; he found work as a security guard in Harrisburg, Pennsylvania; and then Muhammad Ali took him on board for a spell, and once again the Kid's pictures were in the newspapers.

But these were only temporary breathers, and the ailing Cuban Hawk no longer had the strength for one last soaring flight. He suffered three strokes, and moved to Miami where he felt he might be welcomed by the large Cuban community. But he lived his last years almost totally blind, sick, desperately poor, and nearly always alone. He died aged 77 on February 13, 2003.

Kid Gavilan was the 'hell of a fighter' that Billy Graham never became, but perhaps the East Sider was none the worse for that. Unlike Gavilan, he never won a championship belt, but throughout his life he earned only the highest respect from all who met him, and one cannot wish for more than that.

The Uncrowned Champion. A very special title for a very special fighter.

CHAPTER TWELVE

Lennox Lewis
v Evander Holyfield

SATURDAY, MARCH 13, 1999

Just before the principals entered the ring, announcer Jimmy Lennon asked the vast Garden crowd to stand in silent tribute as the timekeeper tolled the final bells for baseball legend Joe DiMaggio, whose recent death had saddened the nation. Just over an hour later, after Lennox Lewis and Evander Holyfield had completed their eagerly anticipated twelve rounds for the three major heavyweight championship belts, the timekeeper could have rung out yet another count, but this time in memory of boxing, what it had once been, and what it had become.

In the furious din, however, his bell would have gone unheard. More than 7,000 British supporters, and just as many Americans in the pro-Holyfield overflow audience, were going bananas. A memorable occasion had again been hijacked by judging deemed incomprehensible by the majority of experts, and the sport at large once more found itself on the back foot.

The next few days, stretching into weeks, would prove a hellish nightmare for two of the officials, Londoner Larry O'Connell and Eugenia Williams from New Jersey, and promoter Don King was, of course, the chief suspect – of what, nobody seemed quite certain. But already the conspiracy theories were in orbit and the heavyweight politicians were scenting blood. This one was too good to miss.

Even long before the days of the flamboyant Jimmy Walker who, as Democratic leader in the state assembly, pushed through the bill that legalised the sport in New York, politicians from all persuasions found the fight game irresistible. Far too many of them, however, have zeroed in on the business, armed with bad intentions and a hungry eye for banner headlines and primetime interviews. Nothing new, and not confined to America. In post-war Britain, a sharp-tongued Member of Parliament named Edith Summerskill crusaded for an outright ban on boxing; an equally vociferous MP, Bessie Braddock, chose to champion the sport; and Jack Solomons would have hit the jackpot had the pair ever clashed at Harringay rather than in the House of Commons.

Bessie and Edith would have been at one another's throats over this one.

Lewis and Holyfield had not performed just before the 21,284 who had somehow been squeezed into the Garden. Their fight was a major international event, seen live around the world, and, according to many, the decision had become a dreadful embarrassment. In state governor George Pataki's mansion aides hurriedly boned up on the athletic commission rules and the background of the judges; Mayor Rudolph Giuliani began firing his usual tough questions; and the state attorney-general, Eliot Spitzer, was right there with the front runners, bluntly asserting, 'The fight shows the judges were either guilty of tampering or incompetence.' Spitzer's competence to assess the judges' competence went unchallenged.

Nobody goes to the gallows for being useless at a job and, as we shall see later, no damning charges were ever forthcoming. But that is not really the point. Boxing can no longer afford the litany of questionable verdicts: the utter unpredictability of so many officials' deliberations is fast turning the sport into a sick joke, an increasing frustration for fans worldwide.

Boxing depends on the enormous cash injections it receives from television, and while your average TV fan might not be a Jim Watt or a Teddy Atlas, he knows what his eyes tell him . . . until the ring announcer reads out the cards, and he tries to remember when he last changed his glasses. Nowadays, with so many different camera angles, not to mention close-ups and reruns, a viewer really does have the best seat in the house, but what point is there watching the fights, possibly trying to score them, when so often the loser is called the winner?

There was, of course, no winner in the Garden. Boxing did not win, nor did Evander, and most certainly not Lennox Lewis, who looked shellshocked, then outraged when Lennon announced the draw. Sure, he was still the WBC heavyweight champion, but just seconds earlier Emanuel Steward and Frank Maloney had been congratulating him on adding the WBA and IBF belts to his collection. For once, this was not about money, but pride and prestige.

There were many who could not generate too much sympathy for big Lennox. The guy was already worth millions, and had even made fortunes by stepping aside from a fight when he could have enforced a contract. Hardly the mark of a warrior. His demeanour in the ring often lacked genuine passion, and outside the ropes, he was calm and unflappable. Some said smug. The bulk of the US media had been disparaging about his fighting qualities and questioned his courage. One writer, Ron Borges of the *Boston Globe*, had shamefully described him as being yellow, but that was an insane slur and totally without foundation. Lewis was no wimp, had taken his knocks and paid his dues.

Too bad, if some of boxing's elite were not quite ready for a polite, quietly spoken, chess-playing champ, as opposed to the motormouths and the bad dudes – Holyfield a welcome exception – who were in vogue. But now he was left waiting for the universal acclaim that he felt was his right. It had been such a long haul.

Lennox Claudius Lewis first weighed in at 10lb 10oz on September 2, 1965, in Stratford, London. His mother Violet, who had arrived from Jamaica, was both industrious and ambitious. She looked forward to a better life in Canada, but there were several false starts before she settled in Kitchener, Ontario. Her elder son, Dennis, went to live with his father, and Lennox remained in London, living with an aunt, until Violet had earned the money to send for him.

He was a twelve-year-old, already reaching 6 feet tall and, belying his later reserve, was a boisterous youngster at school and hard to handle. He was often in street fights, and this inevitably led to a visit to a gym and the world of boxing. Lennox was a quick convert.

His early trainers were an ex-amateur, a German called Arnie Boehm, and then a Romanian, Adrian Teodorescu, and they watched his development from being an ungainly, skinny novice into an outstanding and hard-hitting prospect. Naturally, there were disappointing set-backs that might have dented his ambition: just fifteen, he was beaten by the more mature Donovan Ruddock; there was a serious upset in a tournament in East Berlin, where he was stopped by a Soviet; and then, most notably of all, he was outpointed in the 1984 Los Angeles Olympics by the eventual gold winner, Tyrell Biggs. Preparing for LA, he had sparred with the young Mike Tyson, and although the offers poured in to turn professional, he was still only eighteen, and he made the sensible decision to try again for Olympic gold.

The strategy paid off handsomely, and in the 1988 super-heavyweight final in Seoul he created a huge impression and landed some whopping right hands when stopping America's big hope, Riddick Bowe, in two rounds. Lennox and Violet were overwhelmed with pro offers from all over the world, but again they made a wise decision, hiring a Chicago lawyer, John Hornewer, to evaluate the bids.

Hornewer's recommendation came as a tremendous shock to insiders on both sides of the Atlantic. Instead of remaining in Canada, or, as expected, joining one of the major promotional outfits in the States, Lewis announced that he was signing with a London manager, Frank Maloney, a forty-year-old former amateur, who, up until then, had scuffled around the business as a trainer, cornerman, manager and small-time promoter. A little guy, and by no means bigtime, but now he had considerable financial muscle, supplied by a high-profile businessman named Roger Levitt. Lennox's brother Dennis had first suggested the idea of being based in England, and the deal hammered out by Hornewer was a beauty.

The arrangement was for five years and included a £150,000 signing fee, a Mercedes, the use of a house in London, and £500 a week expenses. Lewis would receive a 70–30 split of the purses and marketing revenue; Hornewer would be put on a retainer; and there would be a job in the organisation for Violet. The lawyer and Violet were keen on hiring an American trainer, and John Davenport, a former US marine drill sergeant, was brought on board. Levitt informed the media that Lennox would make £40 million.

Team Lewis was ready to roll, and on June 27, 1989 the giant heavy made his pro bow at London's Albert Hall, stopping journeyman Al Malcolm in the second. By the close of the year he had won his six fights, all inside the distance, and with appearances in the States and Canada. Clearly the plan was to make Lewis a trans-Atlantic attraction, but he was proving a hard sell: in too many fights he was still hesitant and amateurish, and he won few new fans when he landed his first major title, stopping a game but outclassed Frenchman, Jean-Maurice Chanet, for the European title in October 1990 at the Crystal Palace in London.

Little over a month later there was a surprise upheaval in the camp, when the boss went bust. On December 7, 1990 the Levitt Group, estimated at one time to be worth a cosy £150 million, sensationally folded. In the fall-out, Lewis' contract was bought by another moneyman, a millionaire liquidator called Panos Eliades, who formed a promotional company. The transfer was relatively painless: Maloney remained manager; Davenport, despite increasing friction with Maloney, stayed on as trainer; and brother Dennis was added to the payroll as a personal manager.

In March Lennox became British champion, halting Gary Mason in seven rounds at Wembley. Mason had previously been unbeaten in 35 contests but Lewis was never extended, and his confidence was further boosted with quick wins in the States against former world champion Mike Weaver, and his old amateur foe, Tyrell Biggs. No matter that both were spent forces, the Brit was now considered a genuine contender, and he confirmed his status, and added the Commonwealth title to his collection of belts, after beating Derek Williams in London. Time now for the biggest fight of his career . . . against former amateur rival, Razor Ruddock.

The date was October 31, 1992. The venue, Earl's Court in London. The prize, a promised shot at the winner of the Holyfield–Riddick Bowe championship fight, scheduled for Las Vegas just two weeks later. Particularly in Britain, most boxing folk were convinced that Maloney had been suckered into a terrible blunder.

The Razor had given Tyson two rough nights; he was rugged and could hit; no manager in his right mind would consider him suitable at this stage in Lewis' career. The flak made victory all the sweeter. Lennox hammered the Canadian inside two rounds, and knocked him down three times. This was an awesome exhibition of power, and the Brits acclaimed a new hero. But he would win his world title without throwing another punch.

An in-shape Bowe outpointed Holyfield, but his manager, Rock Newman, wanted nothing to do with Lewis. Obviously, memories of Seoul lingered on, and Big Daddy smiled for the cameras as he dumped his WBC belt into a trash can. An affronted WBC immediately granted recognition to Lewis, but he had to prove himself all over again, and his critics were quick to highlight flaws after workmanlike defences against Tony Tucker, Frank Bruno, and Phil Jackson.

And they seemed to be right when, on September 24, 1994, the unheralded Oliver McCall turned him into an ex-champion. One crushing right hand in the second round did the damage, and though Lewis did regain his feet the fight was rightly stopped. The damage to his ego was far more serious than the hurt from the pulverising right, but Lewis now showed his depth of determination.

Changes were made to his training programme. Davenport had been replaced by a Puerto Rican extrovert, Pepe Correa, but this had never been a comfortable partnership, and after the McCall disaster he was replaced by Emanuel Steward, who had been Oliver's chief cornerman at Wembley. The rehabilitation was slow and complicated by intense political manoeuvring in the heavyweight division, but on February 7, 1997 Lewis regained the WBC belt in an extraordinary return with McCall who suffered an emotional breakdown before losing in the fifth.

Since then Lennox had made a lot of money from four defences, but he wanted more: he owned one title, Evander Holyfield held two. There had to be a showdown, and, inching his way towards the Garden ring, struggling to get through the throngs jamming the aisles, he was convinced that this was his night: the night when he would finally become the undisputed heavyweight champion of the world.

Holyfield had already been an undisputed champ, both at cruiserweight and heavy, and despite his enormous wealth he still had ambitions. One thing for sure: he would not suffer a nervous breakdown.

There can be few fighters who have been so single-minded and unwaveringly convinced of their destiny as the man from Atlanta . . . Marciano and Tunney certainly. Muhammad Ali, of course. Ring legends. But such is the intensity of Holyfield's belief in himself and in God that on occasions there have been genuine expressions of concern for his well-being, unease that one day he will push himself too far.

His huge following feared the worst when, after his losing battle with Michael Moorer, doctors diagnosed serious heart problems. Evander, however, had consultations with an evangelist who doubled as a faith healer – and also specialists at the renowned Mayo Clinic! – and was given a complete all-clear. He also stopped Moorer in a return. But even hard-bitten fight veterans fretted for his health and safety when he first faced up to Tyson. Their anxieties later seemed laughable and Holyfield gloried in the occasion. Put simply, the man they call The Real Deal is unique.

He has always pushed his body to the outer limits. In his late teens, thanks to excruciatingly hard work and a special, Spartan diet, he somehow transformed himself from being an average-sized welterweight into a power-packed, 6ft 2″ 170lb 22-year-old. And much later, now under the guidance of fitness wizard Tim Hallmark, he subjected himself to further torture to bulk up first to cruiser, and then to full heavyweight. In the ring, he often called on incredible reserves, and in one fight – when winning the cruiserweight title from Dwight Muhammad Qawi – he lost a staggering 12lb during the course of the exhausting fifteen rounds. Going head-on with Lewis, he was a 36-year-old whose best days were behind him, but the fires were still burning in his soul.

Evander Holyfield was born on October 19, 1962 in Atmore, Alabama, the eighth and youngest child of Annie Laure Holyfield. Annie's marriage to Joseph Holyfield was long finished, and Evander's father was a lumberjack named Ison Coley, but once again the relationship did not work out. The family moved to Atlanta when Evander was five, and although money was tight there was plenty of laughter in the house, and the children were all brought up to read the Bible. Holyfield never lost the habit.

After a year the lad joined the Warren Memorial Boys' Club, and by the time he was eight he was receiving his first boxing lessons from a man called Carter Morgan. Their relationship was a special one, especially in race-conscious Georgia: Morgan and his wife opened their home to the little black boy, helped out with the extras that the Holyfields could not afford, and they were repaid by Evander's efforts in the gym. Morgan died when the youngster was in his senior year at high school and it was as if he had lost a father. The coach's son, Ted, took over training duties, and already a career in boxing seemed assured.

He worked for a spell, fuelling planes at Atlanta airport, but come 1984 and the Los Angeles Olympics he was tipped for gold in an American team packed with great prospects. Nine Americans won gold: Pernell Whitaker, Tyrell Biggs, Mark Breland, Meldrick Taylor, Henry Tillman, Jerry Page, Steve McCrory, Paul Gonzalez and Frank Tate. A desperately unlucky Holyfield had to settle for bronze.

In the second round of his semi-final against New Zealander Kevin Barry, the Yugoslav referee called, 'Stop boxing', but Holyfield had already unleashed a left hook which floored Barry. He managed to get up, but the ref halted the bout and the outcome was a disqualification. There was a considerable uproar, but the fighter accepted the decision calmly and with dignity. This would become a trademark.

Along with Breland, Whitaker, Taylor and Biggs, Evander signed up with the ambitious Main Events organisation, based in New Jersey and run by the Duva clan. On November 15, 1984 all five were showcased for the first time as professionals in the grand setting of the Garden, Holyfield winning a hard-fought six-rounder against a useful Philadelphian, Lionel Byarm. He was on his way and progress was so swift that after just eleven outings Lou Duva reckoned that he was ready for a title shot against the WBA cruiserweight champion, Dwight Qawi, who had first boxed as Dwight Braxton.

This was a searching assignment: ex-con Qawi was short, stocky, extremely resilient and far more experienced, but on July 12, 1986 in his hometown, Atlanta, Holyfield survived several moments of crisis to hammer out a testing split decision. This was the first of many world title nights, and he speedily took care of all viable contenders, owning all the worthwhile belts after stopping Carlos De Leon in April 1998. The fresh challenge lay with the really big guys, the full-blown heavies, and so too did the serious money, always a prime consideration for Evander.

Tim Hallmark got busy, mapping out fitness schedules, carefully building up Holyfield's weight and strength, but never at the expense of his mobility; Lou Duva, meanwhile, had started talking Tyson.

Evander weighed 202lb for his heavyweight debut, a so-so stoppage over the fading James Tillis, and his form would fluctuate in subsequent fights: impressive stopping Michael Dokes in a thriller; no better than pass marks against Alex Stewart.

But suddenly, Mike Tyson was out of the picture, blown away by Buster Douglas in ten dramatic rounds in a remarkable upset in Tokyo. The relatively unknown James Douglas found himself the undisputed heavyweight champion of the world, and Evander was first in line to challenge the man who had destroyed a myth and demonstrated that in boxing anything is possible.

Buster Douglas loved to eat much more than he cared to fight, and in the weeks following his extraordinary performance in Japan his life had been one magic merry-go-round of sumptuous feasts, banquets and personal appearances at the best fast-food joints in town. An unashamed orgy of self indulgence, and Douglas could never regain either his fitness or his desire. On October 25, 1990 in Las Vegas he clambered into the ring against Holyfield weighing a monster 246lb – 15lb more than he had scaled for Tyson – and he managed to offer token resistance for two rounds. But in the third he flopped to the canvas after a hard right from the challenger landed flush. The Real Deal was the champ.

Offstage, Holyfield's life was less than ideal. There was an acrimonious split with his business manager and adviser Ken Sanders, an Atlanta car dealer. A divorce was in the pipeline from Paulette, mother of his three children. Relations with Dan and Lou Duva were becoming increasingly strained. Evander loved quoting from his Bible, but he was still just a fringe contender when sainthood was discussed.

On April 19, 1991, he beat a fellow man of God, ancient George Foreman, in a rousing first defence, but he looked vulnerable when badly staggered by Bert Cooper in Atlanta, and pedestrian against another oldie, Larry Holmes, in Vegas. And though he fought one of his bravest fights, his first reign came to an end on November 13, 1992 in Las Vegas when a focused Riddick Bowe took his title after twelve memorable rounds.

A shattering experience, and Holyfield's first professional defeat, but just short of a year later he stunned the boxing world by outfighting and outpointing Big Daddy Bowe in the return. This was the fight that was sensationally interrupted for more than twenty minutes after a nutty paraglider got hung up in the lights above Bowe's corner. Perhaps he was trying to deliver a special message from somewhere.

Holyfield's form was now erratic. He lost his WBA and IBF belts to Michael Moorer, and after he had satisfied everyone that his heart was sound, he proceeded to run out of puff and was stopped in the eighth of a non-title decider against Bowe, having had Riddick on the canvas in the sixth. Time to wind up a fabulous career? Not The Real Deal.

There were still chapters to be written in the Book of Evander. On November 9, 1996 he secured his long-awaited match with Mike Tyson. Holyfield was a big betting outsider and there were many good souls who had their fingers crossed that he would be able to enjoy his $11 million purse, but the veteran was a revelation, dropping Tyson in the sixth and battering him so badly that the referee had to rescue Mike in round eleven. Thinking dollars, he welcomed a return, and looked all set to do a repeat number when Tyson totally lost the plot and took a chunk out of Evander's ear, prompting a disqualification. Holyfield forgave him, and proved he was none the worse when gaining sweet revenge over Moorer, stopping him in eight rounds and adding the IBF belt to his WBA title.

Now there was only Lennox Lewis barring his path to undisputed championship glory. The Brit was three years younger, three inches taller, and 31lb heavier, but such stats did not concern Holyfield as he marched towards the Garden ring, smiling and singing gospel songs. Lewis watched him, expression-less and distant, perhaps a trifle miffed that Evander had predicted a third round victory.

The referee was Arthur Mercante Jr, son of the most famous ref of all time. The judges: Stanley Christodoulou, South African and vastly experienced; Larry O'Connell, English and equally seasoned; and Eugenia Williams, American and a surprise nomination, new to this level.

They were a happy family for the opening three rounds, all in agreement that Lennox had edged a quiet, cautious first; had clearly taken the second, thanks to some heavy rights that backed Holyfield on to the ropes; and had lost the third, Evander scoring freely with hard left hooks and solid rights, but never looking close to making his pre-fight prediction come true.

Both fighters enjoyed some success in the fourth, Lewis spearing out lefts and following up with clubbing eye-catching rights; Holyfield getting in close, scoring with hooks. Stan and Larry gave the benefit to the Brit, Eugenia saw it as another Holyfield round. She was not doing too badly, but the fifth was her downfall; the round she went haywire; the round that she would lamely try to explain away to a Senate committee just a few days later.

This was a massive round for Lewis. In control in the centre of the ring, he deftly turned Holyfield and banged home a big right that landed on the back of the American's head, stunning him, and propelling him into the ropes. Lennox could have finished the fight right there, but he seemed in no great hurry as he drove home power-packed left hooks and fearsome right hands, picking his shots with great deliberation. One vicious right uppercut almost did for Evander, but courage and conditioning kept him upright until the bell.

Londoner Mickey Duff, who has spent a lifetime around ringsides and who admitted to a big bet riding on Lewis, later claimed that the fifth could have been scored 10–8, such was the Englishman's dominance. The lady from New Jersey, however, awarded a 10–9 to Holyfield.

Lewis was controlling the fight, and a revived Holyfield just could not get inside where he always did his best work. He was outboxed in the sixth and soaked up plenty in the seventh, as Lennox landed sharp uppercuts and more hard rights. Manny Steward was urging his fighter forward, scenting an early finish, but again the big man refused to go for broke.

Nonetheless, he clearly won both rounds, and Christodoulou and Williams concurred. But now it was O'Connell who was out of step: he awarded the sixth to Holyfield and made the seventh level. In fact after round five Larry did not give his countryman another round until the twelfth.

Lewis was doing himself few favours. To use a horseracing expression, he was idling in front, doing just enough and stead-fastly refusing to take any risks, as if remembering Oliver McCall's thunderous right from five years back. Steward kept imploring him to step up the pace, apply serious pressure, but Lennox had decided to do things his way.

Stanley and Eugenia both scored rounds eight, nine and ten for Evander. O'Connell gave two to the American, and called the tenth level. In that round, Evander had ducked inside, scored with a good left hook and a hard right which prompted Lewis to grin. No points for smiles or smirks, and he returned to his corner with a nick on his left eyelid.

Nor did he earn any plus marks in the penultimate round. O'Connell and Williams opted for Holyfield, Christodoulou could not separate two very tired fighters. And yet, without doing much, Lewis appeared to be in charge, never in any difficulty, while Evander seemed to be fast running out of ideas. But the Brit's stubborn refusal to exert any sustained pressure was proving a turn-off with the officials. In the corner, Manny Steward was none too happy either. He desperately wanted his man to finish in style.

Everybody in the Garden had to give the final three minutes to Lennox. He completely outboxed a flagging, bruised Holyfield who continued to plod forward. He picked him off with accurate lefts, jarred him with rights, but he was still too leery to try for a knockdown or a knockout. At the final bell he raised his arm, assured and triumphant. Evander returned to his corner exhausted, and with the air of a man expecting the worst.

The fight had been honestly contested and never dull, but aside from the fifth, there had been few moments of electrifying excitement. Lewis must take responsibility for that, as he nullified a one-dimensional opponent, opting for the safe route, playing the percentages. Great tactics for a budding chessmaster, but a mite dodgy in boxing.

And so, ladies and gentlemen, time to go to the scorecards. Stanley Christodoulou, 116–113, Lewis – nods of agreement from all but the American corner. Eugenia Williams, 115–113, Holyfield – cue for shock, horror and disgust. But the English judge would put matters right. Larry O'Connell, 115–115. Blimey! A bleedin' draw, and in the high tiers his countrymen went barmy.

Poor O'Connell was also stunned. Judges hand over the result of their deliberations at the end of every round, leaving no room for adjustments as the fight progresses. As round followed round and O'Connell passed over his scores, he actually believed he had Lewis marginally ahead. He was concentrating, rightly, on each three minutes as an entity, and his fault was in trying to be too fair, too neutral, subconsciously being too generous to the American.

A bad mistake from such an experienced official, and Larry would pay dearly.

When he returned to England he was hounded and vilified by a media fuelled with righteous indignation, bombarded with abusive and obscene phone calls to his home, spat upon and accused of taking bribes. Sports minister Tony Banks described the decision as a disgrace. He would, wouldn't he? But the FBI could find not the slightest shred of evidence implicating O'Connell in any shady deal and quickly closed their file.

The Feds, however, got far more mileage out of single-mother Eugenia. Just seven weeks before the fight, she had filed for voluntary bankruptcy, but in her declaration she had somehow omitted to disclose a bank account containing $20,000. Much ado about that money.

Just as interesting to the FBI was the fact that Williams had been nominated by the International Boxing Federation. The Bureau was in the middle of an in-depth investigation into the IBF and its chairman, Bobby Lee, and her shock appointment fired fresh suspicions. Certainly, her track record as a judge did not qualify her for such a high-profile gig, and she had landed the job on only 24 hours notice. There were rumours that Lee was doing a favour for a friend. Enigmatic.

Williams made a sorry witness before a hastily convened New York senate investigating committee. She claimed that photographers had repeatedly blocked her view, and that at one stage she had climbed on to a table to gain a better look. Weird. And when invited to review the notorious fifth round on tape, she conceded, 'From what I've now seen on television, it looked like Lewis was the winner of that round.' She tried to counter. 'But what I saw on TV was not what I saw on the night. I viewed the fight from a different angle.'

The newspapers had also seen the fight from different angles.

The *New York Post*'s Wallace Matthews, previously a harsh critic of Lewis, wrote, 'Lennox Lewis beat Evander Holyfield from here (New York) to London – with stopoffs in Jamaica and Canada along the way.' Ron Borges (*Boston Globe*) disagreed. 'The *Globe* card had Lewis taking a razor-thin 115–114 decision after giving away rounds 8 through 11, simply choosing not to punch and then coming on to win the final round and the fight.' And what about the *New York Times* veteran, Dave Anderson? 'I agreed with the draw verdict of the British (and WBC) judge, Larry O'Connell.'

And the referee? Mercante Jr pulled no punches. 'This is a crime for the sport I've been around all my life. Lewis won the fight easily. I'd have given Holyfield no more than three rounds.'

Nobody was closer to the action than Junior, and by now everybody and his uncle – from the New York state governor to the British sports minister to the drunk slumped over the bar – had said his piece and could move on . . . next business, please. And at last, the media had calmed down and Eugenia Williams, innocent but incompetent, was allowed to drift back to obscurity. But once again, boxing was left battered and bloodied from self-inflicted injuries.

Naturally, there had to be a rematch, and on November 13, 1999, Las Vegas gave New York a lesson on how to treat important guests from another land. This time, a much more lively Holyfield stretched Lewis throughout the twelve rounds. Many at ringside reckoned that The Real Deal might have nicked the verdict; others were predicting another draw. But not these judges: they awarded the Englishman a unanimous decision, and by flatteringly wide margins.

Since then, Lewis has raked in many millions and has finally achieved his lifelong ambition, pulverising Mike Tyson in Memphis in June 2002 to receive general acceptance as the outstanding heavyweight on the planet. Before doing that, however, he had been forced to come back from a stunning defeat of McCall proportions, against Hasim Rahman in South Africa. Lennox, it would appear, needs to be lifted by a special challenge.

As does The Real Deal. Evander continues to be captivated by his peculiar Holyfield Trinity: The Lord, The Loot, and The Love Of A Good Fight. As this is being written, he can still command top dollar, and we must only hope that he does not stay around for that one fight too many.

And finally, what about this judging business? Facile to talk about raising standards and increasing scrutiny on the capabilities of potential officials. In a sport already so dreadfully fragmented, just who is fit to judge the judges? Next question.

Nights of Shame

Boxing demands discipline and dedication, and in these sick times of increasing juvenile and teenage anarchy it would be no bad thing if the tearaways spent their community service hours banged up in a gym. Only a pipedream, of course, but there just might be the chance that some of the nutters could learn the real meaning of respect.

Only some. One of boxing's most hackneyed vindications is a history of giving hope to the hopeless, and turning around lives headed for the gutter and the slammer. And there have been countless shining examples.

But boxers are just like the rest of us: vulnerable, unpredictable, sometimes weak, often just plain bad guys. The pity is that when a fighter goes off the rails, the media has a ball.

No surprise that some of the best jigs have been danced in the Garden.

CHAPTER THIRTEEN

Fritzie Zivic *v* Al Davis

FRIDAY, NOVEMBER 15, 1940

The one difference between Abraham Davidoff and the rest of his ragged street gang was the fact that young Abe would always rise early, race down to the market, pile his pushcart high with choice fruit, and then start on the hustle. His pals preferred the easy way: a lightning swoop on a cart, and bingo! Free fruit and a few bucks robbed from some frightened old pedlar.

That in-born work ethic set the youngster apart from the rest of the budding hoodlums. That willingness to toil, plus an incredible dig in his left hand, would direct Abraham Davidoff into the world of boxing, and for a few fleeting helter-skelter years wrote his name in bright lights on the Garden marquee and in the headlines on all the sports pages. By now, however, the name was Al Davis, Bummy Davis to the hacks, and the champagne years would pass all too quickly.

But the boy who had answered to Boomy Davidoff on the rough streets of Brooklyn's Brownsville section could never become a choirboy. Like his friends, Boomy's boyhood heroes were the guys in the wide-brimmed hats, the trigger men like Abe Reles – a founder member of what the press called Murder Inc. – who could often be seen strutting around the neighbourhood. And the teenager was proud that he was on good terms with Bo Weinberg, a top gun for Dutch Schultz until Bo displeased his boss and went missing, believed to be asleep somewhere at the bottom of the East River, his feet encased in cement.

Boomy (an affectionate nickname bestowed on little Abraham by his family) swaggered the streets with the rest of the young hoods, and trouble was never too far away. He was hot-tempered,

quick to lash out with that left hook; the police were often on his
trail, and he developed a nasty reputation in the neighbourhood.
Boomy Davidoff was a regular Brownsville tough guy.

But as Evander Holyfield, recalling his early poverty, once said,
'You don't have to go to jail to be tough.'

Evander was spot on. There is another kind of tough guy, a far
more admirable sort, who does not require back-up from knuckle-
dusters and ice picks and guns. This tough guy hauls himself out
of bed every morning to punch the clock at a backbreaking job
which he hates, because he chooses to earn his money the honest
way, and he is always looking to make some extra dough. If that
means fighting in the ring, then he will tug on the gloves and take
his chances. Fritzie Zivic was that kind of tough guy.

He shared only one trait with Al Davis. Inside the ropes, both
were vicious and ruthless, with an absolute disregard for the
Queensberry Rules. Zivic is still remembered by many as the
dirtiest fighter who ever laced an eye or dented a foul protector
(an honour that must make Harry Greb spin in his grave) and yet,
in a career that spanned 233 pro bouts, never once was he
disqualified. That illustrates just how expert and cunning he was
at conning referees.

Fritzie Zivic came from sturdy Croatian stock. He was born on
May 8, 1913 in Pittsburgh, on the same day that a report was
published telling how 900,000 immigrants had entered the States
since the previous July. Fritzie was first-generation American, the
youngest of five brothers reared in a district called Lawrenceville,
a melting pot of blacks, Jews, Italians and Poles, within walking
distance of the giant steel mills.

All five Zivic brothers tried their luck in the ring, and with great
success. There was Joe, who was a middleweight; two lightweights,
Eddie and Jack; and bantamweight Pete, who initiated the family
interest in boxing. Pete had injured himself in the mills – apparently
a regular occurrence back then – and as part of his recuperation he
began working out at a local gym, the Willow Club, where he fast
developed into a talented amateur: talented enough that along with
brother Joe, who had followed him to the Willow, he was selected
to represent the US in the 1920 Antwerp Olympics. It was only a
matter of time before Fritzie also decided to become a fighter.

The old *Ring Record Book* says that Zivic was beaten no fewer
than 65 times as a pro; *Boxing Register* claims that the tally was

only 64. No matter who is correct, this remains an embarrassingly high number of defeats for a fighter who held the welterweight championship, and suggests that Fritzie might have been only a fair fighter who landed lucky. His 1993 elevation to Hall Of Fame status tells us otherwise.

Zivic started out during the years of the Depression when so many young men turned to the fight game to earn their eating money. In all divisions there was bitter competition; boxers could not afford to pick and choose their opponents like today's crop can; the wages were small and they fought as often as they could, regularly going into the ring with a cut barely healed, a bruise still visible from the last job.

That was the way things were. There was no smooth path to glory or the Garden, and when the Pittsburgh youngster began he did not have to worry for too long about protecting an unbeaten record. In only his second fight – on November 16, 1931 – he was outpointed by Steve Senich in front of a local crowd. Senich beat him again the following year, as did Jerry Clements, but Zivic accepted those set-backs as part of his education and refused to become discouraged.

Persistence paid off and in 1933 he finally got the better of Senich, stopping him in two rounds. After a heartening string of wins he headed west for California, staying for six months, and remaining undefeated in twelve fights. But those were only prelim bouts, the money was poor, and he returned to Pittsburgh to reinvent himself.

Luke Carney was a capable manager and could always find Zivic plenty of work. Despite his increasing use of the rough stuff – perhaps because of it – win or lose, Fritzie was a great draw, but then, inexplicably, his career went into sharp reverse. Beginning with an unremarkable defeat against Joey Ferrando in Jersey City on August 8, 1935, Zivic hit the skids, losing eight in a row, eventually stopping the rot with a one-round knockout over Billy Celebron in St Louis in May 1936. Celebron had outpointed him during the horror run, and this emphatic revenge encouraged both the fighter and the manager that there just still might be a future.

By Christmas, his fortunes had revived so dramatically that Carney was able to book him for a high-profile showdown with Billy Conn.

A clash between two Pittsburgh favourites. The crowds always turned out to cheer or jeer Fritzie, but they idolised Conn, the fabulous Pittsburgh Kid, who had never boxed as an amateur and who would later give Joe Louis such nightmares. Four years younger than Fritzie, Conn was currently on a 22-fight winning streak (Zivic had gone five without mishap) and the Dusquesne Garden was sold out a week before the date. Zivic conceded considerable weight, but he was always convinced that he won a very close, terribly hard fight. The referee and most of the newspapers agreed with him, but the two judges thought that Conn had done just enough.

Many years later, Conn described the Zivic fight to Peter Heller.

That was like going to college for five years, just boxing him ten rounds. He'd do everything in the world to you. The minute you did something to him, he would holler and scream, you'd have to have the police to keep him quiet. He put an awful face on me, busted me all up with everything. He did everything but kick you. I beat him.

Despite the huge disappointment, this was a crossroads fight for Zivic. His $2,500 purse was easily his biggest, and looked great in comparison to 75 cents an hour in the steel mills. He determined to give boxing his best shot.

In the next three years he packed in 48 fights, losing only five, and two of those defeats were delivered by another great Pittsburgh attraction, the marvellous Charley Burley. Archie Moore named Burley as the best man that he ever fought; Eddie Futch regarded him as the finest fighter he ever saw. Charley was that good, but he had boxed only seventeen times when he first faced the ringwise Zivic on March 21, 1938, and he dropped a close decision. In two subsequent bouts Burley was a clear winner, badly punishing Fritzie in their last meeting in 1939, but the losses did not impair Zivic's march towards a title shot.

Burley was black and lacked the connections to secure a championship challenge; Zivic was white, and anything was possible. That was how the game was played, but at least the tough guy from Lawrenceville was fearless enough to share the ring with Charley three times. Ray Robinson and Jake La Motta were just two legends who could always find an excuse when Burley's name was mentioned.

After outpointing the infuriatingly clever lightweight champion Sammy Angott, Fritzie found himself rated the number one contender to face Henry Armstrong. He was a battle-hardened, flat-nosed pro who had boxed 129 times over ten years, and now he was getting his chance against one of the greatest fighters who ever lived. Many believed that he and Carney were only getting a well deserved paynight in the Garden. Almost a benefit.

The all-action phenomenon that was Henry Armstrong had held the featherweight and lightweight titles, had boxed a draw with Ceferino Garcia for the middleweight championship, and was now the outstanding boss of the welters. A small, compact bundle of ferocious energy, he had blossomed on the West Coast before taking New York by storm. In the four years leading up to the Zivic defence he had fought 61 times, losing only once, to Lou Ambers in a hotly disputed rematch in August 1939. Only the longshot gamblers were attracted to Zivic.

On October 4, 1940 an astonished Garden crowd watched an inspired Zivic go fifteen rounds for the first time, outfighting and outfouling Armstrong who, in close, was no angel either. Fritzie copped a tight but unanimous decision, and the very last punch of the fight was a straight right hand which sent little Henry to the canvas, the final bell ringing at the count of four. Just how brutal were the exchanges can be gauged from Zivic's vivid recollection to Peter Heller for *In This Corner*.

I busted him up, cut him here and cut him there. I'd get him in a clinch. He'd have his head down, trying to give you that head. I'd come up on the side. When the eye was cut, I'd rub it with the laces to open it up a little more. Then he's watching this cut, and I'd cut this (other) eye. His mouth was cut real bad. He was too proud to spit the blood out. He swallowed it. Swallowing the blood made him sick. His mouthpiece fell out of his mouth about five or six times in the last five or six rounds. He was a little tired I guess. He kept opening his mouth and I was banging him with uppercuts.

Has there ever been a more stark and chilling account of the grim business of winning a boxing championship? No Golden Boys here; no classic one-punch knockouts; no dazzling footwork. Just one extremely mean machine clinically dismantling another.

After all those lean years Fritzie had struck gold. He had been paid only $3,500, but there was a return contract and in the rematch he was due to pocket $25,000. In the meantime he could earn top money fighting a few non-title bouts. Carney got busy. Just over a month after he had shocked Armstrong, Zivic was back in the Garden, booked for a ten-rounder against the tough guy from Brownsville, Al Davis.

Bummy had also come a long way, but in a far shorter time. His crushing left hook had made him one of the hottest attractions in town. The Mob turned out in force to shout on Bummy; the more legitimate citizens of Brownsville also turned up in droves, many hoping to see young Al take a beating. Those were the ones with long memories.

Abraham Davidoff was born on January 26, 1918, just a couple of days after President Woodrow Wilson had ordered that all industry – except food production – must shut down for five days, and then close every Monday for three months because of a chronic coal shortage. In the Davidoff household, with five girls and three boys, there was a chronic shortage of everything, and from a very early age little Boomy fended for himself on the streets. He knew the truant officers better than he knew any of his teachers and by then he had learned always to throw the first punch, and so he also became well acquainted with the local law.

Most of his boyhood associates continued their education in Riker's Island and Sing Sing; a few got their fifteen minutes of fame and went to the electric chair. Boomy was lucky: discovering boxing did not save his soul, but at least it distracted him enough to avoid any seriously heavy wrongdoing. He had always been a great street fighter, and the few dollars he could make in the neighbourhood bootleg fights were a strong enticement.

It was soon obvious that he was far better than the usual scrappy bootleg standard, and important managers started making overtures. The teenager was advised to sign up with an experienced partnership, Johnny Attell and Lew Burston, two hardcore boxing men with all the important connections, right up to Uncle Mike Jacobs. Attell was an experienced teacher, Burston would progress to become the Garden's international representative, and both knew how to develop a young prospect with a dynamite punch.

'Abraham Davidoff' would never have fitted in large type on a poster, and so 'Al Davis' became his *nom de guerre*, and Boomy conveniently transformed into Bummy. There were those who said the nickname was most appropriate, that he was still a hoodlum bum . . . but he was a bum with a punch.

Burston and Attell started him off in the small clubs, building up his experience and a fan base in the Broadway Arena, the Ridgewood Grove and the Fort Hamilton Arena, and the youngster, with his wild, attacking style, was an instant hit. In his first three years as a pro he went unbeaten in 39 fights, and now the managers gambled that he was ready for the big money, and a top spot on a Garden card.

On All Saints Day 1939 he destroyed the once-great Tony Canzoneri inside three rounds. Canzoneri was a sorry shadow of the wonderful fighter he had been, and many Italians never forgave Davis for the vicious manner in which he brought an end to Tony's incredible career, but there is no room for sentiment in boxing, and the name looked good on Bummy's record. As did that of Tippy Larkin who, just over a month later, lasted into the fifth.

The New Jersey ace was far from washed up, and would later win the junior welterweight title, but his fancy boxing and sharp hitting failed to discourage Davis. After chasing and missing for four rounds, he landed the convincer in the fifth.

Just how far could this little terror from Brownsville go? Bummy, Burston and Attell were convinced that he was ready for any lightweight in the land. They took aim at Lou Ambers who, having beaten Armstrong, was the 135lb champion for a second time. Lou's best days were behind him, but he was still a fine all-round performer and as hard as concrete – Zivic had broken his jaw back in 1935 but Ambers had still won the fight. His manager, Al Weill, loathed taking risks, but despite Bummy's well-earned reputation as a fearsome puncher, he reckoned the outcome was a formality. As in most matters pertaining to boxing, Weill was on the mark.

Anyway, The Vest was not risking the title: this was only over ten rounds and as he forecast, Ambers dished out a painful lesson to the upstart. Lou was not shy of the left hook, but he did not have to take too many. Every time Davis set himself to let fly, the champ would bang home a hard left, upsetting Bummy's timing, making him miss by ever-increasing margins. He never gave up hope, always kept searching for that one clean shot, but by the middle rounds he had become an easy target, and at the final bell there could be only one winner. He had not been disgraced, but his limitations had been exposed.

Time to regroup. Davis displayed no signs of a hangover when beating the veteran, Joe Ghnouly, then Tony Marteliano and Johnny Rinaldi. Once again, Mike Jacobs and the Garden beckoned: Bummy had been outclassed against the lightweight champ; how would he fare against the newly crowned welterweight holder? A large, noisy Friday night crowd were willing to pay good money to find out.

The fans jeered and whistled when referee Billy Cavanagh brought the fighters to centre ring for their instructions and called for 'a good clean fight'. Cavanagh expected a strenuous night, but nothing like the extraordinary six minutes that were about to unfold.

Right from the opening bell the pace was as hot as the tempers, the exchanges savage and wild. Within seconds the Garden headliner had transformed into a violent free-for-all, a riotous punch-up and wrestling match that would have graced any waterfront bar, but which was bang out of order within these hallowed walls. Who started the rough stuff? Even money each of two, and naturally the following day both camps pointed the accusing finger at the other.

Davis came out fast, tossing trademark left hooks; difficult to say if the follow-up forearm or elbow was intentional when the punch failed to find the target. Zivic replied with counters, many of which strayed low, but these were early days, and probably he was still adjusting his range and timing. His bobbing head frequently halted a Davis rush, and invariably Fritzie would steady himself by grabbing Bummy's throat. His thumb seemed drawn to his opponent's eyes, but this was one rap to which the Pittsburgh villain would ever plead not guilty.

Zivic would confess to butting, lacing, choking, deliberately hitting low, but never to using his thumb. He maintained that he never thumbed anyone, because he would not like to take one in return. Fair enough, but somebody's left hand was busy around Bummy's face, Cavanagh was hoarse from bawling out warnings, and the fans were out of their seats, booing and whistling. And as the bell rang out for the end of round one Fritzie signed off his recital with a hard and late shot that surprised Davis.

Bummy was incensed and had to be dragged back to his corner, screaming and cursing and vowing vengeance. During the minute's break, he had to be forcibly restrained, totally ignoring his seconds' pleas to calm down and concentrate on his boxing.

The bell for round two, and out charged Bummy, a snarl twisting his lips, murder in his eyes. This was Boomy the street thug now, and as a shocked Zivic tried to cover up, he shot home one low blow after the other, with no attempt at concealment. One pressman counted thirteen consecutive punches, all designed to make Fritzie sing top Cs. Bummy would have ignored Cavanagh's frantic warnings had he heard them, but he was no longer hearing anything. At last the referee managed to tear him off Zivic and bellow right into his face that he was disqualified.

Is there a difference between mad and crazy? Davis went totally berserk and started kicking and flailing out at Cavanagh and anyone else that came into range. Now the Garden cops were in the ring, the cornermen had joined the melée, and around the ringside some of the best punches of the night were being thrown.

When some semblance of order had been restored the official decision was read out: Al Davis had been disqualified after 2 minutes 34 seconds of round two for persistent fouling. Cue for another thunderous chorus of boos. Bummy, under escort, made it back to the dressing room, but his troubles were just beginning. The New York State Athletic Commission chairman, General John J Phelan, also had blood in his eye.

At the subsequent inquiry, Bummy was fined $2,500 and banned for life from boxing in the state. But the story had not run its course. Shortly after his exile was announced the bad boy from Brownsville received more upsetting news: the army wanted to fit him for a uniform. Davis was aghast: soldiering was not his brand of fighting, but his managers thought that they might salvage something positive from this latest twist.

Feelers were sent out: if private Davidoff was prepared to box in aid of the Army Relief Fund charity, would the New York Commission relent over the ban? Phelan harboured misgivings, but he was also a patriot and a general, and he grudgingly gave the okay for Davis to fight again in New York.

And so, just eight months after he had been barred for life, Bummy was back boxing in The Apple, and once again sharing a ring with Fritzie Zivic, this time in the Polo Grounds. Zivic was delighted. On January 17, 1941 he had again upset the odds when stopping Armstrong in the twelfth round of their rematch; the

Polo Grounds would provide another healthy purse, and there were scores to be settled. Nobody escaped after mugging the Pittsburgh hardcase.

On Wednesday, July 2, Zivic enjoyed the fresh air and a cruel revenge. Davis was completely outclassed, made to look like the wild-swinging club fighter that he really always had been. No question, he was brave, but he suffered a humiliating beating, absorbed tremendous punishment, and from the sixth round Fritzie could have finished the fight any time he cared. Typically, he chose to wait until the tenth and final round before putting Bummy out of his misery. Who was the tough guy now?

Certainly not the Brownsville terror. He had taken a bad physical beating; mentally he was in far worse shape. Screw the army! He took off absent without, and the MPs did not catch up with him for more than a week. General Phelan was outraged and immediately reimposed his life ban; the army was none too happy either, and after being held at the stockade on Governor's Island, Bummy was drummed out of the forces with a dishonourable discharge. Not good enough for the army, not good enough for New York, not good enough for Fritzie Zivic.

But he was still a money-maker, and he could still fight. There were other towns and cities where the crowds would turn out to see this bad guy.

He gave value for money in Philadelphia and Chicago and Pittsburgh and Washington, losing some, winning more, and he could still electrify when landing flush with that stunning left. His equaliser. And, boxing being boxing, by the summer of 1943 everyone was prepared to shake hands and forgive and forget – Davis was reinstated in New York. He started off back in the small clubs, cramming the Broadway Arena, thrilling the fans like the old days, and once again he received the call from Uncle Mike.

He was just turned 26, but promoter Jacobs no longer considered Davis potential championship material. He did, however, sell bundles of tickets, was never dull, and would provide a good workout for his stars. Jacobs booked him to face Bob Montgomery on February 18, 1944: The Bobcat had already signed to challenge Beau Jack for the lightweight title the following month; Bummy would be the ideal tune-up, and everybody would make a few bucks. Some tune-up! Montgomery never saw the lightning left that exploded on his chin, and the fight was all over inside a round.

But that was to be Davis' last night of glory in the Garden. Beau Jack outpointed him on St Patrick's Day, and while the Allies were still cleaning up the Normandy beaches, a fast-fading Henry Armstrong stopped him in the second. On May 25, 1945, Bummy still had enough zip to dump a younger and heavier Rocky Graziano on the canvas, but The Rock climbed back up, and virtually brought Davis' career to a close, thanks to a fourth round knockout.

Bummy and Rocky had got to know one another briefly on Governor's Island while awaiting their dishonourables, and by 1945 Graziano was heading straight for the top and lifetime fame and fortune. Nobody could have forecast what the year still had in store for Davis.

In the meantime, Fritzie Zivic had not been idle. Just over three weeks after destroying Davis, he had lost his championship to Red Cochrane in Newark. Judges were not employed in New Jersey and only the referee's vote counted. Zivic swore he was swindled, and became even more convinced when the contract for the return was not honoured. There was only minor satisfaction in beating Cochrane in a non-title rematch, but he remained a red-hot attraction, fighting the best.

Sugar Ray Robinson . . . On the night when Fritzie won the title from Armstrong, a slender Sugar Ray had made his professional debut on the undercard, stopping Joe Echevarria in the second round. Exactly a year later Robinson topped a Garden bill for the first time, against Zivic, and he learned plenty, scraping a split decision after ten rounds. By the return Ray had learned enough to halt Fritzie in the final round. After he retired, Zivic would always nominate Sugar Ray as the best he ever fought.

Jake La Motta . . . A big hardcase and a little hardcase, head to head. Through 1943 and into 1944 they clashed four times, Zivic always conceding lumps of weight. Three fights resulted in split verdicts, and Fritzie's only victory came over fifteen rounds, a curious trip for a non-title affair. He dismissed La Motta as neither a great puncher nor boxer, but paid tribute to his courage and durability.

Though still a rugged opponent, Zivic was on the downhill: in one depressing run starting in June 1945 he won only once in twelve outings. Now he was just another journeyman with a name, always turning up on time, doing his best on the night, collecting his wages, and then moving on. Fritzie, however, still loved the life, much preferring fighting to punching his time-card at the steel mills.

He had a solid marriage to Helen; there were two sons, Fritzie Jr and Charley, and a daughter, Janis; and a good year on the circuit provided the family with a comfortable lifestyle. His last serious year came in 1946 when the 33-year-old boxed eighteen times, losing ten, but always going the full distance. In the following three years he gradually broke the habit of a lifetime, fighting only five times and winding up, on January 17, 1949, with a points win over Eddie Steele in Augusta.

Out of 233 bouts he had won 159 (80 inside the distance); lost 64, fought nine draws and one no-decision. He had lost only four fights inside the distance, and despite his reputation he was always quick to mention that he had never been disqualified. The record mirrors the fighter: nothing came easy, nobody did him any favours, and though the Conns and Armstrongs, the Burleys, La Mottas and Robinsons could never recall Fritzie with affection, all spoke of him with great respect. Even awe.

After boxing, he proved as busy as he once was in the clinches. He owned properties and represented a distillery; he tried his hand as a house painter and worked as a boilermaker. In his later years he would prove popular as an after-dinner speaker, reminiscing over the old days. He died on May 16, 1984, a week after celebrating his 71st birthday.

There would be no well-planned drift towards domesticity for Bummy Davis. That had never been on the cards since his wild, early days as Boomy Davidoff, but this script could only have been written in Hollywood.

After Graziano, Davis was disillusioned with the business. There was one more fight – on September 11, 1945, against somebody called Johnny Jones – and the irony was that Bummy won on a second-round disqualification.

He was married with a son, and there were still a good few bucks stashed away in various places. The Graziano fight had been a great earner, and he had never been too rash with his cash. Al Davis felt confident that he could afford to retire from the fight game and direct his energies elsewhere.

Right back to his earliest days, hustling with the pushcart, Bummy had always loved doing deals, and shortly after the Jones debacle he bought a bar in Canarsie. He quickly discovered, however, that his tavern's trade was not what he had been led to expect and within a month, on impulse, he sold on the business to a man called Art Polansky. Such was the speed of the transaction that Polansky could only come up with a down payment; the balance would be paid out of the receipts.

At the same time, Bummy also held an interest in several racehorses being trained in Florida. He had planned a November visit to look over his string, and on the night before the trip he was a late caller at his old bar. At that hour business was quiet and there was only a handful in the joint, including an off-duty cop. Bummy had a drink and talked repayments with Polansky and everything was nice and friendly, until around 2.45 on the morning of November 21, 1945, when the four stick-up merchants burst into the bar.

The gunmen already had a big reputation. In recent weeks at least a half-dozen taverns all over Brooklyn had been held up and robbed, and in one heist a sixteen-year-old girl had been shot.

Serious bad buys, but that meant nothing to Bummy who had grown up around such desperados and feared nobody. He tried reason, explaining that the owner was just starting out and there were only peanuts in the register. No dice. One of the gunmen warned him to keep his mouth shut, and a bell rang somewhere in Bummy's head. With one left hook he dropped the startled robber and then, just like that night in the Garden against Zivic, all hell broke loose.

A shot rang out, and the fighter fell to the floor, but the bullet had just grazed his neck. As the blood started to flow and the robbers hauled their unconscious partner out of the door, an outraged Bummy rose to his feet and charged. Out on the street, the bandits were pushing their pal into the getaway car; they turned and fired, and Bummy was hit three times. The off-duty cop was now out on the pavement, and as Davis stumbled towards his own car he emptied his gun into the escaping vehicle. One hood died from his wounds, the remaining three were caught and did life in Sing Sing.

Bummy was dead before the ambulances arrived. Apart from the neck wound, one bullet had cracked his spine, another had pierced a lung, and a third was lodged in his right arm.

Perhaps this was always the way the Fates had planned things for Boomy Davidoff, the bad boy from Brownsville. But at least he bowed out on the side of the good guys. He was 27.

CHAPTER FOURTEEN

Billy Fox *v* Jake La Motta

FRIDAY, NOVEMBER 14, 1947

Dickens said it first, but Charles was long gone. Had the sharp social observer still been around in 1940s New York, however, he might have been tempted to rehash his opening words to *A Tale of Two Cities* and shoot off a piece to *Ring* magazine. The forties were truly tremendous and turbulent years for the fight business: years that were both great and ghastly.

'It was the best of times, it was the worst of times.'

The best of times? Just take a quick glance down the names in *Ring*'s middleweight ratings for November 1947. Rocky Graziano was the champ, ex-holder Tony Zale the leading contender; then came Bert Lytell, Marcel Cerdan, Fred Apostoli, and Jake La Motta. Former champions and future champions, apart from the smooth and accomplished Lytell, whose colour made him a big outsider even to get a sniff at a title. There was equal strength in depth in the light heavy, welter, light and featherweight divisions, and most Fridays the Garden was buzzing.

The worst of times? Our old friend Frank Carbo and his merrie men were extorting an intolerable tax from the sport, and nobody seemed able or willing to stand up against them. Following a stroke in 1946 Mike Jacobs was a permanent invalid; the New York State Athletic Commission, chaired by Eddie Eagan, made plenty of noise but time and again ducked the Carbo issue; and the *Ring*, the voice of boxing, was hobbled by the libel laws and, perhaps, a reluctance to delve too deeply.

In 1947 the world of boxing was reverberating from the after-shock of a major scandal which, ironically, might have been brought about through a trumped-up charge. New York District

180

Attorney Frank Hogan had instigated a highly publicised investigation into an alleged $100,000 bribe made to Graziano to throw a fight against Cowboy Rueben Shank. Rocky had cancelled the bout, claiming an injury in training; Hogan insisted that he pulled out rather than take a dive. He and his aides beavered away and issued a torrent of statements, but they had zilch. No charges were brought against the middleweight or anyone else.

Colonel Eddie Eagan, however, fancied some good press for himself, and his commission initiated a fresh inquiry, found nothing concrete, but still slapped a life ban on Graziano for failing to report a bribe. And when the news broke in a Chicago paper that the fighter had been dishonourably discharged from the army, the commissioners could afford to pat one another on the back and congratulate themselves that they had rid boxing of an evil character. Eagan got his spread in the newspapers, but many influential columnists wrote that the middleweight champion had been railroaded by New York.

Bum rap or not, one would have imagined that even Carbo and his cohorts might have been persuaded to lie low until the storm died down; instead they arrogantly set about choreographing a high-profile phoney fight, unaware at the time that they were organising the most notorious fix ever: Blackjack Billy Fox and Jake La Motta starring in *A Funny Thing Happened on the Way to the Garden*.

And, unlike the Graziano affair which eventually saw the fighter reinstated, more popular than ever, the sordid events surrounding the night of November 14, 1947 are still cited whenever boxing's warts are put under the microscope . . . the blackest night in the history of Madison Square Garden.

We have already detailed how Carbo bossed a network of compliant managers which grew by the year, and how Blinky Palermo was one of his most energetic and loyal aides. At that time Frank Palermo operated from the Shubert Building on South Broad Street, Philadelphia, and he was a little big man in the city's flourishing numbers racket. He also handled a string of fighters, most notably the lightweight champion Ike Williams, a welter, Billy Arnold, and a lean light heavyweight called Billy Fox on whom he had spent a little money and a lot of time and imagination. Come the final accounting, Blinky always recovered his dough and invariably charged heavily for his hours. This was the year when the investment in Fox was scheduled to pay off in blue chips.

Palermo and Carbo had already engineered for Fox one crack at the 175lb championship over far more deserving challengers like Archie Moore and Jimmy Bivins, but the 21-year-old had been beaten by Gus Lesnevich. They were confident, however, that they could squeeze another title shot for Blackjack Billy, but first he required a big name on his win record to re-establish his credibility. Carbo chose Jake La Motta.

A surprise choice, because Jake was not affiliated to any of the right faces: the Bronx Bull was a surly, suspicious loner; a tough, popular middleweight who would be a strong favourite to beat Fox if the fight was on the level. But La Motta was not a kid any more and had spent six hard years trying to beat the system without success. He knew the score, and Carbo figured that Jake was now ripe for an approach: a $100,000 bribe plus a shot at the middleweight championship if he lost to Fox was an attractive package.

The mobsters were covering all the angles. Blinky's kid would get another title shot and the boys would cut up another big purse. They would also make a killing from betting Fox against La Motta at good odds, and, equally satisfying, Jake would be brought into the fold at long last. He had been an independent for far too many years.

Because of La Motta's highly charged nature, negotiations were more delicate than usual. Jake's brother Joey, who fronted as his official manager, acted as the intermediary, but the final details were thrashed out in La Motta's own fight club, the Park Arena in the Bronx. To honour the occasion Carbo arrived in person, accompanied by Palermo and another familiar face, Bill Daly, then managing Lee Savold among others. The trio departed happy and also relieved, because even the toughest of the tough stepped warily when dealing with the moody middleweight with the hair-trigger temper.

And that had always been the way around Jake. Nobody dared tell him what to do, not on the street, nor in jail, nor in the ring.

He was born Giacobe La Motta on July 10, 1921 on New York's Lower East Side. His father hailed from Messina in north-east Sicily; his mother was city-born of Italian parents, and the youngster's earliest days were spent running wild around Tenth

Street, which also happened to be the playpen of another local terror, the infant Rocco Barbella, who would later become Rocky Graziano. La Motta Sr, with his horse and cart, toiled as a street pedlar and for a few years the family tried its luck in Philadelphia, but life was no easier there, and the La Mottas resettled in New York, only this time in the Bronx, where Giacobe resumed his juvenile crime wave.

By his teens he was a veteran street thug, thief and mugger, with the inevitable result that he was packed off to the State Reform School at Coxsackie where he renewed acquaintances with the young Barbella, and also joined the boxing programme. On his release he decided to pursue his boxing, quickly built a fresh reputation as an amateur light heavy, winning the prestigious Diamond Belt competition, and fought in the bootleg clubs before making the transition to full-time professional.

There was certainly no shortage of available managers. The nineteen-year-old did most of his training at the Teasdale Athletic Club in the Bronx, and he hooked up with one of the regulars, a young man called Michael Capriano, who was starting to make a name. But almost from the outset the partnership was doomed: La Motta trusted nobody and was unmanageable, but he could deliver in the ring.

He made his debut on March 3, 1941, beating Charley Mackley over four rounds in New York, and started trimming down to middleweight – he weighed as high as 174lb in his third fight against Johnny Morris but scaled just 162lb for his final fight of the year, a points loss against Nate Bolden.

Jimmy Reeves also beat him twice in Cleveland during that first twenty-fight year, but both Reeves and Bolden were quality opponents, and nobody was doing Jake any favours. More of the same in his second year, when he drew with and lost to José Basora and was outpointed in the Garden by Ray Robinson on October 2, 1942. That was the first of the memorable six-fight series between the pair, which would climax in a gory finale nine years later in Chicago. Sugar Ray and the Bronx Bull never failed to provide terrific action, and in their second meeting in Detroit La Motta dropped Robinson on the way to a points verdict. This would be his only win over Ray, but every bout was bitterly contested.

Those early epics, not to mention a gruelling four-bout war with Fritzie Zivic, elevated Jake into the middleweight ratings, where he would languish, year after year, with little hope of a title shot. His parting with Capriano had been acrimonious and now he was handling his own business, stubbornly refusing to cut the Carbo people in for a share, and so, time and again, his claims were ignored. He was being treated like so many of the great black fighters of the era, and to earn a decent income he was forced to face many of those blacks who were shunned by most of the rated white fighters.

We are talking exceptional fighters. Aside from Robinson, La Motta took on such untouchables as Lloyd Marshall and Holman Williams, Bert Lytell, Jimmy Edgar and Bob Satterfield. A less durable customer might have wilted under such a fearsome programme, but Jake was proud of his astonishing capacity to absorb the heaviest punishment, even boasted that he was impervious to pain. By the close of 1946 he was a battle-hardened 25-year-old with 75 fights under his belt. An outstanding contender with little hope of landing that elusive title shot.

La Motta had to resort to desperate gimmicks to ensure high-paid fights. He contracted to scale down to 155lb to secure a bout with the popular Garden headliner Tony Janiro; not only that, but he would be forced to stump up a $15,000 forfeit if he failed to make the weight. The task seemed impossible: between fights his weight frequently ballooned to more than 180lb, but when Jake set his mind to something . . . On the night of June 6, 1947 La Motta went into the Garden ring a full pound under the required limit and still found the strength to batter the youthful Janiro in the closing stages to win the decision.

This amazing feat was as much a tribute to his stubborn streak, his wonderful constitution, and his love of a buck as to his boxing prowess. He received a sensational press, but in his very next fight he slipped up badly when dropping a decision to the unheralded Cecil Hudson in Chicago.

This was a huge upset and a massive blow to any dwindling championship aspirations, and it was the result that persuaded Carbo that The Bull would at last be willing to talk business. In *Ring*'s November ratings he had slipped to fifth; in the light heavies Fox was listed one behind Ezzard Charles in the queue of prospective Lesnevich challengers. Curiously, the magazine would make no adjustment to either boxer's ranking following the Garden fraud.

And so the dirty deal was in place, although Billy Fox himself remained an innocent, unaware that his opponent was about to go into the tank. That guaranteed authenticity from at least one corner and may not have been the first time that, without his knowledge, Fox had been given help. In later years, shattered by the ugly reality of the scandal, he protested that he never even knew that Palermo was tied in to the underworld.

Billy was born on January 29, 1926 in Tatum, Oklahoma, but the family soon moved to Richmond, Virginia, where life was not great for the youngster. He remembered writing away for a copy of Nat Fleischer's textbook, *Training for Boxers*, and read and reread Fleischer's words of wisdom until he decided that he must become a fighter. Unhappy with his home life and determined to realise his ambition, the fourteen-year-old hit the road, travelling first to Washington, then briefly to New York before winding up in Philadelphia. A long and hard journey for one so young.

In South Philly he met a fight trainer called Jimmy Reed, and the pair formed an instant rapport. Reed was a patient coach and the boy was a natural mover with a good punch; next step was to find him a manager, and Reed introduced Billy to Palermo who, after a cursory appraisal in the gym, signed him to a contract. All Fox knew from Reed was that Blinky was a character who could get things done, and that was certainly no lie. He was also a guy who played fast and loose with the facts and figures, and he began putting together a bizarre record for his light heavy.

Going into his February 1947 title fight with Lesnevich, the record books credited Blackjack Billy with an incredible winning streak of 43 straight knockouts. Not so, according to Fox. In a 1981 *Ring* interview with E J Gary, Fox was adamant that he had boxed only 36 times before challenging for the title.

He told Gary, 'Boxing was my life. I kept track of my fights. I know how many fights I had. I had 36 fights before I met Gus Lesnevich for the championship of the world.'

Fox's staccato sentences have a ring of the truth, and there was no good reason for him to claim fewer wins than he had really scored. The inventive Blinky had merely indulged in some creative padding, adding seven knockouts that never happened. As for the real kayoes? Billy also recalled that he fought the same opponent twice, with the guy using different names; other opponents could, at best, be described as dubious. Palermo was fashioning a masterpiece to impress the big boys in New York: Fox's pedigree was definitely not kosher, but he was on his own when he went into the ring with the veteran Lesnevich, and perhaps he did well to last into the tenth round.

But there was still big money out of playing blackjack. Billy quickly put together six more knockouts and, according to Blinky, the La Motta fight would prove beyond doubt that Fox was a genuine contender, worthy of another crack at old Gus. There were, however, some anxious moments along the way.

In a tune-up before facing Jake, Fox was booked to box one Augustino Guedes in Allentown, Pennsylvania. Billy, his connections, and the 5,000-plus crowd got far more than they expected. Guedes, billed as the former light heavyweight champion of Portugal, dropped Fox for a nine count in the fifth and for another nine in the eighth, before Billy miraculously stormed back in the same round to floor the Portuguese twice and force a stoppage.

A very close call, and one that demonstrated the 21-year-old's vulnerability. The conspirators remained unfazed: who cared what went down in a backwater like Allentown Pa.?

The rumours started a few days before the fight and built up to a crescendo. Al Silvani, then working as La Motta's trainer, was not party to the plot yet feared the worst a full two weeks before the contest. He told author Ronald K Fried, 'A fixed fight, you smell it . . . You smell that weeks before the fight. I told that to La Motta. You smelled it all over.'

La Motta remembered differently. He told Fried, 'Was he in my corner? See, I don't even remember. I don't think he knew anything, but he knew something was wrong . . . I think I fooled him, I fooled everybody. Nobody knew.'

Not true, Jake. A privileged few were in on the secret, many more were suspicious, and come fight time the Garden was a frenzy of speculation.

The betting odds, of course, signalled that a stroke was about to be pulled. As expected, the bookmakers had opened with La Motta their clear favourite, but all the serious money, the inspired money, was for Fox. The bookies reassured themselves by recalling that the same Philadelphia mob had dropped a bundle betting Fox to beat Lesnevich, and they could be wrong again. Jake's fans regularly staked heavily on their man, enough to shore up his price, and on the morning of the fight, he remained an uneasy 6/5 on favourite. In the afternoon, however, an avalanche of dough sent Fox's price into freefall, Billy finishing an astonishing 12/5 on before the bookies raised the white flag. No more bets on Billy Fox.

Only the drunks, the deaf and the blind were still punting on Jake, and at the ringside some hardnecks were looking for even money that La Motta would not last the distance – the same Bronx Bull who had never been stopped or even put on the canvas!

Most definitely something was screwy, and the almost-capacity 18,345 crowd was prepared to pay $102,528 to discover just how the plot would unfold. Hot rumours of a fix always brought out the curious.

At 167lb, Jake weighed 5lb less than Fox but considerably heavier than his norm since becoming a headliner. The extra pounds, however, looked no handicap in round one as, with his usual gusto, La Motta subjected an extremely tentative Fox to a withering body attack, with a few good head shots thrown in for good measure. The Bull's mind seemed to be on business as usual.

Jake painted a more dramatic picture in his autobiography. 'The first round, a couple of belts to his head, and I see a glassy look coming over his eyes. Jesus Christ, a couple of jabs and he's going to fall down? I began to panic a little. I was supposed to be throwing a fight to this guy, and it looked like I was going to end up holding him up on his feet.'

Over now to *Ring* correspondent Jersey Jones for rounds two and three. Jersey, as you will see, believed the fight was on the square.

In the second, Fox whipped over a right to the chin. La Motta's legs buckled and he reeled backward. Billy, following up his momentary advantage, jolted Jake several times with left hooks. La Motta grimaced viciously, and made threatening gestures with his fists, but Fox refused to scare. Billy, boxing coolly, methodically, continued to snap left jabs to La Motta's face, manoeuvring Jake into openings for lusty rights.

La Motta came out for the third as though he meant business, and landed two good overhand rights to Fox's jaw. But Billy shook them off, forced La Motta back against the ropes in a neutral corner, and outfought the Bronxite in a wild exchange of body punches.

Jake unquestionably was hurt, and twice was saved by the ropes from falling as he sagged under the thunderous smashes to the midsection.

Jersey Jones, respected and vastly experienced in all facets of the game, was apparently satisfied with what he saw, and even found the action quite thrilling. But La Motta wrote, 'The only thing I could figure to do was just let him hit me, but even that didn't work too good because, like I said, this kid didn't have a punch.'

And now to the fateful fourth, and time to call in the esteemed *New York Times* reporter at ringside, James P Dawson.

Early in the fourth round, a right uppercut sent La Motta back to the ropes in a neutral corner. There he crouched and cowered without attempting to strike a blow as Fox drilled La Motta with numerous rights and lefts to the head and body. Once La Motta's knees sagged, but he fought his way out of the corner.

A right to the head sent La Motta into the ropes near Fox's corner, where the Philadelphian again piled the rights and lefts to the head. As La Motta's knees sagged once more, fighting out of the corner apparently unhurt, Jake ran into another storm of misdirected rights and lefts in midring, and Fullam called a halt.

A few minor contradictions there. Sagging knees? Apparently unhurt? Another storm of misdirected rights and lefts? Clarification is required from Jake's memoirs.

Finally the referee had to stop it – what else could he do? I was against the ropes with my hands down, pretending I was taking a beating, and Fox hit me about fifteen times with everything he had, which wasn't enough to dent a bowl of yogurt.

Far from being contrite, The Bull seemed intent in describing just how difficult Billy Fox and his ineptitude had made it for him to lose convincingly. But just how convincingly?

Jake shed tears in his corner – remorse, relief, who knows? – and had the horrible experience of being booed by a huge and angry crowd. But although there were loud jeers and many cries of 'Fake' there had been far worse demonstrations in the Garden. Jersey Jones remained content that the fight had been on the level; the *New York Daily Mirror*'s Dan Parker, however, was equally convinced that he had witnessed a fraud, and he had plenty of supporters. His renowned column appeared 48 hours after the event, on November 16, 1947, and the short interval did nothing to calm his anger. Time for some vintage Parker.

The art of pretending is one of the most difficult for an honest fighter to master. Jake's first local appearance as a thespian was redolent of Westphalia. The odor of ham was stronger than in a delicatessen. For one round La Motta savagely tore into Fox and threatened to strew his entrails around the ring, so vicious was his body attack. Then Jake went into his act. This bull-like specimen to whom blows from a battering ram would be cause for only minor irritation, suddenly began to buckle up at the knees under ordinary left jabs. Instead of fighting in close as he had done with such good results in the first, he stood off, dropped his guard, bared his tartar-covered fangs and snarled what was supposed to be defiance at Fox.

From that point on, Jake was in danger of being picketed by Equity at any moment for not having an Actors' Union card. He reeled around the ring, let himself be backed into corners and pummelled without making any effort to defend himself, and he pushed his punches as if playing volleyball instead of fighting. Once he forgot himself and threw an authentic right cross. But when it was half way to its target, he applied the brakes sharply and saved the night for Fox – and himself. Referee Frank Fullam stopped it near the end of the fourth round – but not for the right reason. Fullam should have called it no contest.

Naturally, the State Athletic Commission convened an inquiry, and Colonel Eagan once more saw his picture splashed all over the newspapers. But proving a fixed fight was all but impossible, especially as the crafty La Motta already had his excuse off pat to explain away his miserable performance. During training he had been injured in a sparring session, and his personal doctor,

Nicholas Salerno, diagnosed a ruptured spleen, also telling him to forget all about fighting Fox.

As usual, Jake ignored the advice: he was eager to complete the deal and now he had a great story to quieten the suspicions of the commissioners; even better, the tale was true. Dr Salerno, called as a witness, testified that the fighter had indeed injured his spleen, and the investigation effectively collapsed. La Motta was off the hook: the commission could only fine and suspend him for failing to disclose an injury, and considering the circumstances, seven months and a grand was a slap on the wrist.

Although the middleweight was hammered mercilessly in the newspapers, the bad guys had won. Without any qualms, they brazenly pressed ahead with their plans for Fox to challenge Lesnevich again, despite the fact that the youngster had been traumatised by all the horrendous publicity.

More than thirty years after the event, Billy was still reluctant to believe that his greatest fight had, in reality, been a phoney, and he gave *Ring's* E J Gary his own version of what happened.

I threw a lot of jabs and I set him up. I threw about 25 or 30 lefts and rights and I thought he was ready to go down. But just as he staggered, the referee came in and stopped the fight. I think he would have gone down.

I think he said that [La Motta admitting the dive to the Kefauver Committee] afterwards to save face. I don't want to call him a liar, but I don't think he's telling the truth. That fight ruined my career. It ruined my life. It took the heart out of me.

Sad memories. Billy Fox might not have been the greatest light-heavy ever, but he had a fighter's pride and he was honest. Billy was so distraught that he moved base from Philadelphia to New York, where few people knew him or would grill him about the fight. That, however, was no more than an incidental as far as the mob was concerned, and Palermo merely transferred Fox's contract to another of the boys, Herman Wallman, better known as Hymie The Mink because of his profession as a furrier.

The light heavy had lost heart but he still had to obey orders and less than four months after the La Motta fiasco he found himself back in the Garden, once again challenging Gus Lesnevich.

The contest, on March 5, 1948 lasted two seconds short of two minutes. Fox first took a six count, then went down for the full ten from a heavy right hand. He said later that because of his state of mind he had not prepared properly, but more likely there was a grain of truth in La Motta's assertion that he had a glass head. The mob were not exactly devastated or embarrassed by the fast finish: they had made a pile out of Fox and now the 33-year-old Lesnevich was being hyped as a genuine heavyweight contender, which was no bad thing as far as the boys were concerned.

Billy's one-time sensational career rapidly went down the tubes, and he lost most of his remaining fights. He also separated from his wife in 1952 and never again saw his son, who had been two at the time. Working at labouring jobs, he drifted into lonely obscurity, but was never allowed to forget the fight with Jake.

The 1960 Kefauver Committee investigation into boxing brought the bad memories flooding back; same again, when Martin Scorsese's masterpiece, *Raging Bull*, created a stir around the world.

La Motta, naturally, was on the movie payroll as an adviser; Al Silvani acted as technical consultant; Billy Fox's services were not required. Billy never would have understood the nuances of dramatic licence, and he was amazed and hurt when he saw the picture and heard De Niro talk to his character throughout the infamous four rounds. According to Fox, 'He never egged me on like that. He never said, "Come on, come on, hit me." He never whispered in my ear. We never said a word to each other in the ring.'

Fox had just learned another bitter truth: directors and movie stars were just as cavalier with the facts as Blinky and the boys. His final years were spent living in the Bowery, occasionally doing a stint as a dishwasher, and he passed away some time in the late 1980s, unmourned, and one of boxing's casualties.

La Motta was determined not to become a casualty. He impatiently served his suspension and returned to action in June 1948 with a stoppage win over Ken Stribling in Washington, but a year would pass before the mob honoured the promise and handed him his long-awaited crack at the title.

The holder was Marcel Cerdan, a wonderful French fighter who had become a huge favourite in the States, as much for his bubbling personality as his tremendous all-round ability in the ring. Marcel had been fighting for sixteen years and had been beaten only three times – twice on disqualification – but on June 16, 1949 in Detroit he was forced to concede on his stool before the start of round ten. At long last, Jake was the middleweight champion of the world.

In the very first round Cerdan had injured his right shoulder after a tumble, and he had been badly handicapped throughout, until his corner retired him, already with an eye on the rematch.

But there would be no rematch. On October 27, 1949, flying back to America to face La Motta again, Cerdan was killed when his plane crashed in the Azores. He was 33 years old, and the entire French nation was rocked by the tragedy.

Jake was still only 27, not a particularly fresh 27, but he might have expected many lucrative years enjoying the spoils of his skulduggery. But, largely because of increasing weight problems and a guy called Sugar Ray, his championship reign was brief.

There were two successful title defences against the Italian, Tiberio Mitri, in the Garden and the Frenchman, Laurent Dauthuille, in Detroit – the Dauthuille victory made memorable for La Motta's remarkable last-round stoppage when trailing badly on points. Next up came his old enemy Robinson, and they fought for the sixth and last time in Chicago on St Valentine's Day, 1951, and yes, there was a massacre. A weight-drained La Motta held his own for ten fierce rounds until Robinson turned up the heat, and Jake took an awful beating before referee Frank Sikora intervened in round thirteen.

Note to Scorsese students. La Motta did not utter the immortal lines: 'You never put me down, Ray.' Trainer Silvani remembers Jake collapsing in his arms, just seconds after hostilities ceased.

That was The Bull's last really meaningful fight. He lost then won against Irish Bob Murphy, a light heavyweight prospect, but he took a count for the first time when stopped by Danny Nardico in Coral Gables, and in his final bout, on April 14, 1954, he was outpointed by Billy Kilgore in Miami Beach. His controversial career record shows nineteen losses and four draws from 106 fights, and there is no asterisk beside the Fox defeat.

Jake should have been all set to sit back and enjoy the good life. He was now living in Miami Beach with his second wife, Vickie. He owned expensive houses in New York and Florida, still had the Park Arena up in the Bronx and a valuable parking lot near

Yankee Stadium, and had just invested in a nightclub. The club was his undoing, and his dream world shattered when he was charged and found guilty of procuring an under-age prostitute for his clients. The case was complex, the evidence sketchy, and just this once La Motta might have been the innocent, but he wound up serving six months inside.

Whatever popularity he had once taken for granted now plummeted to less than zero, and there were still more horror headlines to follow.

In 1960 Senator Estes Kefauver headed a committee investigating corruption in boxing and on June 14 Jake appeared as the star witness. Thanks to the Statute of Limitations he was safe from prosecution when admitting that he had thrown the Billy Fox fight, but he was still reluctant to spill all. He hedged when asked to repeat the names of the three men that he had disclosed to a New York assistant district attorney only the previous month as the gentlemen who had propositioned him. In fact, he would not confirm any $100,000 bribe, insisting that he went in the tank only to secure a title shot. Then he further muddied the waters when revealing that he had still been made to fork out $20,000 to clinch the fight with Cerdan. Very strange. Brother Joey, the intermediary, was much more straightforward: he pleaded the Fifth Amendment no fewer than 53 times.

Jake had reached the bottom of the barrel: he was broke and earning only small change working as a club compere and comedian. Even many of his old boxing buddies shunned him, and he did not get an invitation when the former middleweight champs, Basilio, Fullmer, Turpin and Olson, helped pay tribute to Sugar Ray in 1965. The Garden was yet to forgive and forget.

If nothing else, Jake knows how to put up a battle, and he was not prepared to disappear meekly into a foxhole. His 1970 autobiography, a highly coloured version of his life, rekindled interest in The Bull; his club act improved into an acclaimed theatre gig; he made some movies; and after *Raging Bull* hit the screens he became a worldwide personality.

In 2003 old Jake, with his trademark Stetson and cigar, has transformed into the benign elder statesman of boxing, still recycling the old gags, still in great demand as an after-dinner speaker. He has travelled a long, long way from his early days as a thief and a mugger, but the Billy Fox scandal remains a terrible stain on an otherwise admirable career.

Madison Square Garden finally relented and now he gets a big hand when he is introduced from the ring: Jake La Motta . . . the Bronx Bull . . . the Raging Bull . . . the former middleweight champion of the world. The Hall Of Fame saw fit to honour him, and perhaps the time has come for the rest of us to award Jake his parole, pay tribute to a great fighter, and at last forgive him that one night of shame in the Garden. None of us is perfect.

CHAPTER FIFTEEN

Riddick Bowe
v Andrew Golota

THURSDAY, JULY 11, 1996

There are those precious moments when the boxing enthusiast can sit back, survey the rest of the sporting world with a degree of smug satisfaction, and come to the conclusion that the much-maligned old game is not doing too badly in comparison. But, please, never too much smugness, too much satisfaction.

In boxing there have been very few instances of performance-enhancing drug taking, a blight that is endemic in both athletics and cycling and has even tainted swimming and skiing; none of the high-profile inquiries into betting machinations that have embarrassed soccer, cricket and horseracing; and the sport has yet to be engulfed by the hooligan hordes who seem to be thriving, as mindless and vicious as ever, throughout English soccer.

We can never afford, however, to be complacent, particularly with respect to the yobs who have infiltrated all walks of life. They have gained a toehold in fight arenas all over Britain; small bands of lager-swilling, banner-waving morons, chanting obscenities and the soccer hymns, obstructing views, at times hijacking rows of seats. They have not become a major problem yet, but only a policy of zero tolerance stewarding can hope to keep the cancer from spreading.

End of lecture, and in fairness, nothing of late comes close to matching the terrible scenes at Wembley Arena more than twenty years ago when Marvin Hagler won the world middleweight championship from Alan Minter. There were nutcases back then too.

Before that fight in September 1980 the atmosphere in the sold-out arena bore an uncomfortable resemblance to the bad old days when Hitler was rallying the masses in the beer halls: fanatical support, national flags everywhere, lashings of drink, and an unflinching belief in ultimate victory.

The riot kicked off when Minter was stopped on cuts in round three. Immediately the bottles rained down on the ring, and battles broke out all around the ringside. Hagler's cornermen, the stewards and police shielded the new champion from serious damage. Fleeing to the safety of the dressing room minus the title belt, Marvin had been denied his unique moment of celebration by the madness of the crowd.

In the States, the scenes were viewed with slack-jawed disbelief. Sure, there might be the odd dust-up at a fight, but never anything like this. Americans as a rule work hard at enjoying their sports: ball games provide a family day out, a chance to gorge on hotdogs, hamburgers, popcorn and Pepsi; they cheer their heroes and jeer the villains, but with a brand of good nature that never managed to buy a ticket into Wembley.

Such an ugly fracas would never happen in the US – but never say never.

Exactly a week after Independence Day 1996, and in the Garden of all places, the television millions throughout the land and across the world witnessed horror pictures of brutal mayhem that made the Wembley riot appear like some silly schoolkid fight. This was the law of the ghetto jungle, live, in colour, and replayed on all the newscasts. Craziest of all, the winners were attacking the losers!

The sheer senselessness and viciousness of the assault made by Riddick Bowe's team on Andrew Golota's corner was astounding and brought into focus another sore that boxing would do well to address – the almost exclusively American phenomenon of the small armies of minders and sycophants, loud and violently aggressive, who nowadays plague weigh-ins and media conferences, trying to outdo one another in demonstrating loyalty to the boss.

Sugar Ray and Ali, possibly the greatest two boxers of all time, may have been the first to employ a retinue of camp followers: Robinson's was born out of vanity and a desire for style, Ali's out of a sense of mischief, coupled with a shrewd understanding of the media's wants. When it suited, Muhammad could be cruel in trash-talking his opponents, but his was a unique routine that his successors could never hope to emulate. Ali bounced his material off Bundini Brown; today, the wannabes feel lonely if they are not packing a dozen Bundini clones, gophers and minders for back-up. No more fun, only dark intimidation.

Weigh-ins have become the stage for macho showdowns: loads of insults, much jostling and shoving, an occasional slap or a punch. Hackneyed and predictable, unless a Tyson is on the premises and develops a taste for leg of Lewis.

There were no scuffles when Bowe and Golota weighed in for their Garden date, only a row over the duration of the fight. The Golota camp was under the impression that this would be a ten-rounder. But Bowe's manager Rock Newman and his company, Spencer Promotions, had the final say, and Rock decided on twelve rounds.

The abrasive Mr Newman also intended to have a goodly number of Bowe loyalists close to the corner, and so freebies, granting access to the media enclosure, were dished out with gay abandon. The gang would make their presence felt, and Big Daddy Bowe would not feel alone. The irony was that right from his earliest days the former heavyweight champion had always shunned the gang and drug culture that were rife in his Brownsville, a decaying wasteland, barely recognisable from the days of Bummy Davis. Now he was hanging out with a gang of his own.

Bowe was born on August 10, 1967, the second youngest of a family of thirteen children who were raised single-handed by their mother, Dorothy. Daddy Bowe Sr was seldom seen around the area, but the birth records tell us that he must have turned up now and again. He was, however, almost a stranger to most of his brood.

The tenement in which the Bowes lived also housed a crack den. In fact most of the crumbling neighbourhood was one giant crack supermarket: dealers, their messengers and their lookouts commanded the street corners; ragged junkies littered the dark hallways; muggers prowled endlessly in search of the price of their next fix. One of Riddick's sisters was actually murdered by an addict whose attempted robbery went terribly wrong, and yet, somehow, young Bowe refused to be sucked under by this desperate environment of drugs and despair.

In so doing, he showed a tremendous determination and character, an inner strength that, sadly, has eroded alarmingly in his later years.

Riddick was no saint but he listened to his mother, and regularly turned up at PS 396 where he got to know Mike Tyson, who spent about six months as a schoolmate. By the age of thirteen he had met Judy, who would become his first wife, and who would exert a good influence. He had also started to box, almost overnight discovering that he could handle himself well. Early on, however, there was no burning ambition to make fighting a career; indeed, he had always harboured vague notions of joining the army, but before too long his ring exploits prompted a drastic rethink.

When reviewing Big Daddy's amateur career, the first image to mind is that of Bowe being knocked all over the ring by right hands from Lennox Lewis in the 1988 Olympic super heavyweight final in Seoul. He was stopped in round two, seemed to accept the referee's decision meekly, and earned fierce criticism from the disappointed American media who questioned his courage.

Bowe, however, never lacked for bottle, and his laid-back style – both in and out of the ring – could be deceptive. He enjoyed a successful if sometimes erratic stint in the amateurs, starting out as a gangling light heavy, and the cups and medals soon became routine: four times a winner of the New York Golden Gloves, a world junior champion, and a veteran of the Pan American Games and numerous international bouts, the future looked bright until Seoul.

Had he won gold, of course, Riddick would have been sifting through mega-buck contracts, mind-blowing offers of luxury cars and elegant homes, and blueprints detailing his path to the championship. Big Daddy discovered that silver did not fetch nearly as much, but the medal did get him Rock Newman, and then Eddie Futch, and eventually the heavyweight title and guaranteed riches. In the circumstances, he did all right.

Only a few in the business had heard of Eugene Roderick Newman when he emerged as the surprise manager of the 21-year-old from Brooklyn, who was now married to Judy and the father of two children. Back in 1981 Rock had befriended the WBC light heavyweight champion, Dwight Braxton – later known as Dwight Muhammad Qawi – and as the pair grew closer, he became his manager in all but name. He was now part of the circus, perhaps only a bit player, but fascinated by the huge sums that could be generated out of bigtime boxing. He picked up valuable experience working for the flamboyant promoter Butch Lewis, but, post-Seoul, after Butch declined to make a bid for Bowe, Newman decided to go it alone.

Perseverance was one of Rock's strong suits. A graduate from Howard University, this strange guy with the large forehead, tiny nose and razor-sharp tongue, had been a car salesman, a student counsellor back at Howard, and then a minor radio personality with his own talk show. Now he wanted to be a major player in the fight game, and he was certain that Bowe could be his ticket to the top.

The fighter was not even certain that he wanted to turn professional. His confidence had been badly dented by the hostile reaction to his loss against Lennox. He was again mulling over a life in the army to provide security for his young family. Rock had sold cars, now he was selling himself and a dream. He cleaned out his bank account, haggled a good price for his treasured BMW, and started sweet-talking. The amiable Bowe admired his chutzpah, and eventually agreed to try his luck and not long after that, the hustling Newman roped in ten investors, who brought a much needed cash injection of $250,000.

Rock retained outright control, and the investors showed a good return on their outlay when the manager, exercising a clause in their arrangement, finally bought them out. When Bowe became champion there was only one boss.

Newman also had to use all his persuasive powers to attract Eddie Futch aboard. The renowned mentor of champions was a sprightly 78, had a young wife, and did not intend to waste valuable time on a fighter who was not fully committed. The old man had heard reports that the 6ft 5″ giant could be diffident, often had to be cajoled in the gym, and was a glutton at the table. Futch wanted no hassle, but was, in fact, pleasantly surprised when first introduced to Big Daddy.

The young giant was easy to like and clearly there was much to work on. Despite his size, Riddick moved far better than most of the lumbering heavyweight monsters who made the old heroes such as Marciano and Patterson seem like pygmies. And he already possessed a hard jab and a decent shot in his right hand.

Though Bowe did not smoke, drink or do drugs, mentally Futch thought him immature and lacking in direction. Eddie could provide that direction, and the motivation to become his sixth heavyweight champion, but he warned the youngster that any signs of slackness or disobedience meant he would have to look for a new trainer.

Bowe, almost in awe, promised to be a model student, and on March 6, 1989 he made his pro debut in Reno, stopping Kevin Carter in the second, scoring three knockdowns. An unbeaten year later he headlined a card for the first time when beating a hard puncher called Art Tucker in three rounds in Atlantic City, and then followed the traditional path of being carefully matched against an assortment of fading stars and journeymen. Riddick was obeying instructions, and by 1992 both Futch and Newman were convinced that Big Daddy was now fit to spank the best.

He demonstrated his resolution when outfighting Pierre Coetzer in Las Vegas, and then four months later – on November 13 and again in Vegas – he took the world title from Evander Holyfield. That night his size and his superior firepower were the deciding factors, and he dropped Evander in the penultimate round, but there were times during the hard-fought twelve rounds when he was made to dig deep, and he did not disappoint. No longer could his spirit be called into question.

The new champ was undefeated in 33 fights (only six had lasted the full route) and he held all three major belts but right off Newman started flexing his muscles. Rather than honour an agreement to defend against old enemy Lewis, the manager decided that the WBC belt was worthless, and had Riddick dump the prize in a trash can for the benefit of the photographers.

Was this shrewd boxing politics, or were Newman and Bowe running scared of Lennox? The Seoul stories were rehashed, and doubts about Riddick's courage resurfaced.

Newman laughed off the charges, and countered that twice he had made offers to the Lewis camp; in fact those offers were derisory, insulting, and could never have been accepted. Instead, Rock opted for the easy money, and to hell with the media.

Bowe's first two title defences were non events, embarrassing mismatches against a spent Michael Dokes and a journeyman, Jesse Ferguson, who were both blown away inside a total of three meaningless rounds. Newman was just sticking to the time-honoured managerial credo of getting the best wages for the least possible risk, but those defences were the cue for more flak.

Big Daddy, however, was not too fussed. He was enjoying himself, raking in serious dough from easy fights and lucrative endorsements; building his dream home in Fort Washington, Maryland, and buying a nearby property for his mother; and working hard – not, alas, in the gym, but on his image. Riddick had a vision of himself as another People's Champion, loved and respected throughout the world, and so he hit the road . . . an audience with the Pope in the Vatican, a sitdown with Nelson Mandela in South Africa, a huge charity donation to the poor folk of Somalia. The full shtick. But during the tour his weight had ballooned, Futch had not seen him in the gym for months, and the return date with Holyfield was fast approaching.

A week short of a year after winning the title, Big Daddy returned to earth with a bump.

In the Vegas return – the one interrupted for twenty minutes by the crazy antics of the paraglider – Holyfield ruined all the plans for canonisation and sporting immortality. The exchanges were hard-fought and always close, and Futch was convinced that Riddick was just finding his rhythm when the guy dropped out of the sky. Perhaps. But the bottom line was a majority decision for Evander.

The road back would be tortuous. Nobody was in a hurry to do Newman any favours, and this time Bowe had to take the slow road. He beat Larry Donald and won Herbie Hide's WBO belt, which he did not consider worth much. He stopped Holyfield in a return non-title third match, but had to come off the canvas, and he did a number on the huge Cuban, Jorge Luis Gonzalez, who had beaten him as an amateur.

There were huge fights out there, but as usual the lawyers were busier than the boxers. Though Tyson was back in circulation, Lewis was flying high and Michael Moorer was in the shake-up, Bowe was many people's favourite to become champion again. But he was forced to mark time, and the match with Golota was only a payday, an appearance to maintain both his profile and his ranking.

According to Newman, Spencer Promotions were paying Riddick $5 million, which seemed extremely generous; the big

Pole would receive a career-best $600,000 and terrific exposure, and his veteran trainer Lou Duva – an arch enemy of Newman – believed that he had pulled off a masterstroke. Duva had watched Bowe up close from his amateur days, had never rated him highly, and had heard all the stories about Big Daddy's binges. He was sure that his heavyweight had the tools to spring a huge upset.

There were few to share his enthusiasm: outside the trade Golota was practically an unknown; within the business the Pole was regarded as tough but temperamental, and nowhere near Bowe's class. More than one source suggested that he might be a loose cannon.

Andrzej Golota had packed much into his 28 years. Being dragged up poor in Warsaw was not all that different from being down and out in Brownsville but, unlike Bowe, neither parent was there for the infant Andrzej, who was reared in foster homes. He grew into a large, rough youngster with very little to say, and he got himself into the usual scrapes. Boxing was recommended as the natural outlet for his energies and, like Bowe, he quickly found that he had talent.

A successful amateur was a celebrity in Poland, and Golota became a four-time national champion, a European and world junior medallist, and he too just fell short in Seoul, winning a bronze in the heavyweight class.

In 1990 Golota's cosy world exploded. Attending a disco with several of his boxing team-mates, the heavyweight became embroiled in a scuffle that escalated into a serious incident. The story goes that his shirt was ripped, punches were exchanged, an air pistol was produced and, though no shots were fired, one guy was made to strip down to his socks. It was not Golota. The upshot was that the fighter faced serious charges. Rather than take his chances before a court, he fled Poland and six years would pass before he was able to return.

We might discover how Andrzej escaped to Chicago if he ever pens his memoirs, but the Pole must have had influential allies. In the Windy City he found work as a truck driver and, naturally, his boxing record created interest around the gyms. In February 1992 the new Andrew Golota made his professional debut, stopping Roosevelt Schuler in the third round. He had, however, won around eight fights before he was brought to the attention of Duva and the powerful Main Events organisation.

Little Lou had been in Seoul and remembered Golota as big and raw. He had not improved much since then, but Duva reckoned he had possibilities and decided to take him on. The Pole passed all his tests; going into the ring against Bowe he had extended his unbeaten sequence to 28, including an impressive 25 wins inside the distance, and he was ranked by all the major bodies. But there had been two worrying lapses in character which raised questions about the Pole's frame of mind under fire.

After being rocked in his bout against a so-so Samoan, Samson Po'ouha, Golota turned nasty, bit Samson on the neck, and was fortunate not to be disqualified. And then, in his last fight before facing Bowe, he turned caveman again, deliberately butting Danell Nicholson and hitting him perilously low before forcing a stoppage.

Big Daddy remained unworried. He was no angel either, and when the going got tough he was well able to throw them low or late or round the back of the head if necessary. In the pre-fight hype he spoke menacingly about what he would do if Golota strayed offside. His real objective, of course, was to help shift some tickets.

Rock Newman was struggling in that department. New Yorkers were refusing to get excited about a fight where Riddick was an unbackable 12/1 on, and Spencer Promotions were not stingy in handing out blocks of freebies: bad for Bowe's image if a Brooklyn boy could not attract a big crowd into the Garden. In the end, the official attendance was given as 11,252.

Many knowledgeable fans would have been put off buying a brief when, two days before the fight, the former champion weighed in at an astonishing 252¼lb, his heaviest ever, and damning evidence that he was not treating the occasion too seriously. Come ring time Bowe must have been even heavier, and he looked soft around the middle. In contrast, Golota had scaled 243lb, and at 6ft 4″ he looked rock-hard and ready.

Nobody was quite sure what to expect from the Pole when the bell signalled round one. A raging bull? A timid tiger, paralysed by Garden nerves? He was neither. This Golota came out smartly and confidently, banging home excellent lefts, already doubling up on the jab, scoring with hard rights, and easily evading a cumbersome Bowe who lumbered forward but did little. A couple of Andrew's shots were borderline but they were unintentional, and referee Wayne Kelly's reminders to keep 'em up were mild.

Golota had boxed an almost perfect round, but in the second there were signs that, at last, Big Daddy was coming to life. Kelly had to warn him for clubbing Golota behind the head, then he landed two terrific left hooks, which momentarily stunned the Pole. Golota fought back furiously, and the crowd roared as the pair exchanged punches, Bowe just missing the ref with a wild right on the bell. Kelly had again spoken to Golota about the low ones, but at this stage the ref was not becoming too uptight.

Already Riddick was beginning to mark up and he was much more businesslike coming out for the third, slamming home accurate lefts. Surprisingly, the Pole retained his composure, though in one flurry he again landed low, and this time Kelly got serious: one more low blow, he warned, and Golota would be deducted a point. Big Andrew seemed unimpressed, and just before the bell he connected with a sizzling left hook to the head, which gave Bowe something to think about during the break.

Only the fourth, and Riddick was tiring, while Golota, his confidence growing with every minute, was threatening to take total command. Aside from the off-limit blows, he was boxing a textbook fight. Bowe was visibly wilting and without a gameplan. A hard right to the jaw sent Big Daddy stumbling back into the ropes, hurt and in trouble. And then, quite calmly, Golota dug a hard left hook into Bowe's groin. The crowd gasped, Bowe sunk to the canvas, as promised Kelly deducted a point, and the stricken fighter used two minutes of the allotted five to recover. The house was in an uproar but Golota showed no emotion. The foul had looked really bad, but even if the punch was not deliberate, why was the Pole still throwing so many body shots, having been warned so often? It was not as if he was experiencing any difficulty finding Bowe's head.

The loss of the point seemed to have no effect on Andrew. In round five he caught Bowe on the ropes with a blistering cluster of rights and lefts, and though the New Yorker bravely came back, scoring with a hard right-hand left hook combination, the blows just bounced off Golota, who was clearly in peak condition.

The action was exceeding all expectations, and now a huge upset loomed as a distinct possibility. Bowe had cheated in his training, had badly underestimated his opponent, and now he was paying the price.

He was constantly being beaten to the punch, and in round six he was again under the cosh as Golota kept up the pressure. And then, unbelievably, Golota fired another low left – not a chiller to the groin this time, but clearly below the belt, and Kelly fined him another point. Bowe took a minute out to compose himself, and he looked as if he needed all the breathers he could get. He might still escape this torment on a foul, and the Pole appeared to be the only person in the Garden who did not realise how close he was coming to losing on a disqualification. Was this guy dumb?

The answer had to be in the affirmative. Golota was in control in round seven, beating up Bowe, then bang! a right uppercut landed low, and for the third time Kelly deducted a point. Undeterred, Golota resumed the attack, battering Riddick to the head with left hooks and short rights, and Big Daddy was in dire trouble, on the verge of a stoppage. And that is when the pride of Poland, for a reason that only he knew, again made the groin his target for a left hook. Bowe collapsed on his back and a disgusted Wayne Kelly, who had toiled valiantly all evening, had no option but to disqualify Golota. Time: two minutes 33 seconds.

The fight was over, the war about to break out.

In the tiers, the fans were booing: some because of Golota's persistent fouling; others because they believed that Bowe had exaggerated the damage and had got himself out of jail. But almost immediately they were struck silent in disbelief, as they watched all hell break loose down in the ring.

Bowe was still on the canvas when his entourage charged. Not the official cornermen, of course, but the gang of thugs who had been allowed access to the media enclosure, and who had been the cause of increasing disquiet all evening. But Rock Newman was right there in the van.

As the mass of bodies rushed forward the prime targets were Golota and Duva. The giant Pole was struck from behind, and as he turned to face his attacker another maniac violently lashed out with a walkie-talkie, hitting Golota three times, gashing his head. Later, his wounds would require thirteen stitches. And little Lou, 74 years young and with a history of heart problems, was felled by another madman, stretched out on the canvas amid a sea of threshing legs, and in a bad way. Paramedics fought to reach him, but that was far from easy.

As the outnumbered stewards and a few saner heads tried to break up one battle, another fierce skirmish would erupt, and the heaving mob would lurch across the ring, threatening to collapse the corner posts and the ropes. The beleaguered Golota faction fought a rearguard action to get their fighter to safety and at last Duva was strapped to a stretcher and hurried on his way to hospital. Miraculously, his condition was described as stable the following morning.

But by now the brawling had spilled out of the ring into the press section, and from there throughout the huge hall. Golota supporters, and there were plenty in the Garden, seeing their countryman under attack, surged forward to his defence. Now it was black fighting white, and there was hardly a cop in sight.

Author Thomas Hauser wrote a detailed summary of the shameful events for *International Boxing Digest*:

The incident began at 10.43 p.m. Eighteen New York police officers had been assigned to detail outside the Garden, but none were inside the building when the trouble started. MSG's fifty ushers and seventy security personnel were quickly overwhelmed, and five minutes passed before the police were notified. The cops arrived nine minutes later. At its peak, 150 police officers were assigned to the operation. Finally, at 11.19 p.m., the officer in charge of the site declared the disturbance 'under control'. Fifteen spectators and nine cops were treated for injuries at local hospitals. There were sixteen arrests.

The media hung the rap on Rock Newman for being the principal instigator of the mayhem, but the manager vehemently denied the accusations: 'What was written in the paper about Rock Newman, truly makes Rod Newman seem as if he is either Satan or the next thing to Satan . . . I did not precipitate, or in any way encourage the thought that anyone would conduct themselves in the way so many people did on that night.

Newman, however, had a prior history.

Back in 1991 in Washington a deranged and outclassed Elijah Tillery had started kicking Bowe at the end of round one. First up on the ring apron was Rock, grabbing Tillery from behind in a choke hold and hauling him backwards over the top rope. A serious disturbance had ensued. And Big Daddy's hoods had already demonstrated their eagerness and expertise with both fists and boot when the paraglider unexpectedly dropped in on the Holyfield fight. They took their best shots while the guy was still tangled up in the ring lights.

The reasons for the length of the Garden riot were obvious: far too few security men and not nearly enough police. But why the violence exploded in the first place remains a mystery: Bowe had been beaten comprehensively and had been saved by the disqualification. One would have thought this was an occasion for Big Daddy's crew to mop their brows and raise a glass to Wayne Kelly.

The enormous publicity guaranteed a rematch, but the Garden wished no part of a rerun, and so the battleground was switched to Atlantic City's Convention Center, the date December 14, 1996. In the intervening five months Bowe had trained into good physical shape, and he weighed in at a promising 239lb, his lightest since winning the title, and 13lb less than he carried into the first Golota fight. But he had lost much more than the pounds: his skills had vanished, and only his courage remained.

Big Daddy suffered a frightful beating, although he did succeed in flooring Golota in the fourth round. But he was dropped himself in the second, again in the fifth, and was headed for certain defeat when, yet again, the erratic Mr G experienced that familiar rush of blood. The Pole had already had points deducted for butting and hitting low, and just before the bell to end the ninth he banged home a three-punch flurry, each blow landing well below the belt. Another disqualification, another win on Riddick's record, but at least no carnage this time.

Lou Duva was in despair: he had a hot property, a powerful fighter, but one who had a total disregard for the rules. Golota, however, was extremely marketable, and when two dates fell through to box Ray Mercer in 1997, out of the blue he was offered a shot at WBC champion, Lennox Lewis. A marvellous opportunity, but on October 4, once more in the Convention Center in Atlantic City, Andrew proved that he was neurotic as well a nasty.

He turned up at the Center barely an hour before fight time and marching towards the ring he stared straight ahead, as if hypnotised. The Pole still had not wakened up when the opening bell rang and he headed, robot-like, in the direction of Lewis, who looked him over and then started pot-shotting. A terrific right sent Golota crashing, his eyes horror-wide, as if for the first time he knew where he was. He rose uncertainly, Lennox delivered another salvo, and that was that. All over.

Golota had frozen, and further character flaws surfaced in November 1999, when after flooring Michael Grant twice in the opener, he began to struggle, took a count in the final round and then just quit. And any lingering doubts about his mental fragility were dispelled the following October in Auburn Hills, Michigan, when he surrendered in round two in what was supposed to be a battle of the bad men with Mike Tyson.

Who can tell what passes through another man's head in moments of extreme crisis? And no doubt Andrzej Golota can find plausible explanations for his weird antics in the ring. But Golota's woes are nothing when compared to the demons that have haunted Big Daddy Bowe since his retirement.

Riddick never fought after his second bout with the Pole, and most observers were relieved. True, he was only 29, which was still youthful for a heavyweight, and his record showed only one official loss, but his skills had deserted him at an alarming rate, training had become a mind-numbing chore, and, most worrying of all, he was beginning to slur his words quite badly. Time for the big man from Brooklyn to bid farewell while he could still enjoy his wealth.

Since his early days in Brownsville, Bowe had hankered after a life in the army, and to the world's astonishment, in 1997 he enlisted in the Marines, but lasted only three days in boot camp. Embarrassing, and evidence of his confused state of mind, but far worse, his home life was falling apart. There were highly publicised spats with a sister and a nephew, and then in 1998 wife Judy and their five children left the dream mansion in Maryland and resettled in South Carolina.

Bowe went in chase, and he was arrested after abducting the family at knifepoint and driving them 200 miles to Virginia. Fortunately nobody was harmed, but the former champion also had in his possession a pepper-gas spray, handcuffs and masking tape. Found guilty on several charges, Riddick's life has become an endless catalogue of court appearances: plea bargains and appeals, mitigation hearings and parole violations and ultimately jail.

A living hell for this once gentle man and, sadly, this story may not yet have run its course.

Don't Come Late!

This is her first time at the fights, and so far, all has gone brilliantly. He has been nursing her along on a diet of TV action, she thinks that De La Hoya and Calzaghe are 'gorgeous' and she just loves all the old Ali tapes. But this is the big test.

Dinner had been superb, and they arrive as planned, only a half hour before the main event. Their seats are terrific for the price, and the atmosphere is amazing as the boxers come into the ring.

The bell for round one, and he settles forward in anticipation. She gently tugs his arm and he turns towards her, trying to hear what she is saying through the din. She looks stunning. Then, a huge, triumphant roar, and he frantically jerks his head back to the ring, but too late . . . eight, nine, out!

No refunds and no reruns, and he has forgotten to set the video. That's boxing, baby.

CHAPTER SIXTEEN

Jock McAvoy *v* Eddie Risko

FRIDAY, DECEMBER 20, 1935

Old Archie Moore used to meet with as much trouble memorising the eye charts at the medical as he did figuring out many of his opponents. Sometimes the lightweight banger Lew Jenkins would stash a pint of brandy in the corner bucket to help him make it through a rough night, and the great Graziano would always snatch one last soothing drag on a cigarette before heading out for business. The great and the good all have their own peculiar ways of handling the awkward moments.

Of course, some boxers never learn to hack the hard times, drop out early, then spend the rest of their lives agonising . . . what if? For others, the love affair becomes an obsession, and they linger for far too long. And then there is another band: the guys with the bad hands or the tender skin; the fighters with the iffy chins or the suspect stamina, no matter how hard they train, who all soldier on, grimly determined to make good no matter what.

Some of them have been inspired by earlier tales of courage over adversity; others have chosen simply to ignore a serious handicap or have amended their style to suit. And all deserve special recognition for bucking the odds.

Notorious bleeders like Vito Antuofermo, Henry Cooper and little Walter McGowan are just three who spring readily to mind, and that trio did not do too badly. And nobody was more frequently stitched up than Frankie Ryff, a Bronx lightweight contender from the 1950s, who always seemed to be on television or in a doctor's surgery. Although Frankie's act was not for the squeamish, and his accumulation of cuts prevented him travelling all the way to the title, for nine years he staged one of the most

211

popular shows in town and, thankfully, he suffered no permanent damage to his eyes.

Boxing crowds are not especially bloodthirsty, but when a cut opens up they recognise that the contest is about to enter a crucial stage. They are rarely given a similar insight, however, when a fighter bursts his hand. In fact, if the injured man is brave enough and smart enough, he might even con his opponent out of ever suspecting that anything is wrong. But that is far from easy.

The fist is the boxer's tool, both his hammer and his scalpel, and it is an exceptionally delicate implement with all those bones just waiting to be broken. Remember, gloves were adopted to protect the hand and not the head, but they do not come with a guarantee. And even when snug in carefully wrapped bandages, the fist will come off second best if a wayward shot strikes the top of the skull or an elbow.

A hand fracture is a disaster and can put a fighter's entire career in peril. But some have brittle hands from birth.

Muhammad Ali often finished his bouts facially unmarked but with sore and swollen hands. Johnny Bratton and Paul Pender were two other champions regularly sidelined with breakages. The oldtime featherweight Bat Battalino remembered bursting both hands in the fourth round against Andre Routis, yet he battled on and won a fifteen-round decision. The fans thought Bat was crying with joy at winning the featherweight title, but the tears were prompted by pain.

Jock McAvoy, a contemporary of Battalino, often shared Bat's experience of feeling the excruciating pain shoot from the glove right up the arm, but this Englishman would have preferred a slow death to shedding tears in public. And on the freezing night of December 20, 1935, when he ducked through the Garden ropes to face the reigning middleweight champion, Babe Risko, he already anticipated further abuse to those treacherous mitts. That was the way things had been for the last nine years, and not once had he cried.

This night, however, he planned to have assistance – a shot of novocaine in the right hand just before he left the dressing room – because this was one fight he did not intend to lose. His manager, Dave Lumiansky, had failed to deliver on his promises, and Risko's title was not on the line. A defeat, and Jock would be shunted to the back of the queue, but if he beat Babe the

Americans would have to agree on a championship rematch. Wouldn't they?

The middleweight division had been thrown into chaos when Mickey Walker relinquished the 160lb title back in June 1931 to hunt bigger game, and had not yet made a total recovery.

The National Boxing Association was first out of the traps in January 1932, granting recognition to Memphis-born William (Gorilla) Jones who stopped Oddone Piazza in Milwaukee, but just five months later the Gorilla left his title in Paris, after losing to the French hero, Marcel Thil, on a disqualification. Then in January 1933 New York entered the fray, backing the claims of local boy Ben Jeby after he beat the Canadian, Frank Battaglia, and that is when things really began to muddy up. Take a deep breath.

In August 1933 Jeby dropped the New York crown to another Canadian, Lou Brouillard, and the NBA brazenly added its blessing to this match. The official NBA champion was still Thil, but he had been summarily dumped by the Americans, although throughout Europe he was still considered the top man.

A terrible shambles, made worse by the fact that none of the champs seemed able to keep hold of the title for more than a few months. Brouillard's brief reign lasted only until October when he was outpointed by Vince Dundee in Boston, and less than a year later Teddy Yarosz took over the lease, outpointing Dundee in Pittsburgh.

Enter Eddie (Babe) Risko, a 23-year-old, and something of an in-and-out performer. On New Year's Day 1935 Risko caused a major upset when he stopped champion Yarosz in the seventh round of a non-title match in Scranton. Teddy was given some time to recover from the shock and notch up two easy knockouts before the pair met again for the championship. And on September 19 Babe travelled to Yarosz's home town, Pittsburgh, and came away with a fifteen-rounds decision and the title.

So many title claimants in such a short space of time. Jones . . . Jeby . . . Brouillard . . . Dundee . . . Yarosz . . . and now Eddie Risko. All hard and competent pros, but scarcely Hall Of Fame material. Of course, they should have been recognised only as American champions, because throughout the middleweight musical chairs Thil had done nothing wrong in Europe where he was still regarded as the boss.

In fact, back in January, when Risko was first beating Yarosz, the bald Frenchman was facing McAvoy in the Palais des Sports in Paris, not for his world middleweight title, but only with his European light heavyweight belt on the line. Extremely weird. McAvoy lost a tight verdict, although he earned the vote of the English judge, W Barrington Dalby, later to become the upper-crust voice of British boxing on radio. At 160lb, Mac would have stood a far better chance against the hardcase from Saint-Dizier.

All of which concerned Babe Risko and his connections not one whit. Paris was a long sail away.

The Babe was born Henry Pylkowski on July 14, 1911 in Syracuse, the son of hard-working Polish-Lithuanian parents. As a teenager he toiled for a time as a coal miner before joining the navy, where he was soon introduced to boxing. Competition in the navy was both enthusiastic and tough, if somewhat short on the finer arts, and the young Pylkowski quickly built up a big reputation, eventually becoming the champion of the Atlantic Fleet, and performing in seaports all over the world.

A great life and an ideal grounding for a professional career. The twenty-year-old made his debut on April 14, 1932, out-pointing Joe Smallwood over six in Philadelphia. The *Ring Record Book* informs us that for the first two years he appeared as Henry Pulaski, retaining his Polish identity but with a name that fitted better on a poster, and, having switched operations to the West Coast, he became a minor attraction in San Diego, which was always a lively fight town. At 5ft 10″, he was a good height for a middle, was a cagey boxer with a busy style, but despite scoring four consecutive stoppages in 1933 he was never regarded as a particularly big hitter. He was, however, considered good enough to warrant a match with Johnny (Bandit) Romero, then considered a hot prospect around San Diego. Five years later, The Bandit still had enough on the ball to beat Archie Moore, but Risko proved too good after ten testing rounds.

Just when Risko seemed to be blossoming, his Californian campaign came to an abrupt halt, after he was stopped in four rounds by the more experienced Swede Berglund, a loss that persuaded Babe that this might be the time to head back home.

And so in 1934 he was back fighting around Syracuse, boxing six- and eight-rounders. He had acquired a new manager, a gentleman named Gabe Genovese who, in a twinkling, changed both his name and his life. One year later Babe Risko was the middleweight champion of the world – at least, America's idea of the world.

Gabe Genovese, not to be confused with the more illustrious Don Vito, was yet another rackets guy, a gambler, numbers operator, and all-round bad egg. Aside from handling Risko, he should also be remembered fondly in boxing folklore as the man who introduced one Paul John Carbo into the business. Perhaps that is a slight exaggeration: Carbo already had many contacts in many places, but prior to Risko he had been too busy to become seriously involved.

Frank had been occupied with more pressing matters, including several shootings, one of which brought about the death of a New Yorker called Albert Weber. Carbo had split to Philadelphia, but misbehaved there also, and eventually he was taken back to New York, stood trial for the Weber shooting, and was convicted of first-degree manslaughter. He had not long been paroled from Sing Sing when Genovese generously offered him a half share in Risko, and ever after, Carbo always expected 50 per cent when he put the arm on a manager. Boxing would never be quite the same.

Mr Gray, as he would become known, had not yet laid down his pistol, and in the 1930s he was implicated in two high-profile murders, one in New Jersey, the other in Los Angeles, but he still had time to organise his new deal for the fight game. And call it coincidence if you like, but that was when the partnership of Babe and Gabe took off like Jesse Owens out of the blocks.

After returning from California, Risko stayed unbeaten in fifteen fights – including three draws – and then came the shock New Year's Day stoppage of Yarosz. Overnight the championship beckoned. Even subsequent losses to former champion Dundee, then two in Cleveland against Jimmy Belmont and Paul Pirrone, failed to queer the script. Nothing was going to stop Risko getting his shot, and the Babe duly did the business in Pittsburgh. Money time.

Despite the fact that the new champ had been born in the state, Genovese had never attempted to build up Risko as an attraction in New York. Curious, and perhaps wisely cautious. Surprisingly, the Dundee loss had been Babe's debut in The Apple, and the knowledgeable Garden clientele were probably better acquainted with Jock McAvoy, who earned rave reviews following his victory over the Canadian, Al McCoy, in November. The Englishman had arrived in the States expecting to land a title shot, and he thought that his tremendous performance against McCoy would guarantee him his chance. He was being naive.

No way were the Americans about to risk the title leaving the States – bad enough that Thil remained an embarrassment – and Genovese would only okay a twelve-rounds overweight match, with vague assurances of a second fight depending on the outcome of the first. Risko, it was pointed out more than once, had been made to go through exactly the same procedure with Yarosz, so why should McAvoy be so special? Take it or leave it, and, finding himself in a corner, Jock had little option but to sign terms, but he was far from happy.

That, however, was nothing new for McAvoy. The 28-year-old British middleweight champion was a truculent, quick-tempered bully and womaniser, domineering, suspicious, and with a string of petty convictions, mostly brought about by his arrogance. On the plus side, he may well have been the greatest 160lb fighter ever born in Britain, and one can only imagine how good he might have become had he been blessed with two sound fists.

McAvoy was born Joseph Bamford on November 20, 1907 in the Lancashire town of Burnley. His father, Joe, was a labourer, but tried his hand at anything that might bring in money; his mother, Nellie, had worked as a weaver in the cotton mills; they were not married and times were hard. Still, they provided the boy with a stable and caring upbringing: in fact, from a very early age Joe was allowed to do as he wanted – a trait that would remain with him for the rest of his days.

The family moved first to Manchester to find a better living, and then on to Rochdale, but money was always scarce. Joe left school at fourteen to find a job, but he could never keep one for long, mostly because of his temper and his willingness to throw the first punch. Earning a living by fighting appealed to him.

At that time the area around Rochdale was a hotbed of boxing, boasting many accomplished professionals and staging regular promotions. Orchestrating much of the action was an incredible livewire named Joe Tolley. At one time or another Tolley performed as a promoter and gym proprietor, a manager, trainer and second, a referee, ring announcer, and last, but not least, a boxing reporter. An aficionado, and then some!

He promoted Sunday afternoon shows at the Royton Boxing Club, and one November Sunday morning the nineteen-year-old Bamford turned up with a pal, both looking for a spot on that afternoon's card. Joe had been learning some moves in the gym, and Tolley insisted that the teenager must first box a trial to prove that he could fight. He passed the test and in the afternoon he made his professional debut, knocking out local boy Billy Longworth in round two. The date was November 6, 1927, and he was paid in coins.

A humble start to a career that would continue until 1945. Before very long, Tolley had become his manager.

On that first Sunday afternoon the promoter had been unintentionally responsible for changing the youngster's ring name. Uncertain as to his mother's reaction to him boxing, Joe asked Tolley to announce him as Jack McCoy, but probably listening with only one ear, the man of many faces introduced him as Jock McAvoy. The name stuck.

Jock was a terrific puncher and as hard as nails, but he was raw and untutored. In his third fight he was badly outclassed by the much more experienced Billy Chew, being forced to retire in the eighth. He was a fast learner, however, and after three further wins he was able to turn the tables on Chew, and by the close of an unbeaten 1929 that loss was the only black mark in nineteen outings.

One of the wins had come at a price. Boxing Jackie Jukes in Morecambe, a fierce right hand went astray and caught Jukes on the top of his head – blinding pain, and although McAvoy went on to stop Jukes with some smashing left hooks, this was the start of his hand problems. In the dressing room the hand was badly swollen, the pain unceasing, yet three weeks later McAvoy was back in the ring. Perhaps Mac invented macho, but he was doing himself no favours returning so quickly, and the right would prove a chronic handicap for the rest of his career. His left could also be vulnerable.

In his definitive McAvoy biography, *The Rochdale Thunderbolt*, Jack Doughty recounts that several people claimed that Jock did not have particularly strong hands to begin with; they were even described as small and delicate (remember De Niro's lines in

Raging Bull about his small hands?) The fighter himself said that
his thumbs were so short that he could never get a glove to fit him
properly, and that was the reason he developed the habit of
repeatedly tugging at the thumbs of his gloves with his teeth
during a contest.

Gnawing on his thumbs became a McAvoy trademark, a
curious sight to behold. When the Americans first saw him
chewing leather, they reckoned that rage had taken hold and Mac
was about to explode. Opponents too must have wondered just
what kind of guy this was heading in their direction.

Despite the constant worry over his hands, the middleweight
was improving fast, and it was time to change managers. Joe
Tolley's influence did not stretch far, and he lacked the important
connections – a familiar tale in the fight game. The parting was
reasonably amicable, and McAvoy signed with Harry Fleming,
who worked closely with the powerful outfit which ran boxing at
Manchester's Belle Vue Arena. Jack Madden made the matches,
while behind the scenes Britain's leading boxing journalist,
Norman Hurst, exerted huge influence – a kind of benign Frank
Carbo without the menace or the rap sheet, but what about the
conflict of interest?

Fleming was a conscientious manager and trainer. He worked
on McAvoy, tightening his defence, encouraging him to box as
well as punch, and experimenting with different methods of
taping the fragile hands. McAvoy continued to improve, but in
March 1932 he was outpointed by Len Harvey, another all-time
great Brit, in a bid for the national middleweight title. A year later
Jock reversed the decision, won Harvey's championship,
extending an unbeaten run that would stretch to 26 before Thil
snatched the verdict in that European light heavyweight joust
in Paris.

That was in January 1935, and despite the set-back, ambitious
plans were being put in place for the year. First order of business
was a revamp of the backroom team. An American called Dave
Lumiansky, who, a few years earlier, had visited Britain with the
fabulous beanpole bantamweight champion, Panama Al Brown,
arrived in Manchester and began working on Hurst, telling
him just what he could do for McAvoy over in the States, and
how his countrymen would love the middleweight champion's
all-action style.

The journalist, who was nobody's fool, was impressed by the smooth sell, and he got busy. Fleming's contract was about to expire, but Harry would be retained as trainer; Lumiansky would become business manager; Harry Levene, later to become a leading promoter, would act as London agent; and Hurst would continue as Minister Without Portfolio. Look out, America!

McAvoy arrived in the States in November, his right hand still sore from a victory the previous month over Frenchman Marcel Lauriot in Manchester. Lumiansky shrugged off his concern, promising to take care of the problem, but it soon became clear that the glib talker had problems of his own, trying to organise a title showdown with Risko. In fact, he could not even secure a fight at middleweight.

The Garden matchmaker, the renowned Boy Bandit, Jimmy Johnston, was only too happy to headline the Englishman – but at light heavyweight, and against a high-flying contender, the 22-year-old French Canadian, Al McCoy. Johnston was doing the visitors no favours, but Jock never backed down from a challenge.

In the dressing room shortly before fight time Lumiansky unveiled his solution to Mac's hand worries: a guy introduced as a doctor, complete with a syringe loaded with novocaine. As the doc started to inject between his knuckles of the right hand, McAvoy keeled over in a faint. Panic stations, but after Jock was revived his nausea gradually receded, and after some shadow boxing he was as ready as he was ever going to be. There was no feeling in his right hand.

Long term, of course, Lumiansky's ruse was far more likely to cause further damage, but the American never looked too far into the future, and there was a job to be done. On the night of November 29 the British champion was a revelation, surprising McCoy, delighting the fans, and astounding the press.

The hand felt great as he outboxed and outpunched McCoy to take a clear decision. Afterwards the old hero, Jack Dempsey, proclaimed, 'Jock McAvoy is the greatest British fighter I've seen in twenty years. We want more like him in America.'

Nat Fleischer added his seal of approval, saying that Jock would be his choice to win both the middleweight and light heavyweight titles. He did not elaborate on why he did not even include the Englishman in the *Ring*'s 160lb ratings, ranking him only as a 175lb contender, although there was no question that Mac could make middleweight comfortably. After Lumiansky's fruitless negotiations with the Risko team, however, there would be no need to train down to the limit for his next fight. A non-title twelve: take it or leave it.

Johnston, Lumiansky and the Riskos were eager to cash in on Mac's new celebrity, and the date was agreed for just three weeks after the McCoy fight. Johnston anticipated a bumper gate, but his hopes crashed when a blast of sub-zero temperatures and heavy falls of snow hit New York.

McAvoy had more to worry about than the weather. Because of the injection he had made plenty of use of his right hand against McCoy, more than usual, and now he was paying the penalty. The hand was tender, could be used only sparingly in training, and on the night would require another shot of novocaine if it was going to hold up for twelve hard rounds with the champion. Mac was aware that he was doing himself harm but felt he had no alternative, and a troublesome chill added to his dark humour.

Confidence behind Risko was high. Since acquiring the championship three months earlier he had won all three of his fights, the most recent – a points verdict over rugged Frank Battaglia in Philadelphia – coming just eleven days before the Garden date. McAvoy had been ringside in Philly and had a good idea of what to expect from the bustling Babe.

Risko weighed in at just 1½lb over the title limit; McAvoy was 7lb heavier, but the weights would have no bearing on this massacre. Pacing his corner, gnawing on his gloves, McAvoy looked like a man bent on venting his spite on anyone handy, and right across the ring was this champ who would not risk his crown. At the bell the Englishman rushed across the ring, tossed a sizzling right hand which landed bang on Risko's jaw, and down went the Babe. Maybe stunned, perhaps embarrassed, he bounced straight back up without taking a count, only to walk into an avalanche of leather. A few seconds on the canvas would have served him better because, with the crowd going wild, Mac gave him no chance to regroup.

Risko desperately tried to grab hold for a few seconds' respite, but McAvoy was powering in with all guns blazing, and two great head shots – a left hook and a follow-up right – sent the American crashing for the second time. He stayed down for seven, but when

he rose there was nowhere to hide as a furious McAvoy drove him
back across the ring. All the demons inside The Thunderbolt
had been unleashed, and twice more Risko went down for counts
of five.

The Babe may not have been one of the great middleweights,
but he sure was one of the gamest. Now battered, bleeding, and
totally bewildered, he swayed helplessly before the British
champion who teed off with another two-handed salvo. For the
fifth time Risko crumpled to the floor. He was as beaten as a
fighter could be, but from somewhere he found the will to struggle
up at eight to face his tormentor.

A crazy display of a champion's pride and defiance, but
McAvoy was merciless. One final thundering right dropped Babe
yet again, and this time, deaf to the count or the roar of the crowd,
he sat on the canvas, utterly exhausted, until his cornermen
rushed to his aid. Time: 2 minutes 48 seconds of round one, and
the Brit was ecstatic. Risko had failed to land one decent shot, and
even if all those rights had worsened his hand, so what?

But Mac's dreams of a title rematch were just that . . . dreams.
Risko's connections would never allow the championship to
cross the Atlantic, and in a frosty meeting in a nightclub just
hours after the fight they resisted Lumiansky's best sales pitch
with a degree of menace. They wanted nothing further to do
with the Limey. More upstanding citizens seemed determined to
build McAvoy into a light heavy. Fleischer, probably because
the Englishman had weighed 8lb over the middleweight limit,
continued to rank him in the 175lb class; and ever the
pragmatist, Jimmy Johnston posed the killer question: who
would pay to see McAvoy face a guy he had already slaughtered
inside one round? Fair point.

The Boy Bandit had been born in Liverpool, but he suffered no
pangs of patriotism. He had, however, become a McAvoy fan, and
offered him a light heavyweight title shot against the slick John
Henry Lewis, who had not long won his belt, thanks to a decision
over Bob Olin. The match would draw well, and a date was agreed
for March 13, 1936.

Jock arrived back in England on New Year's Day for a short
break before beginning preparations for John Henry, and he
received a wonderful reception wherever he went, as if he really
was the world champ. Mac was delighted, and perhaps he felt like

a champion when he sailed back to the States in late January. Lumiansky, however, had a couple of surprises for him.

The manager had booked two tune-up fights to bring in some extra cash, but this was utter madness considering the condition of McAvoy's hands, especially the right. The tools needed protection, not overuse, but on February 17 Jock stopped Jimmy Smith in New York; ten days later outpointed Anson Green in Philadelphia; and two weeks after that, was back in the Garden to challenge the 21-year-old champion. The fighter was risking not only his world title opportunity, but also his future career. The novocaine would be required.

When betting opened on the fight, McAvoy was the book-makers' choice at 11/10, but from certain quarters there were leaks about the Englishman's bad hands, and come the big night all the serious money was for John Henry. His camp had been brought up to speed about the dressing-room injections, and planned a counter measure. Being the challenger, Jock was first into the ring, prowling the square, releasing the tension, chewing on his thumbs, anxious to tear into Lewis. But where was the champ? As the minutes passed the crowd started to become restless, and McAvoy's impatient rage neared the boil before the Lewis faction at last appeared, making its way slowly down the aisle.

They were taking their time, figuring the longer the delay, the more chance the injection would lose its effect before the rounds were completed. The strategy paid off bigtime.

Lewis was a smooth, classy operator with a wide variety of punches, but in the early rounds he was stretched to keep the aggressive McAvoy at distance. The exchanges were hot, and the champ's counters stung the challenger, but Lewis was cut and perhaps trailing slightly by the close of seven entertaining rounds. The novocaine, however, was fast losing its magic, and by the ninth Mac was practically a one-handed fighter, a searing pain shooting up his arm every time he connected with a right. Sensing the predicament, Lewis stepped up the tempo, and at the final bell he was a clear winner. But a tired and sore McAvoy had let nobody down.

Now the smart move was for him to enjoy a lengthy rest and listen to some expert advice about the hands. McAvoy, however, was headstrong, feared no fighter no matter what size, and was ever hungry for money. Incredibly, just a month after losing to

Lewis, The Rochdale Thunderbolt was back in the ring, challenging Welshman Jack Petersen for his British and Empire heavyweight titles in London. Heavyweights!

Dave Lumiansky, no longer looked upon as the American genius, worked his corner for the last time, but Mac was done with syringes and injections, and his hands gave out after five rounds. Outreached and outweighed, only his courage and stubborn streak enabled him to survive until the final bell. But this was a crazy way to pocket four grand.

He was still only 28 and, despite the huge handicap of the hands, many memorable nights lay ahead. In April 1937 he won the British light heavyweight crown, stopping Londoner Eddie Phillips, and then he proved all the doubters wrong by scaling down to middleweight to defend successfully his other title against Jack Hyams in Manchester. As he had insisted all along, Mac was a natural middle, and even two years later he was still able to make 160lb when beating Ginger Sadd. There were two losing light heavyweight battles with his old foe, Len Harvey, the second being for the British version of the world championship, and he did not retire until 1945, bidding goodbye with a points victory over Tommy Davies in Swansea.

McAvoy finished with a wonderful career record. He was beaten only fourteen times in 147 contests, and of his 132 wins, no fewer than 91 came inside the distance. He was an aggressive, all-action fighter with a great chin, an indomitable spirit and a tremendous punch, and he must be included in the top ten British boxers of all time. We can only wonder how great he might have become with two sturdy hands.

Unfortunately, he was as quick to lash out with those fists away from the ring. McAvoy had a short fuse, a huge ego, an apparent grudge against fellow motorists, gamekeepers, and coppers and, as a result, his court appearances for minor offences were depressingly frequent.

At home, he was no prize either.

He married Eliza Jarman when he was 21, but he regarded all women as fair game, and the relationship was stormy, ending in divorce in 1937. Two other marriages followed, first to Joan Lye and then to Renée Garrett, and he remained on reasonable terms with the wives, if only to maintain contact with his children. But he would always be a wild rover.

McAvoy had a wide variety of interests aside from women. He owned a string of horses and was an able rider; he was a pub landlord, dabbled in second-hand car dealing, and for a time owned a caravan site.

But just two years after his last contest his life was shattered when he was diagnosed as suffering from polio which robbed him of the use of his legs. Try as he might, this was one opponent Mac could not lick, and he spent the rest of his days hobbling around with the aid of two sticks, the useless legs encased in callipers. The old champion was still seen at the big fights, still had not mellowed, and incredibly, would still get into scraps. But he could never come to terms with being a cripple.

He died on November 20, 1971 – his 64th birthday – and at the subsequent inquest the cause of death was revealed as barbiturate poisoning. A verdict of suicide was returned.

Eddie Babe Risko had died fourteen years earlier, on March 7, 1957, in his home town of Syracuse. Following the terrible hammering from McAvoy, Gabe Genovese's middleweight held on to the title for just six months before losing to Freddie Steele in Seattle. After that he lost more than he won, was stopped in his last five fights, and retired in 1939 with a record which shows only 28 wins from 66 contests.

The Babe was just another in a long line of so-so champs who got lucky – until that night in the Garden when he was struck by a thunderbolt.

CHAPTER SEVENTEEN

Gerry Cooney *v* Ken Norton

MONDAY, MAY 11, 1981

The era of the White Hopes was just a dim memory, a grim reminder of the sorry, racist dogma that had festered throughout the States some seventy years earlier, and when Joe Louis stepped out from the giant shadow cast by old Jack Johnson he emancipated black fighters for all time. And how they had flourished once the shackles were shaken free! Especially among the heavyweights, where the extraordinary exploits of Ali, Frazier, Foreman and Norton electrified the world of boxing and beyond like no other time.

And yet, this golden age only intensified the search for a great white heavy . . . little to do with blinkered prejudice any longer: money was the name of this game, and though the division was already awash with moolah, a slight change of colour would send a buzz through the closed-circuit market. Promoters and managers drooled when dreaming about the big white heavy who could really fight, and the vast sums they would rake in through purses and endorsements. If only.

Marciano had been such a long, long time ago; the Swede, Johansson, and the South African, Coetzee, had turned out to be false alarms; and the contenders had been mostly pretenders – guys like Henry Cooper, Jerry Quarry, George Chuvalo and Joe Bugner. Good, but not that good. The latest hope to taste the resin had been Duane Bobick, a much-hyped sailor from Minnesota who had built up a flattering 38-fight unbeaten streak. But despite being managed by Joe Frazier and coached by Eddie Futch, Bobick survived for only 58 seconds with Ken Norton in the Garden. The hunt was still on.

225

Larry Holmes was now the champion, and he was a fine standard-bearer who barred nobody, but even after seven defences of his belt he was still seeking the acclaim and affection that had been lavished on his predecessors. And when, in 1980 in Las Vegas, he was railroaded into facing his one-time sparring boss, Ali, Larry found himself in a terrible no-win situation. Only Muhammad's magic tongue had sold the fight as feasible, but within a matter of minutes Ali's sad secret was out. In the circumstances, Holmes dealt with him as compassionately as possible, before The Greatest failed to come out for round eleven. A humiliating night all round, and more than ever the undefeated Easton Assassin desperately needed a defining fight, as much for his ego as his bank balance.

In New York, two successful real estate brokers were becoming increasingly convinced that they held the contract on a young man who could not only provide Holmes with the mega fight that he craved, but also come away with his championship. Mike Jones and Dennis Rappaport no longer dreamed every manager's dream: now they were dealing with the reality that they had unearthed a genuine white heavyweight star, the hottest ticket in town, and the millions they forecast making rocketed far into the realms of funny money. They had Gerry Cooney.

In the trade, Rappaport and Jones were dubbed the Whacko Twins, thanks to their eccentric brand of management. Their first signing had been Ronnie Harris, a lightweight gold at the 1968 Mexico Olympics, and Rappaport in particular pulled out all the stops to get the southpaw meaningful fights and bags of publicity. He spun the idea that Harris was Jewish and threatened to sue the New York State Athletic Commission to allow the fighter to wear a *yarmulke* (a skullcap) in the ring. Ronnie earned plenty of column inches from this nonsense, and same again when the manager assembled the media in the Garden lobby, then paraded a guy dressed in a gorilla suit for the cameras, claiming that at last he had found an opponent willing to face Ronnie Harris. The Garden security guards were not impressed.

The Whackos, however, had the last laugh. Their sheer persistence broke down doors, and in August 1978 Harris – undefeated in 26 fights – was awarded a title shot in Buenos Aires against Hugo Corro. Ronnie was outpointed, but the Twins had delivered their end with their first fighter and could do no more. They also struck the crossbar with another Olympic hero, lightweight Howard Davis, negotiating a phenomenal television deal with CBS, estimated at over $1.5 million, and guiding him to a lightweight title challenge against Jim Watt in Glasgow.

Within a matter of days the managers were the two most detested men in Scotland, renaming the champ Jim Who, bickering over every minor detail surrounding the promotion, hellbent on securing every possible edge for their fighter. Davis was also outpointed, but again Messrs Jones and Rappaport had done their job.

They were still aggressive, still hustling for any advantage, still trying to squeeze every last dollar from a deal, but now they did not have to pull any stunts to drum up publicity. The newspapers, the radio, the television, everybody wanted an angle on giant Gerry Cooney who was just one fight away from a crack at the heavyweight championship of the world. And if the big guy could lick the ageing Kenny Norton in the Garden, then Mike and Dennis felt they could name their own price for the privilege, something unique for a challenger.

Gentleman Gerry Cooney, or Irish Gerry Cooney if you prefer, was born on August 4, 1956 in Huntingdon, Long Island, one of four brothers, the sons of Tony Cooney, a tough construction worker, a stern disciplinarian, and a man who decided early that Gerry must learn how to fight. He hung a heavy bag in the basement, and when the youngster began to box competitively Cooney Sr would arise at six in the morning to ensure that his son did his roadwork. He also imposed an evening curfew, but the boy often skipped back out to meet his friends after his dad had gone off to bed. From his earliest days, Gerald Anthony Paul Cooney experienced a love-hate relationship with boxing that would cause him much anguish in later life.

No lack of enthusiasm was ever apparent in the ring. The hulking 6ft 6″ 220lb novice was no dancing master, but he carried a left hook of tremendous power, and in 57 amateur bouts he was beaten only twice, collecting two New York Golden Gloves titles in the process. Jones and Rappaport were just two of a posse of managers eager to sign the twenty-year-old, and their bid was surprisingly modest: an interest-free advance of $200 a week and a guarantee that he would be allowed to train full-time. No overnight financial security, no fancy cars, but the Cooneys seemed satisfied, as did their lawyer. The formalities were completed, and then they started talking trainers.

Several names were mentioned, but the Whackos strongly recommended a Puerto Rican named Victor Valle who worked at Gleason's gym and after he and Gerry took a cautious first look at one another in a Manhattan restaurant, Valle agreed to train the young heavyweight. In the mid-1930s Victor had been a busy teenage featherweight, losing only twice in forty starts, according to the *Ring Record Book*, one of the defeats coming against the future lightweight champ, Sammy Angott. But recurring hand troubles forced him to retire early, and in 1938 he switched to teaching fighters.

Around Gleason's, he had earned a good reputation as a shrewd and diligent coach, and he quickly formed a rapport with Cooney, a willing student. There was much to learn, and Valle went to work, tightening the heavyweight's slack defence, improving his footwork, shortening his punches, and building up his fitness levels. The left hook was always there, and on February 15, 1977 the big man was deemed ready to debut against someone called Bill Jackson. All over inside a round, and the Cooney bandwagon was rolling.

In his first three years campaigning, Gerry won 22 straight, only Matt Robinson, Sam McGill and Eddie Lopez lasting the full course. Over the next eleven years, Gentleman Gerry would grace the ring just nine more times, but those were the money years, the years when, with a mere mention of his name, the cash registers would start belting out 'Galway Bay'. But even back in 1980 the dough was getting serious, as were the chess moves that would lead to a title shot.

Both the WBA and the WBC featured Cooney high in their ratings, and Rappaport and Jones found themselves negotiating a minefield: who to fight next, who to avoid? Gerry was still learning; one rash choice, and they might have to start all over again.

After much nail-biting, arguing and poring over record books and studying tapes, they finally accepted Jimmy Young, a 31-year-old from Philadelphia, who had done several laps of the block. Young was a smart boxer and a decent puncher, and back in 1976, in his only title challenge, he had given Ali fits for the full fifteen rounds in Landover. He also had rung down the curtain on George Foreman's first career, thanks to a stunning points upset in Puerto Rico; had twice outpointed the dangerous Ron Lyle; but the signals suggested that, with four losses in his last seven fights, Jimmy had lost his ambition. Still . . .

On May 25 the giant from Long Island demonstrated that he had added a powerful right to back up his vicious left hook; proved himself under fire, when Young scored with some good hooks of his own, plus several borderline shots; and though the contest was halted in the fourth because of Young's cuts, Gil Clancy, commentating for CBS network TV, was impressed enough to call Cooney 'The hottest fighter in the heavyweight division.'

There were many who echoed his sentiments, and five months later, in Uniondale, New York, hot was turned up to red-hot after Gerry wrecked the once-feared Lyle – now boxing from memory – inside one round. Following those two wins, Jones and Rappaport feared nobody: not WBA champion Mike Weaver, nor Holmes, the WBC boss, and certainly not old Ken Norton, who was being pencilled in for a lucrative engagement, no more than a filler, until the mega deals had been thrashed out to the Whackos' satisfaction.

Everyone wanted to buy lunch for the Twins, but right then every manager awaited a call from a mysterious black guy named Harold Smith, the head of a promotional outfit called Muhammad Ali Professional Sports, Inc. (MAPS) and although Muhammad had been paid a considerable sum for the use of his name, he had absolutely nothing else to do with the organisation.

Smith had the boxing world in a whirl. A one-time rock entrepreneur, he arrived on the scene with satchels of readies, paid well over the rate for his fights, and although, more often than not, his shows were box-office flops, back he would come with even more dough and even more grandiose plans. Rumours abounded: he had billionaire backers; he had inherited a fortune; he was putting mafia money in the washing machine. The fight mob was curious, but nobody really cared where he found his loot.

Harold wanted Cooney and Norton to head a super, sensational, multi-mega extravaganza which he scheduled for the Garden on February 23, 1981. Also on the bumper bill were Thomas Hearns against Wilfred Benitez; Alexis Arguello facing Hilmer Kenty; and Matthew Saad Muhammad fighting Eddie Mustafa Muhammad. Wow! But just three weeks before the big night, Harold Smith did a runner when the news leaked out about his connection to a sum of $21 million which had gone walkabout from a Beverly Hills branch of the Wells Fargo Bank. All this time, Harold had been holding up the stagecoach!

Naturally, the grand promotion collapsed, but the Garden executives decided to press ahead with only the Cooney–Norton showdown, and that suited a relieved Jones and Rappaport just fine: the rescheduled date was May 11, and Norton would be another three months older. In actual fact, although the *Ring Record Book* listed Kenny's birth for 1945, he had been born two years earlier, and going into the ring with Cooney he would be a wealthy 37-year-old, picking and choosing his final fights in a fabulous career.

The former champion, however, was too proud to present himself as a sacrificial offering. True, in Vegas in 1979 Earnie Shavers had dropped him twice when scoring a one-round knockout, but Earnie could poleaxe anyone if he connected. True again, he was floored twice when scraping a draw with Scott LeDoux in Bloomington, LeDoux's home town. But he was still no patsy as he showed when outpointing tough Randall (Tex) Cobb in a split-decision thriller in San Antonio on November 7, 1980 – his last appearance before fighting Cooney.

Jones, Rappaport and Valle were encouraged by the four knockdowns, and Norton's gruelling battle with Cobb, and figured that Ken's time had come. Still, they anticipated a few hard rounds before Gentleman Gerry started to unload with his bombs: everyone knew that Norton always came to fight.

He was born on August 9, 1943 in Jacksonville, Illinois, the result of a teenage liaison between a boy called George Florence and a sixteen-year-old named Ruth. The kids went their separate ways but in June 1947 Ruth married John Norton; her three-year-old son became Kenneth Howard Norton; the marriage would survive for more than fifty years; and only child, Ken enjoyed a boyhood that bordered on the idyllic.

His father regularly held down three jobs to provide the extras that so many neighbouring black families had to go without; his mother was the activities director at the local hospital. Ken wanted for nothing.

Not the traditional upbringing of the hungry fighter, and everything seemed to come to Ken without too much effort. He was a bright, if none too industrious student, and on the sports fields he was amazing. A career beckoned in football or baseball or basketball, and he was even better at track and field. Al Rosenberger, his coach at Jacksonville High, later claimed that Norton was easily the best all-round athlete he had seen in thirty years, good enough to reach the very top as an Olympic decathlete. From a deluge of college scholarship offers, he chose Northeast Missouri State, but he dropped out in the second year – a huge disappointment to his parents.

Next stop, the Marines! The twenty-year-old had grown into a muscular 6ft 3″ body beautiful, and he was a stand out for the Marine football team, but he quit the squad after a dispute with an officer and took up boxing, where the perks were equally attractive. In all other sports, he had been naturally gifted, but boxing did not come easy. Still, he learned enough to become the All Marine champion three years running, finishing with a record of only two defeats in 26 fights. He also started to learn about life.

Ken was always dynamite around the ladies, and in 1965 he became a father for the first time, but he would see little of Keith Anthony Norton, who was raised by his mother, until much later in life. And then he married his first wife Jeanette, and there was soon another son, Kenneth Howard Norton Jr who would go on to become a famous linebacker for the San Francisco 49'ers and the Dallas Cowboys. The marriage, however, failed to click, and this time it was Ken who kept the boy.

He did not discover domestic stability until he met and married Jackie Halton, and they had a daughter, Kenisha. By then he was a headliner, his name known all over the States. But when he completed his stint in the Marines, he was a 24-year-old nobody, a single parent with few career options, and now he was that hungry fighter.

A San Diego businessman helped him make up his mind. Art Rivkin had refereed Norton in the amateurs and liked what he saw. He and his partner, Bob Biron, owned a Coca Cola distributorship, and they made Norton an offer to turn pro – $100 a week and a share of the purses: not much to keep big Ken and little Ken. Moving to Los Angeles to train at the Hoover Street gym, he was forced to take a job on the assembly line at the Ford Motor plant to supplement his earnings.

The record books say that he stopped Grady Brazell in the ninth on his debut in San Diego on November 14, 1967, but in his autobiography, *Going the Distance*, the fighter insists that the end came in the third, pointing out that he would never have been given a ten-round job for starters. Fair enough, but Ken's own version of his record includes an eighth-round knockout over Venezuelan, Jose Luis Garcia, in July 1970, when in fact Norton was the one who was stopped. None of us is perfect.

Certainly not Norton that night in LA. After sixteen consecutive wins (only one on points) he was growing cocky, and only doing enough in the gym to get by. Eddie Futch pinned a newspaper picture of Ken taking the count on the door of the fighter's locker, and smiled his wise smile. The ubiquitous Eddie, then a youthful 57, had taken over as Norton's trainer after three fights, and that was when the heavyweight really started to make strides.

At the time, Futch was also training Joe Frazier for his friend Yank Durham, but the rewards could not have been all that hot because he was moonlighting with a job in the post office. Nevertheless, he had two million-dollar fighters, and he knew how to draw the best from them. Norton and Frazier sparred vigorously and often, and Ken probably picked up more from his sessions with Smokin' Joe than he did from his carefully selected real fights. There was also a fateful three minutes sparring with Ali.

The year was 1970, and Ali's banishment from boxing was nearing its end. As was his habit in any city where he touched down, Muhammad arrived at the gym on Hoover Street, looking for Futch to provide him with some quality sparring action. Last man in with him was Norton, and in the final minute of their round, Ali turned on the style, but Norton surprised him with stiff counters. Only a spar, but the exiled champ was somewhat miffed, and returned the following day, looking to pursue the argument. Eddie, however, told his fighter to keep his clothes on: the next time they shared a ring, the trainer told Ali, Norton would be earning big money.

Three years later, and $50,000 still represented huge money to Norton when they finally got it on in the San Diego Sports Arena on March 31, 1973. Even better, managers Biron and Rivkin generously waived their cut of Ken's biggest purse by far. Outside California, Norton was virtually unknown: promoter Bob Arum feared that the fight might not last two rounds, and his television paymasters would start asking questions; sportscaster Howard Cosell, sage as ever, forecast the worst mismatch of all time; Norton was 5/1 in the betting, and few expected him to survive the twelve rounds for Muhammad's North American Boxing Federation heavyweight championship.

Sensation! Ali lost a majority verdict, his tinpot title, and suffered a broken jaw. An inspired Norton constantly outjabbed him, then outpunched him to both head and body, and although one judge thought otherwise, the verdict was just. Chief corner-man Angelo Dundee and Ali were adamant that the jaw was fractured in round two; Norton and Futch were equally positive that the damage was done in round eleven. Both camps had obvious agendas.

Two things were certain. There would be a rematch, and Ken Norton was no longer a fifty-grand fighter. His handsome face was flashed around the world, strangers arrived with all sorts of propositions, but first business was to buy a bigger house in a better neighbourhood. Big Ken and Junior were on their way.

Norton was every marketing man's midnight fantasy. Here was this great-looking guy with that terrific physique, and he was not one of those loudmouthed nuts either: he was articulate, spoke sense, he was rearing a kid on his own, and he could deliver in the ring. A natural for major TV exposure – even after Ali exacted his revenge in their September return in Los Angeles.

Again the twelve rounds were agonisingly close, the verdict, another majority, but the consensus was that Ali – significantly lighter this time – was just about value for his win. Muhammad would never quite master Kenny's awkwardly effective, wide-footed style, and three years later, in their championship epic in New York's Yankee Stadium, once more the pair could barely be separated. The cards were unanimous in favour of the champ, but the margins showed just how little there was between them: 8–6–1, 8–7 (twice) and the arguments raged for weeks. If anything, however, those hotly disputed decisions only enhanced Norton's prestige.

The fans were even willing to forgive him his miserable first challenge for the heavyweight title against Foreman on March 26, 1974, in Caracas. That night, Norton left his fight plans in the dressing room, and Big George destroyed him in two rounds. But there would also be glory nights: taking Jerry Quarry's best shots before halting him in five rounds in the Garden; getting even with José Luis Garcia in St Paul; exposing Bobick in less than a minute in the Garden again; and squeezing through on another split decision against Jimmy Young in a 1977 final eliminator in Las Vegas. Big paynights, important wins.

The Young victory should have set the scene for a fourth Ali–Norton clash, but instead Muhammad opted for a defence against Leon Spinks, and the World Boxing Council had little alternative but to remove its recognition of The Greatest. On March 29, 1978 WBC president Jose Sulaiman, in an unprecedented step, proclaimed Ken Norton as the new WBC heavyweight champion of the world. A champ without throwing a punch!

And no more than a caretaker champ. On June 9 he lost the prized belt after a titanic fifteen rounds against the 27-year-old Larry Holmes at Caesar's Palace in Las Vegas. Larry had been done few favours on his slow march to the top, and Norton gave him a ferocious argument before surrendering the championship. The final round is still remembered as one of the most brutal and thrilling ever fought, with the Vegas crowd going insane as the two huge gladiators battered one another into a state of exhaustion, both looking about to topple during the tremendous exchanges. A magnificent three minutes, and nobody could be sure about the outcome, but once again Ken's luck was out with the judges: 143–142 (twice) for Holmes, 143–142 Norton. Larry would always recall Norton as his toughest opponent.

Kenny had never enjoyed a love affair with the business, and not for the first time he contemplated retirement. This might be the perfect time to walk away, but there were still bundles of offers, and the money was so difficult to turn down. He had proved against Randy Cobb that there still was a trickle left in the tank, and an $850,000 payday helped dispel any doubts about tackling Cooney. Who knows? If he could pull out a win, millions would be on the table for a return with Holmes.

Over the years there had been changes in the Norton camp. Eddie Futch had split after the second Ali fight in LA – quit or been fired, depending on who told the story. Futch had taken over as manager of Frazier following the death of Yank Durham, and this did not sit well with Biron, who also maintained that Norton had been overtrained for Ali II, a view which, in turn, offended the proud and prickly Futch.

Ken was caught in the middle and said little, but he deeply regretted Eddie's departure. Although his replacement, Bill Slayton, became a loyal and shrewd adviser, there was only one Eddie Futch.

And then, a month after Ken's draw with LeDoux, Biron died after a lengthy illness. The manager was 66, had always treated Norton like a son, and he would be sorely missed during the countdown days.

The fight and the death of reggae king Bob Marley at the age of 36 were the main stories across the New York airwaves that May Monday, but at the Garden there was much gnashing of teeth because ticket sales had failed by a long way to live up to expectations, and the executives were steeling themselves for a mighty loss. Two factors here: a charge of $200 for a ringside seat to see a fight in which Gentleman Gerry was a 4/1 on favourite was optimistically steep, and equally significant, pay-per-view coverage had not been blacked out in the New York area. In the end, 9,436 aficionados, most of them decked out in green, filed into the Garden, and several insiders estimated the MSG loss as high as $1 million.

Norton was first into the ring, a sheen of sweat covering his body, perhaps a trifle nervous; only a quarter of a pound separated the pair but Cooney looked immense and assured. At the first bell he strode forward, eager to get down to business.

The boxers exchanged tentative jabs, trying to loosen up, trying to find the range, then Cooney got busy. He hooked a left into Norton's body, followed up with a searing right to the jaw – remember, that right was still supposed to be Gerry's dummy hand – and finished the combination with another sizzling left to the body. Norton, uncharacteristically, backed off, surprised by the ferocity of the attack and more than a little hurt. Cooney powered after him, crashing home more hooks to the body, and now Kenny was in real trouble, frantically looking for a bolt hole.

He had planned to outbox the New Yorker early on, but already, after just a few seconds, he was in the trenches and fighting for his life.

He managed to turn Gerry on to the ropes, landed two left hooks, missed with a wild right uppercut, then walked into a chilling Cooney special, followed by another dynamite hook that spun his head on his shoulders. Crisis time.

Instinctively, Norton tried to grab Cooney's arms until his brain stopped rattling, but Gerry was too quick and too strong, and manhandled Ken round on to the ropes. From then on the Long Islander might have been banging the heavy bag in Gleason's. Scenting the bonus of another early night, he battered Norton with both hands: a few shots went astray, but the hooks were landing with a sickening frequency, and then a terrific right almost lifted Ken off his feet. He slowly collapsed on to the bottom rope as Cooney's merciless shots rained down on his unprotected head. At last, referee Tony Perez jumped in between the fighters to rescue the stricken Norton, and not a second too soon. The old champ was unconscious, but still supported by the bottom rope. The carnage had been completed in 54 seconds – four seconds less than Norton had taken to thrash Bobick in the same ring – and Kenny was lucky to still be in one piece.

Cooney later told the reporters, 'I got a little bit frightened because I kept hitting him and he was unconscious.' Norton was equally sure that a tragedy had just been averted. 'I had erred by trading punches with a puncher, but I felt fortunate just to be alive. The fight doctor said I was four seconds away from death.'

There were, actually, three doctors quickly in attendance in his corner, but Norton recovered quickly and thankfully there was no lasting damage. He was even brave enough to put in an appearance at the post-fight media grilling, but now there was no question about Kenny ever boxing again. His farewell was not especially sad: Cooney's violent assault would have finished off any fighter, Norton had been paid top dollar, and now there were far safer ways to earn a buck.

He left boxing with a fine record of just seven defeats from fifty contests; had earned in the region of $16 million from the ring, although in today's inflated market he might have been paid that sum for a single superfight; and he had his health, his family, and a wide range of business interests.

He had already featured in two movies, *Mandingo* and *The Drum*, and though Ken was no Sidney Poitier and the films were far from classics, he showed enough talent to guarantee future work. There were also his stints as a sportscaster, and he became a sports agent, cutting deals for younger heroes. Ken was doing all right, until a February night in 1986, when his world shattered around him, and the Associated Press rushed out a terse bulletin over the wires:

> Los Angeles, CA – Ken Norton, former boxing heavyweight champion of the world, is in critical condition at Cedars Sinai Hospital today. Norton was involved in a mysterious car accident when his car veered off the Santa Monica Freeway off-ramp late last night. Medical experts are stating that his chances of survival are slim.
>
> —Associated Press
> February 23, 1986.

In hospital, doctors removed skull fragments from his brain; his jaw was fractured in three places; there was a broken leg and a litany of other injuries, but somehow, he pulled through. When Ken was released four weeks later, however, he was 52lb lighter and was paralysed down his right side; his vocal chords had been badly damaged and his memory seriously affected. Norton still has no recollection of how the accident came about.

But the guy for whom everything had come so easily found inner powers, and after two years in a wheelchair he began to walk again. He also learned how to talk again, though his words are sometimes slurred. His memory would still cause him problems.

In 1989, during his rehabilitation, Norton took part in the excellent video documentary *Champions Forever*, along with old buddies Ali, Frazier, Foreman and Holmes. This served as a huge lift, and there was further good news in 1992 when he was inducted into the Hall Of Fame. The comeback from the dead was complete.

While Kenny Norton had been fighting for his life, Gerry Cooney was battling his personal demons. The 1980s had turned sour on Gentleman Gerry.

After the demolition job in the Garden, Cooney found himself the most famous sportsman in America. He was featured on the covers of *Time* magazine and *Sports Illustrated*, and the *New York Times* described him as 'potentially the highest-paid athlete ever'. Lending credence to that forecast was the fact that, even though he was the challenger against Holmes in the much-hyped showdown scheduled for June 11, 1982, the New Yorker would enjoy purse parity with the champ. Not surprisingly Holmes was furious.

Nor was the champion happy that the contest was being sold on the colour angle. Cooney also hated being made a pawn in the race game, and was finding the White Hope pressure hard to handle. But this was such a monster promotion: a 32,000 crowd outdoors at Caesar's Palace; more than 800 reporters and photographers from all over the world; an estimated 50 million closed-circuit audience; and wages of $8.5 million for the fighters.

The fight lived up to the ballyhoo, and Cooney survived until round thirteen, until little Victor Valle decided that his man had taken enough. But Gerry had performed heroically against a champion at the top of his game, and had hurt Holmes in several rounds. He had given his best, and nobody can do more. Cooney, however, felt that he had let everyone down and went into a deep depression.

He spent days, which stretched into weeks and then months, apologising to strangers for losing to Holmes. He stayed away from the gym and avoided his great friend, Victor, ignored calls from his manager, started drinking heavily, and two years passed before he fought again. But after tune-ups against Phil Brown and George Chaplin, he once more went awol. Hand and shoulder problems were laughed off as excuses by the same writers who had tipped him as the next champ; columnists and comedians paid high for the latest Gerry Cooney gag. Life was hell.

There would, however, be two more blockbusters, but he was a poor second best in both of them. In 1987 in Atlantic City Michael Spinks comprehensively beat him up in five rounds, and a full three years later he was still considered an attraction, but was stopped in the second by ancient George Foreman.

He was 33, probably relieved that he was done fighting, and now it was time to get on with his life. He had plenty of money, married in 1994, and a son, Jackson, was born in 1998. Now, he and his wife Jennifer devote much of their energies to running a non-profit organisation called FIST, aimed at helping former fighters make the transition from the ring to new careers away from boxing. He also teaches conditioning and boxing, and is at ringside for the big fights.

Gerry Cooney no longer goes around saying sorry, and Kenny Norton is just happy to be walking around. Nothing wrong with a happy ending.

CHAPTER EIGHTEEN

James Smith
v Tim Witherspoon

FRIDAY, DECEMBER 12, 1986

Terrible Tim and The Bonecrusher – two of the great nicknames from the 1980s, catchy enough to ensure that memories of their owners survive that shambolic time when heavyweight boxing was down on its knees and attention shifted to the spectaculars provided by genuine superstars such as Hagler and Duran, Hearns and Leonard. The business owed that foursome much back then.

Do you remember? Larry Holmes was widely regarded as the real champ, and as first the WBC boss and then the IBF holder, his longevity, coupled with his undoubted skills, gave the division a degree of respectability. But Larry's status was sadly and badly undermined by the hotchpotch collection of rival champions who came and went at such a depressing and bewildering rate of knots that perhaps only Don King could keep track. And only with the assistance of his lackeys, the late Al Braverman and Paddy Flood.

Please try to remember. There was Mike Weaver and Michael Dokes and Gerrie Coetzee and Tim Witherspoon and Pinklon Thomas and Greg Page and Tony Tubbs and Trevor Berbick and James Smith and Tony Tucker. Not counting Holmes and his successor, Michael Spinks, a grand total of ten world heavyweight champions, all within the space of six years. Talk about devaluation!

Terrible Tim Witherspoon and Bonecrusher Smith and Dynamite Dokes and Tony TNT Tubbs. If for nothing else, boxing will always owe an eternal vote of thanks to the young Iron Mike Tyson for clearing up the sorry mess.

The sanctioning organisations, their insatiable greed and their total absence of ethics, must take the rap for the disgraceful farce. Co-defendant has to be Don King, who played the alphabet game with breathtaking skill and nerve, while on his farm, which doubled as a training camp, his herd of heavyweights grazed on the Ohio acres, being fattened up for the championship market. Thanks to his unscrupulous scheming, allied to an incredible energy and ambition which easily surpassed that of any of his fighters, King owned all the major players . . . the heavyweights who would become known as the Lost Generation.

So easy to blame this buccaneer of a promoter for all the ills that befell those far-from-happy campers, and there is no doubt that time and again he shamelessly ripped them off and denied them their rights.

His serfs were obliged to accept King's stepson, Carl, as a manager and Carl's whack was 50 per cent (one third was the legal managerial deduction) and he often represented both boxers in the ring, a blatant conflict of interest. Purses were reduced as a matter of course, and the fighters were made to train at King's camp before being billed heavily for the privilege. Then there were the contracts, perhaps three or maybe four, concerning just one fighter, and available for all emergencies. There was no question that the members of the Lost Generation were fleeced bigtime.

Larry Holmes had been one of the first to suffer the machinations of The Don, but Larry persevered, kept his mind on business, and eventually made his millions and won his independence. And Michael Spinks went down a different road with another promoter, Butch Lewis, and Michael requires no handouts. And what about Gerry Cooney or Mike Tyson? King was never allowed close to Tyson until after the deaths of first Cus D'Amato, then Jim Jacobs.

Difficult, indeed extremely challenging, to reach the top of the heavyweight tree without the goodwill of the one-time Cleveland numbers boss. But not impossible.

So what about King's band of brothers down on the farm? Many were poorly educated and thus were easy marks for the maestro's trickeration, his special word for the glib explanations which could bewitch far sharper minds. Others figured that this must be the only game in town, and so meekly played along; and because of King's violent history, some may have been just plain scared to rebel. If the troops were continually bitching, at the same time some were snorting the odd line of coke or passing around a toke, or stuffing themselves full of fast foods and candy bars, comfort eating away a career. Can we blame King for not employing counsellors?

Those so-called lost boys were very often lazy, self-indulgent and delinquent young men, regularly turning up in the ring with layers of belly fat evidence of their indifference, equally uncaring about the fans who had forked out their hard-earned. Some of the championship fights were woeful, laboured exhibitions, but nevertheless the big guys took their dough, still very welcome despite the deductions, then returned to their whingeing. All down to King?

Terrible Tim Witherspoon will be remembered as the heavy-weight who cried 'enough', and finally stood up to the promoter; the fighter who bravely defied the threats and a total freeze-out to take his case to the courts, a marathon six-year struggle which eventually resulted in The Don agreeing a settlement, said to be in the region of $1 million.

Witherspoon deserves huge credit for his dogged courage and determination, but that was the hardest he ever battled in his life. What a pity that he seldom displayed similar single-mindedness during his fighting career.

In the gym and in the ring, Terrible Tim could be as big a loafer as the rest of the gang, routinely cheated on his training, and often short-changed his many fans. And never more so than on the December Friday in 1986 when he surrendered his WBA belt to The Bonecrusher in the Garden and then laid all the blame for his miserable showing at the door of The Don.

Granted, Tim was still reeling from the shock of receiving a derisory fee as payment for his London defence against Frank Bruno that summer. And true, he had signed to fight Tony Tubbs in the Garden, only to discover that James Smith would be a late replacement, and he wanted out of the promotion. But were those reasons enough to go into the ring already a beaten fighter, toss away what still could be the richest prize in sport, and turn a title fight into a one-round farce? More like the babe throwing the soother out of the pram.

Witherspoon was a very good fighter with a serious punch, when he bothered to work himself into shape. Some fighters would murder for just one chance at a heavyweight title, but Tim had twice been a champion, and no doubt felt that there would be further opportunities in the future. He never really appreciated his talent or his titles until it was too late, and that vital edge had departed for good.

Tim was born on December 27, 1957 in Philadelphia, and boxing never figured in his adolescence. He avoided trouble on the streets, was a good student at school, excelling in sports, and won a football scholarship to Lincoln University in Missouri, but an injury cut short his playing ambitions and he dropped out of college. Back in Philly, and now an imposing 6ft 3″, he found work, preparing and serving the staff meals at a local hospital and, always partial to a snack or ten, he started frequenting a nearby gym solely to keep his weight in check. But that was when he discovered boxing.

From the start he showed plenty of natural ability, but nobody was looking after him properly and with practically no ring experience he was entered for the Philadelphia Golden Gloves, being drawn against Marvis Frazier. Back then, Smokin' Joe's son was considered an Olympic prospect and floored and out-pointed the novice, but Witherspoon still gave him a torrid time. No question, Tim had a future, and after only a handful of amateur outings he turned pro as a 21-year-old, requiring less than a round to dispose of Joey Adams on October 30, 1979 in Upper Darby, Pennsylvania.

Upper Darby was scarcely a boxing hotbed, and neither was Lynchburg, Va, nor Commack, NY, nor McAfee, NJ, which were the staging posts for his next three wins, but the word was spreading fast about the newcomer, and soon he was on Ali's payroll as a sparmate at Deer Lake, the wages being sufficient for him to quit the hospital shifts.

At that time, Witherspoon was managed by a fast operator named Mark Stewart – soon to be embroiled in a tax-fraud case – but the pair had nothing down on paper until 1981, when a contract was drawn up guaranteeing the fighter a minimum $100,000 a year, and giving the manager a half share of the purses. What Tim did not know was that Stewart had already sold on half his share to Don King, later claiming that his sole motive was to further the heavyweight's career but with his court trials looming, Stewart sold off a further slice to Carl King for a reported $50,000. The Don had completed a secret takeover.

Tim may have had misgivings about large chunks of him being traded off like shares in a racehorse, but right then he was on fire in the ring, and everything was coming up roses. In Atlantic City, he stretched his unbeaten sequence to thirteen when he stopped experienced Alfonzo Ratliff, and in 1982 he had just two fights, but they were significant wins, halting Luis Ascosta in two, before appearing in Las Vegas for the first time, outpointing major leaguer Renaldo Snipes.

After only fifteen fights spread over three years, and following scant amateur experience, the fighter Ali had dubbed 'Terrible Tim' was deemed ready for a shot at Holmes' WBC belt. A huge ask, but on May 20, 1983, at the Dunes Hotel in Vegas, he outpointed Larry in everyone's eyes bar those belonging to two of the judges. One official, Chuck Hassett, actually scored 118–111 for the champion, but Chuck's brain must have gone walkabout. If Witherspoon felt betrayed by the judges, imagine the sickener when he received his wages. Instead of the $150,000 promised by promoter Don, manager Carl presented him with a cheque for $52,750. Welcome to life with the Kings.

The Don was creative with the bookkeeping, but he never fell short on providing opportunities and less than a year later, Tim was handed another shot at the WBC title vacated by Holmes. In the opposite corner, challenging for the vacant championship, was another Carl King representative, a former brilliant amateur named Greg Page. Nobody seemed to care about Carl's glaring conflict of interest and, if anything, Page, a 25-year-old from Louisville, was even more outspoken than Witherspoon when bad-mouthing his bosses. Greg, however, registered his protest by dodging serious gym work, ignoring his diet and staying out late. Self-destructive, one would have thought.

In his remarkable book, *The Life and Crimes of Don King*, Jack Newfield reports a revealing conversation with Witherspoon concerning the Page contest. Said Tim, 'I would say that Don hated Greg even more than he hated me before the fight. I know that because before the fight Don told me that if I didn't get knocked out, he would make sure I won the decision. He said if I'm standing at the end, I'll win.'

But might King not have delivered the same special pep talk to Page? And if Witherspoon distrusted the promoter so much, why should he believe him?

On March 9, 1984 Page entered the Vegas ring, undertrained and overweight; Witherspoon, assuming the fight was in the bag, was no sleek Adonis either, and the contest developed into one long yawn, an unedifying spectacle of two big men, grunting and groaning and leaning on one another for round after boring round. One judge voted a draw, the other two returned identical cards for Tim, but by that time few in the arena cared that the 26-year-old from Philadelphia was the new heavyweight champion of the world.

This time, according to Mr Newfield's book, Witherspoon's contract guaranteed him $250,000, but his take-home was a miserable $44,640. Another horrendous financial mugging, of course, but many unfortunates who bought a ticket for the farce might have ventured that forty-odd grand was generous for what Tim had produced in the ring.

Terrible Tim was being clinically fleeced by the master, and the experience must have been traumatic in the extreme. But in turn, the heavyweight was taking the public for a ride.

If anything, the new champ's mental state must have been even more fragile in the build-up to his August first defence against fellow Philadelphian Pinklon Thomas – yet another of Carl King's endless list of clients – and he spiced up his training routine by smoking dope. Couldn't care less? He admitted to Newfield that shortly before the fight, he had become so desperate that he tried to bribe a judge – an offer of $3,000 'to look out for me'.

Was this the act of a disillusioned, dispirited fighter, or of one who has suddenly recalled that he had taken all the short-cuts in training? Make up your own mind.

Pinklon must have done the better gym work, because he was given the majority verdict, but once more there were no memorable moments befitting a match purporting to be for the heavyweight championship. Just another untidy scuffle.

The contract that King lodged with the Nevada commission was of far more interest. This stated that Witherspoon's purse was $400,000 and claimed that he had 'no manager'. But Carl had not bid *adios*, and the fighter was paid $116,000 after the stepson had taken his normal share and a sheaf of bogus expenses had been debited. The title had also gone, and if ever there was a time for Tim to take stock, this was it.

The amiable Witherspoon was bright and intelligent, and now

knew the score backwards. If he split the camp he would struggle to find meaningful paydays, such was King's control over the ranked heavies. Hiring lawyers to fight his case would be expensive and not guaranteed success, given The Don's expertise and track record in the courtroom. A waste of time appealing to the various sanctioning bodies or the state commissions for justice. Witherspoon was not yet ready to become the shining knight, and the smart move – the only sensible move – was to remain with the promoter and hope, like Larry Holmes, that conditions would eventually improve until he had won some financial clout. King might be a pirate, but even his doctored purses were far better than Tim could hope to earn elsewhere.

That, however, should not have given him the green light to neglect his training, go out on eating binges and dabble in drugs. Not if he still regarded himself as a real professional, not if he retained any pride.

And so he soldiered on. He knocked out James Broad, then comfortably outpointed The Bonecrusher in North American title fights, and King considered those wins sufficient to warrant yet another crack at the world title, this time the WBA version, currently in the meaty fists of TNT Tubbs who, on the crazy merry-go-round, had won over Page. Most likely The Don was beginning to realise that of all his unhinged heavies, Terrible Tim was the best bet to emerge as a marketable and credible champion . . . if he took his boxing seriously.

By now, however, the heavyweight circus had degenerated into a sick joke. On January 17, 1986 Witherspoon became the champ for a second time, outfumbling the grossly overweight Tubbs in a dismal parody of what had once been a wonderful occasion, packed with tradition and memories of great champions of the past. But now? King filled the Atlanta undercard with a choice selection of his other heavies and, without exception, they proved dreary underperformers. A crowd of just 5,000 bothered to turn out, and they left having witnessed one of the worst shows ever. Heavyweight boxing was drowning in a vast vat of lard.

Even worse, after the shambles came the news that new champion Witherspoon had tested positive for traces of marijuana in his urine sample. He was fined $25,000, but held on to his title and escaped more severe censure thanks to King getting busy backstage. Big bad Don had his uses.

And he could still deliver. Next stop was London and a high-profile summer defence outdoors at Wembley against the local hero, Frank Bruno. This would be a huge affair, co-promoted along with Bruno's managerial team, and the negotiations were both complex and lengthy.

For once, Witherspoon was delighted and excited. Even allowing for the detested deductions, Tim figured to come out with as much as a half million. Almost as good, Bruno had been knocked out by The Bonecrusher two years earlier, so should not prove too dangerous. In fact, on the July night in 1986 big Frank proved extremely lively, and Tim was hurt and bruised before he found hidden reserves to come back and batter the exhausted Briton to defeat in the eleventh. Party time for the Americans in Piccadilly, but not for long.

Even by Don King standards, the looting of Witherspoon's purse was monstrous. Tim's final cheque amounted to a disgraceful $90,095, and he had to remind himself that he was the champion and had been the winner. The beaten challenger had been paid $900,000 by his own promotional outfit who had no say in how King divided up his share of the spoils.

Witherspoon was both shattered and furious: now he started talking lawsuits, and he desperately wanted to be free from King at all costs. But the promoter never had demanded love from his fighters, and he was accustomed, almost impervious, to litigation. Terrible Tim was still his champion, and he had plans for him which included a December rematch with fat Tony Tubbs in the Garden.

But this would be a tricky gig, even for The Don. Not only was Witherspoon seething and planning rebellion, but Tubbs was also holding out for more money than he had been offered, and was proving very difficult. Even after New York commissioner Jose Torres threatened a suspension Tony refused to budge, and a week before the scheduled date, he discovered a shoulder injury and pulled out. King hurriedly looked around for a replacement, and decided on The Bonecrusher. He had, after all, knocked out Bruno a round earlier than had Terrible Tim.

For James Smith, a happy, outgoing 6ft 4″ puncher, this was a shock opportunity to resurrect a career that was apparently heading nowhere. Two years had passed since he had knocked out Bruno and battled Holmes for the title. Now he was regarded as no better than a journeyman, but a journeyman who could still hit extremely hard.

He was born on April 3, 1954 in the little town of Magnolia, North Carolina, and built a record that must be unique in boxing: a graduate with a business degree from Shaw University in Raleigh, NC; a sergeant during a two-year stint in the army; a guard at a maximum-security prison; and an ordained minister. Boxing was at first just a hobby, then a means of earning a few extra bucks and dreams of fighting for a world title were just a secret to share with his pillow.

He started boxing in the army, compiling a decent record of only four losses from 35 contests, and it was in the amateurs that he was tagged with the nickname Bonecrusher after one opponent suffered a broken nose, and another fractured ribs. His 25 knockouts were impressive and persuaded friends that he might have a future in the pros, but James remained unconvinced: he was 27, had a steady job at the prison, and now visited the gym only to keep himself in reasonable shape.

One day, however, a local manager contacted him about filling in as a late substitute up in Atlantic City, and Smith decided that the money would be useful. Still there were no ambitions to make boxing a career, and he was far from being in top shape, but he reckoned he had nothing to lose. So, on November 5, 1981 he made his debut against former amateur hotshot James Broad who was being groomed for stardom, and in the circumstances, The Bonecrusher did well to survive into the fourth before running out of steam.

Though he accepted a few more similar late jobs, he still did not regard himself as a proper pro. He had no manager and trained himself, but now he was winning his fights, though he was still being hired as the opponent.

The situation changed following a hard-earned split decision over the previously unbeaten Chris McDonald in Atlantic City, a fight which featured on ESPN's regular Saturday night slot and created a minor stir. Among the impressed viewers were a couple of New York fight buffs, a real estate entrepreneur called Alan Kornberg and his friend Steve Nelson, who made his money as a mortgage banker. When they discovered that the giant heavy had no managerial ties, they decided to try and break into the fight game, and home in on The Bonecrusher.

When Smith next boxed, against Lonnie Chapman, on the Eusebio Pedroza–Bernard Taylor undercard in Charlotte, NC, Nelson was at the ringside. And after James halted Chapman in the second, Nelson fast-talked his way into the dressing room and introduced himself to the fighter.

There were already other offers on the table, but Smith was impressed first by Nelson and then by Kornberg at subsequent meetings, and opted to sign with the New Yorkers. He was taking a risk with such novices, but right off they showed that they meant business by approaching the legendary champion Emile Griffith to become James' trainer. Headquartered at Jimmy Glenn's Times Square gym, Griffith was building a big reputation as a coach and could afford to pick and choose, but after watching The Bonecrusher spar two rounds with Larry Alexander, he was sold.

Smith resigned from the prison service and was put on a salary. In the ring he continued to deliver, and when he knocked out Florida's Nate Robinson in the second, NBC television guru Dr Ferdie Pacheco raved about the performance; Lou Duva, who had seen a prospect or two, described him as 'an unbelievable find and a title threat if he's handled right'. An ecstatic Griffith forecast that Smith would be a world champion in 1984.

Happy days, and they were to get better.

A call came from London for Smith to box Bruno, then being meticulously steered towards a world title. As a rule, matchmaker Mickey Duff never let a big puncher within miles of big Frank, but somehow, the man from Magnolia slipped through the net. On May 13, 1984 – a Sunday, because the fight was being screened live in the States – The Bonecrusher was outboxed for nine rounds but caught up with the tiring Englishman in the tenth and knocked him out. Duff had worked hard to get Bruno priceless exposure in America; Smith should have tipped him a few dollars because now he was the hot ticket coast to coast.

Now was the chance for Griffith's prophecy to come true. On November 9 James was back in the ring, challenging Larry Holmes for his IBF belt at the Riviera casino in Las Vegas. After only fifteen fights he was gambling for the jackpot.

Bonecrusher gave it his best shot: he hurt the champion and he cut the champion, but Holmes had a great chin and an even greater heart. Larry established control, and the fight was stopped in the twelfth because of a bad cut over Smith's left eye. He had never been down and could be proud of his effort. But after that James seemed to lose that vital spark: his big hitting had taken him a long way but he was no more than an average boxer and the following year, Terrible Tim easily outpointed him in a North American title fight. His chance to become the first college graduate to win the heavyweight championship seemed to have gone for good, until the call-up from King.

No heavyweight title fight ever could have suffered a more negative build-up. First Tubbs' controversial departure from the scene, allied to Witherspoon's constant threats to do likewise; and now the introduction of Smith who had proved no match for Tim the previous year. Both media and public were underwhelmed, but King, thinking of the television revenue, kept that famous grin clamped to his face.

One fighter had not bothered to train; the other had not been given time to train. But Bonecrusher was more concerned with his managerial adjustments than the short notice. King may have been in a tight spot, but he was not about to ditch the habit of a lifetime: stepson Carl had to be cut in for a share. Business as usual, and irrespective who won in the Garden, The Don would still have the rights to the champion.

One can imagine Witherspoon's tortured mind. He had squandered all the dough he had earned (even with the rip-offs, the sums were not just a few bucks); he was behind with his tax demands, had seen his car repossessed and his phone cut off. King's fault, or lousy housekeeping? With or without the promoter, boxing was his only way out of the hole, and remember, he still held the title – devalued perhaps, but still worth an awful lot of money.

Just three weeks before the scheduled showdown in the Garden, a young and dynamic Mike Tyson won the WBC title with a devastating two-rounds knockout over Trevor Berbick. Iron Mike against Terrible Tim with their two titles up for grabs would have been a gigantic attraction, and certainly would have solved Witherspoon's cash problems, but the fighter was looking no further than his navel.

He did, however, turn up at the Garden, along with 5,042 souls who came in out of the cold. The referee was Luis Rivera, the judges Samuel Conde from Puerto Rico, Venezuelan Julio Roldan, and American Joe Santarpia, and they warrant a mention if only because they put as much effort into the occasion as the champion. They did not, however, have to take the punches.

Possibly uneasy about his stamina lasting too many rounds, Smith came out fast, and his first thunderous right effectively decided the outcome. The champ remained upright but he was a befuddled standing target and a follow-up left hook dropped him for a count of three. On rising, he threw a desperate, reflex right but Bonecrusher, scenting the early finish, battered him down for a second count. Tim was back up at two – evidence that his brain was scrambled – and Smith kept flailing away until Witherspoon fell for the third and final time.

The official time was two minutes twelve seconds of round one; Witherspoon's wages, after deductions, came to $129,000, most of which was gobbled up by the IRS; and he would never again contest a world title. What a waste of talent!

There was added angst. The New York State Athletic Commission, which had been on his case before the fight, announced that Tim had failed a drug test. Later the shame-faced commissioners were forced to admit a clerical error, but the damage had been done.

As his multi-million lawsuit against King started its long, slow journey through the legal system, Witherspoon tried to kick-start his career. The opportunities were few, only five fights spread over the next three years. But they were all wins – in fact, in the ten years following the Bonecrusher fiasco, he was beaten only twice (by Bigfoot Martin and Ray Mercer) in 22 outings. Different managers and promoters came and went, and there were nights when he looked a slim, trim fighting machine capable of troubling any heavyweight on the planet. But all too often he turned up blubbery, ill-prepared and devoid of motivation . . . the two Terrible Tims.

By 1992 his lawyers had backed King into a corner and The Don decided that a settlement might be appropriate. Witherspoon had won the marathon battle, and though the exact details of the deal remained secret, the fighter received more than one million dollars. One year later, and Terrible Tim was once again broke, and this time he could not blame the Kings.

Meanwhile, Bonecrusher had grabbed his chance, and now he was the graduate champion. On March 7, 1987 he got his money shot against Tyson at the Las Vegas Hilton, but disappointingly settled for survival tactics. Only in the final round did he open up and hurt Mike. Far too little and far too late.

James stayed around for the purses. He was still too heavy-handed for the mediocre and the moderate, but the top men, like Razor Ruddock and Michael Moorer, inevitably were too good. From time to time his name would crop up: boxing in a one-night tournament in Mississippi, then joining the golden oldies circuit, facing Joe Bugner in Australia and old pal Larry Holmes back in North Carolina, but in both of those fights he had to quit because of a recurring shoulder injury. The Bonecrusher finished up with an honourable record of 43 wins from sixty fights, and his sunny nature and sharp mind hopefully ensure many more bright days for the big man from Magnolia.

Witherspoon also remains an engaging personality, and although his career ground to a low-key finish there is no bitterness, not even when Don King's name enters the conversation. The Don gave him much grief and cost him even more money, but deep down Terrible Tim, the nice guy from Philly, must know that if he had eaten less, trained more, and ducked the late nights, he just might have been remembered as a truly great champion.

The report card says: could have done better. Much better.

The Last Hurrah

Increasingly few folk retire these days . . . at least, not with the gold watch and the bouquet for the wife and the presentation pic in the local rag. Now the lucky ones organise an early deal and split; but more often, there arrives that dreaded redundancy slip, or the company goes belly-up, and with it, the pension dosh.

Boxers do not have pension funds and there is no fixed date for making the emotional announcement from the ring. Some, like Ray Leonard and Tommy Hearns, refused to believe that the game could do without them. Others, like Tunney, Marciano and Hagler, had the character to walk away, head held high.

Financially they could afford to, but most fighters hang around for the dough: those last few purses that might set up a small business or clear the back alimony or stave off a repossession. Solid reasons. But there will always come that night when reality hits home like a Ray Robinson left hook. No gold watch.

CHAPTER NINETEEN

Jimmy McLarnin
v Benny Leonard

FRIDAY, OCTOBER 7, 1932

Had the young Jimmy McLarnin and Benny Leonard been around in these enlightened times, they would be a safe bet to find themselves taken into care, their parents tongue-lashed and put on notice, the kiddie counsellors given the red alert.

Imagine! Little lads like Benny and Jimmy – and we are talking really small guys, scarcely into their teens – scrapping in dark, smoky backrooms for a few dollars, egged on by gamblers and gangsters and a cross section of other lowlifes, well able to warp permanently any young boy's mind. My goodness! The traumas, both physical and mental! No internet delights back then.

Very doubtful, however, if owning a laptop would have stopped Leonard and McLarnin and countless other youngsters like them from doing their thing. Certainly Ma Leiner never gave up the struggle to persuade her Benjamin to quit boxing, even after he had become a great champion and the best-loved sports face in New York.

As for McLarnin, he managed, with the considerable assistance of his mentor, Pop Foster, to negotiate those stress-filled teen years without collecting too much baggage. By the time he was nineteen, Jimmy would later recall, he had one hundred grand stashed safely in the bank, and had never once suffered a crisis of identity.

Though there was a ten-year age gap and they grew up on different coastlines, McLarnin and Leonard travelled a similar strenuous journey to the pinnacle of their chosen profession at a

255

time when right across the country there was a host of outstanding competitors, each with his own cheering section. Ethnic rivalries may now be frowned upon as being politically incorrect, but back then they proved magic at the turnstiles. Most of the young boxers were the sons of immigrants; some, like McLarnin, were born in another country, and the very best were idolised by their own.

The Jewish boxers proudly wore the Star of David on their trunks; the Irish boys would sport a shamrock or a harp; many of the Italians adopted more readily pronounceable names (for example, the one-time welterweight champion Young Corbett III was really Rafaele Capabianca Giordano and had been born in the old country) but the *paisans* still flocked to shout on their heroes. Black power, however, was still generations away, and although the blacks could boast many marvellous performers, they were still very much a secret society.

Benny Leonard first learned to bob and weave on the streets of New York, defending his patch against marauding Irish kids and interlopers from the Italian ghetto. Of course, Ben and his band of urchins would, on occasion, do some interloping of their own. The tots were not exactly delinquents and their scuffles were conducted with fists, bats and rocks, almost Marquess of Queensberry compared to today's murderous street clashes, but they earned the same kind of prestige. Little Ben, who never stretched taller than 5ft 5″, was always a standout.

He was born Benjamin Leiner on April 7, 1896 on the Lower East Side, the son of a struggling tailor and a strong, loving mother who reared her eight kids always to do the right thing. She was vehemently against boxing, but Benjamin was equally passionate about the sport and first pulled on the gloves when he was eleven.

There was a neighbourhood hangout called the Silver Heel Club which staged every Saturday afternoon boxing matches between youngsters for the amusement of the members. Two of those worthies were Benny's uncles, and the boy became a regular Saturday spectator in the Silver Heel's backyard, always pestering for a chance to box, until his uncles finally gave him the okay. He duly won his debut contest with the gloves, and from then on Benny Leiner was seldom to be found far from a ring.

He was never an amateur, always collecting a few cents, then a couple of dollars for his efforts. By the time he was fifteen he had his own manager, a local billiards-room proprietor called Buck Areton, and also his new name, Benny Leonard – the result of yet another announcer fluffing his lines.

But his first official match for Areton turned out a disaster when he was stopped in round three by a tough nut called Mickey Finnegan, because of a damaged nose, and there would be two further stoppage defeats (against Joe Shugrue and Frankie Fleming) in those early years. Other teenagers might have become discouraged but Benny merely put the losses down to the learning process. He would lose only twice more from a total of 212 bouts in his remarkable career. Quite astonishing.

Mentally, Leonard was mature far beyond his years. No boxer ever took his craft more seriously and delved more deeply into every aspect of the exceptionally demanding and complex sport. When he was not earning in the ring, he was learning in the gym, experimenting with new moves, trying different combinations, inventing fresh tricks. He haunted the New York gyms, closely studying the top fighters, analysing styles, discovering what made some boxers great, others just good.

Benny was preparing for his own master's degree. As he strengthened physically, he developed a terrific right hand shot to add to his already impressive arsenal, making him the complete fighter. Soon he was a living legend, worshipped by his huge Jewish following who nicknamed him The Ghetto Wizard. Ray Arcel, one of boxing's genuine professors, but back then only a student trainer, was still in awe of the great Benny many years after he had passed on. He told Ronald K Fried:

Leonard was just as great as can be. And he used to talk to me, and I used to ask him a million dumb questions and he used to show me. And naturally, I absorbed all of his knowledge. His main asset was his ability to think. He had the sharpest mind. He was the one fighter that I saw who could make you do the things he wanted you to do. He could feint you into knots. He was the master of the feint.

The early years were marvellous times for Benny and his growing band of fans. On fight nights a fleet of buses would be lined up outside the Silver Heel on Eighth Street, oilcloth signs tacked to the sides of the vehicles declaring, 'BENNY LEONARD,

COMING LIGHTWEIGHT CHAMPION OF THE WORLD!' Nobody, especially Benny, had any doubts.

Buck Areton had done a good job handling the teenager, but he was strictly a small-league operator, and a deal was arranged for Billy Gibson to take over the managerial duties. Gibson owned the Fairmont AC, an important fight club in the Bronx and his influence extended throughout the city. Later he took on another brainy champion, Gene Tunney, and the two deep thinkers became great friends.

In truth, Gibson only had to act as a booking agent: in the final stages of refinement under first George Engel and then Mannie Seamon, Leonard was a dream both to manage and to train, and such was his confidence that no opponent was barred.

Eventually, on May 28, 1917 the inevitable became reality when he stopped Britain's Freddie Welsh in the ninth round at the Manhattan Casino in Harlem to become the lightweight champion of the world. He was in his seventh year as a professional, had boxed for four years before that as a baby pro, and Welsh was his 109th recorded contest. Yet The Wizard had celebrated his 21st birthday only one month before.

In those days a champion did not sit back, accept the plaudits and sift through the endorsement offers. Just seven days after winning the title Benny was back earning, boxing a no-decision six-rounder in Philadelphia against Joe Welsh. From Freddie Welsh to Joe Welsh inside a week; from a title fight to a humble six-rounder: all the same to Leonard if the wages were good and, incredibly, before the end of the year he would fight another seventeen times, travelling as far west as Denver, as far north as Toronto.

An extremely punishing schedule, and often the champ would conserve energy, doing just enough. Some of his matches were no better than glorified exhibitions, but in others he actually got his hair all messed up. Benjamin was vain about his sleeked-down thatch with the immaculate centre parting and could be stung into immediate reaction if an opponent took a liberty with his locks. At least, so the hacks, for whom The Wizard was an endless source of copy, would always maintain.

In the old Garden on Madison Square, Benny packed the house for Tex Rickard, defending his title against Joe Welling, Richie Mitchell and Rocky Kansas. There were other memorable nights in other cities, against Johnny Kilbane and the Philadelphia southpaw Lew Tendler, and he boxed an eight-fight series with the featherweight great, Johnny Dundee, who was burdened with the nickname The Scotch Wop, and who had been born in Sicily.

Nat Fleischer described the Garden classic with Milwaukee's Richie Mitchell as the greatest fight that he ever witnessed – the January night in 1921 when Leonard came within seconds of blowing the title because of a bet. The champion was friendly with the notorious New York gambler Arnold Rothstein, and when Mr R asked Benny for a prediction the fighter cockily replied that he could finish off Mitchell in one round. Rothstein said he would bet $25,000 on his pal doing just that, and Benny would collect 10 per cent of the winnings. All the incentive the champ required.

At the opening bell Leonard raced across the ring and dropped Mitchell with his first punch; twice more, he floored his challenger, but in his anxiety to land the wager he left himself open, and the battered Mitchell got lucky with a tremendous right that flattened the champion. Badly hurt, Benny took a nine count, but his brain was still operating at top speed. He smiled, and motioned Mitchell to come forward and for vital seconds Richie hesitated, and the bell rescued Leonard. He was still recovering in the second, but after that he took control, scoring four knockdowns in a sensational sixth and forcing a stoppage. Only later did he discover that Rothstein had never managed to get the money down!

The gambler's proximity to both Leonard and Gibson might help explain Benny's most controversial fight: the night when he was disqualified against Jack Britton at the Velodrome in the Bronx.

Leonard was a strong favourite to take the welter belt from the veteran Britton but, according to trainer Seamon's newspaper memoirs, Gibson told the fighter that this was one night when he must not win. Leonard, according to Seamon, was distraught, but played along. He was trailing on points in a dull fight until in round thirteen he knocked down the champion with no more than an average shot. Realising his blunder, he calmly walked across the ring, belted Britton while he was still on his knees, and was disqualified.

That was Mannie Seamon's version, but there were many other wild allegations, including one that Britton had actually bet on

Benny and there had been two non-triers in the Velodrome ring! Most of the punters, however, saved their cash because at that time most bets were void if there was a disqualification. Perhaps that was the reason why Benny's public chose to forgive him so readily. In an era when America boasted such sporting giants as Babe Ruth and Bobby Jones and outstanding fighters like Dempsey, Tunney and Mickey Walker, The Ghetto Wizard remained the most popular sportsman in New York, loved equally by the fans and the writers.

After he retained his title against Tendler in July 1923 Leonard had little left to prove. He had bossed the lightweights for more than seven years, had dealt with all comers and, at last, was beginning to grow weary of the long years of hard graft.

Plans for a lucrative showdown with Walker, the new welter champion, had come to nothing; his hands were suffering from wear and tear, and his mother, not enjoying the best of health, was still pressuring him to stop boxing. Benny decided the time was right. There was one final appearance, a no-decision affair against Pal Moran in Cleveland, and on January 15, 1925 he formally announced his retirement.

He had packed a lifetime into his 28 years, and now he planned to enjoy himself and his money. Naturally, he was an immediate target for every shark in town: the freeloaders and the conmen and the guys with the great ideas, all formed a line. Leonard bought into a string of racehorses and a restaurant and then a tyre company, and all cost him bundles. But on the plus side he purchased a luxury home for the family, he was loving the good life and his continued popularity, and most important, the bulk of his money, his pension dough, was safely tucked away in long-term investments . . . until that Black Thursday in October 1929.

Almost overnight Benny was wiped out by the Wall Street Crash. No consolation that he was just one of many who were down and taking the count, and the few bucks that he had managed to salvage only kept up appearances for a couple of years. There was only one solution: a return to the ring.

The old Wizard formed a new back-up team. Wily Jack Kearns, Dempsey's good doctor, would arrange the matches and haggle the terms; Leonard's brother Joey was taken on board as a co-manager and confidant; Ray Arcel was hired as the trainer. But all three were well aware that Benny could never recapture his magic.

In the six years of inactivity his body had taken more punishment than in a lifetime of boxing: he had become soft and flabby; his reflexes and his timing would never be the same; even his hair was beating a fast retreat.

Like an iffy play gearing up in the sticks while preparing for the worst on Broadway, the comeback began low key, with a series of exhibitions in hotspots like New Haven, and then on October 6, 1931 he marked his official return with a two-round knockout over Pal Silvers. No big deal, and Kearns ensured that few risks were taken as Benny remained undefeated, and stretched his sequence to nineteen. But he was only making a living, not a fortune, and the time had come to face a real fighter and shoot for the big money. There were few fighters more real than Jimmy McLarnin.

Coast-to-coast, everyone knew Jimmy McLarnin, the little fellow they called Baby Face; another infant marvel who had developed into a tremendous all-round mechanic and a sure bet to become a world champion, sooner rather than later. Leonard had been Jimmy's role model, and the youngster had been proud to shake the great man's hand when Benny made a stage appearance in San Francisco. Baby Face, however, no longer had any space for heroes, only titles, and Leonard stood in his way. There would be no quarter in the Garden.

James Archibald McLarnin was born in Belfast on December 19, 1907, but he emigrated to Canada with his family when he was just three. The McLarnins settled in Vancouver and, one of twelve children, little Jimmy took odd jobs when he was old enough to put some money into the pot. But boxing became a fascination, and he claimed that he had his first paid fight when he was ten. He weighed 58lb, sprained both his thumbs because he did not know how to punch correctly, but came out the winner and was paid a dollar.

He told Peter Heller, 'I was a professional when I was ten. I always got paid. My first fight I got a dollar for and my last fight I got sixty thousand. But between the one and the sixty, boy, there was a lot of hard work.'

McLarnin never shirked a tough shift and, as an underweight fly, he tackled other tiny terrors, until his path crossed that of Pop Foster, a former pro who could always appreciate talent. According to McLarnin, Foster and his father were acquainted, and the pair constructed a makeshift gym for the now thirteen-year-old. The old fighter began teaching the youngster the basics with heavy emphasis on the scientific aspects: don't get hit and you can't get beat.

Foster told the boy, 'I'll make you a champion of the world if you'll just behave yourself and do as I say.'

Young McLarnin behaved himself and Foster delivered on his end of the bargain. In fact he became something of a surrogate father, and the welfare of his fighter took precedence over all else. Their partnership endured for more than fifteen years, possibly the finest boxer-manager relationship ever, and when Pop died in his eighties he willed his entire bankroll to McLarnin, an estimated $250,000.

Jimmy had not long turned fifteen when his career got under-way in earnest with a four-rounds points win over one George Ainsworth, and although the early records are sketchy, he completed 1923 unbeaten in ten contests against opponents whose expertise remains a mystery. Time to hit the road, and Foster and McLarnin relocated to California where there would be plenty of work – provided the youngster could secure a licence. He had to lie about his age, making himself two years older, and even then promoters were at first reluctant to hire him because he looked so young.

Once he started performing, however, the fans could not see enough of him. Baby Face boxed seventeen times in 1924, including a win and a draw over the future flyweight champion Fidel La Barba. The following year he lost for the first time against the vastly more experienced Bud Taylor, another future champ, but he outpointed the reigning flyweight king, Pancho Villa, who ten days later would tragically die of blood poisoning, and also knocked out Jackie Fields, who would become welter-weight champion before McLarnin. Those names give an idea of the strength of the competition.

Jimmy was still growing from a teeny flyweight, through bantam and feather, and he was a compact twenty-year-old lightweight when he made an electrifying New York debut on February 24, 1928, poleaxing a great Jewish favourite, Sid Terris, in one round in a packed Garden. .

Three months later, on the strength of that one-round blitz, Rickard paid Baby Face $50,000 to challenge the lightweight champion, Sammy Mandell, at the Polo Grounds, but on the night Mandell was just too smart and deserved the verdict. By now McLarnin was struggling to scale 135lb, and although he subsequently beat Mandell twice in non-title affairs, he sensibly moved up to welter. Another tough division.

Jimmy discovered just how tough when he was matched against Billy Petrolle, an exciting puncher billed as The Fargo Express, who handed him a bad beating, with McLarnin performing miracles to last the distance. The following year, however, he twice beat Petrolle on his only two appearances, and then he took a year out to recharge his batteries. The battles with Petrolle had been extremely gruelling and Pop Foster feared burn-out, but after the lay-off came another set-back when the Irishman was outpointed by the former welter and future middleweight champion, Lou Brouillard. He had not looked great.

Doc Kearns and Arcel were gambling that the wars with Petrolle had left their mark. He had produced little against Brouillard, and after nineteen comeback fights Benny was as good as he was going to get. If his legs could just last out, and if he could sucker the Irishman on to that right hand . . .

Of course, the old days were gone for good. Rickard was dead, and now little Jimmy Johnston was making the matches at the Garden. And this was a new Garden, not the grand old house on Madison Square where The Ghetto Wizard had performed his magic for his adoring fans. But those fans remained true, convinced that Benny would somehow fool Father Time as well as Jimmy McLarnin, and a record crowd of more than 20,000 packed the arena to overflowing.

Leonard had done his best to ensure a huge support, shamelessly playing up the race angle. He told his journalist pals, 'One of the reasons I want to lick McLarnin is that I want to wipe out his successful record against Jewish fighters.'

Those words guaranteed a grand exodus from the ghettos to the Garden: the avenging Jew head to head with the upstart Irishman. Indeed, McLarnin had knocked over an impressive number of Jewish heroes: Terris, Joe Glick and Ruby Goldstein, Sergeant Sammy Baker, Al Singer and Jackie Fields, who was born Jacob Finkelstein. But Jimmy had not deliberately engineered a pogrom: this might have been a golden era for Jewish boxers, but Baby Face just happened to have their number.

On October 7, 1932, for the last time, the great Benny received a tumultuous welcome all the way into the ring, but when referee Arthur Donovan called the rivals to centre stage for their final instructions, the immense task facing Leonard was immediately plain. There stood McLarnin, trim, firm, and impatient to be unleashed; and there was The Wizard, pale and podgy around the middle, spindly legged, his bald patch shining under the light. He resembled an old uncle, conned into showing the precocious nephew a few moves, but a mite uncomfortable and wary.

He did not, however, fare too badly in round one. McLarnin recalled, 'He was a pretty fat man when he fought me. He watched me train, and I had a bad habit of leaning under a right hand, and the very first punch that he hit me, I saw a million stars. He'd been watching me for quite a while. I made a mistake, and you can't make mistakes with him. If he'd been a little younger . . .'

A giant if. In the second, McLarnin turned up the pressure, hurrying forward, hands low and menacing. Leonard could still feint an opening but he was no longer fast enough to capitalise. Nearing the end of the round, Baby Face backed him into a corner, then floored him with a hard left hook. Always the dandy, Benny rose and dusted himself down, but the fight was over as a contest: just a matter now of calling the round.

There were still fleeting glimpses of Leonard's skills, but only his defensive artistry. He blocked, parried and ducked, but his legs were leaden and there was no way he could smother all McLarnin's well-placed shots to the head and body. In a matter of minutes The Wizard had transformed from 36 to 63, referee Donovan was looking on anxiously and by round six Benny was spent, and a prime target.

McLarnin opened him up with some sapping body shots, then landed flush with a terrific right hand; somehow, Leonard remained erect, but his brain had flown back to the old Garden. His feet were planted on the canvas, his body bent forward from the waist, as if he might topple face down at any second, and as the Irishman followed up with a rapid cluster of punches, Donovan jumped between the fighters and rescued the old champ. Since the second, the ref had been looking out for Benny, determined that he would not get too badly hurt.

The Garden thousands bid him a generous farewell. They had paid anything from a dollar to five bucks ringside to see Leonard's last hurrah, and his $15,000 purse was enough to get his domestic affairs back on track.

Jimmy McLarnin had never been off track and the big purses continued to swell his bank account. Just two fights after retiring Leonard, and in the eleventh year of his campaign, Baby Face was the welterweight champion of the world, knocking out Young Corbett III (our old friend Giordano) in the very first round in Los Angeles.

Only blockbuster fights from now on: Pop Foster was not interested in exacting road tours, boxing non-title fights for non-title wages, especially as Jimmy's hands were causing increasing problems and required rest between bouts. Retirement was always on the agenda and, in fact, Baby Face would be called upon just six more times – but for serious pay, and against three other boxing legends.

McLarnin held the title for one day short of a year, being outpointed by Barney Ross – the latest Jewish superstar – on May 28, 1934. Barney was a terrific boxer and the styles of the two fighters guaranteed excitement. In the inevitable return four months later Jimmy regained his championship in another cliff-hanger. There had to be a decider, staged in the Long Island Island Bowl – the Garden's outdoor arena and a jinx venue for champions – and Ross was awarded a hotly disputed decision, Gene Tunney being just one ringsider who described the verdict as a disgrace. Tunney's old rival Jack Dempsey had been the referee, and weirdly scored seven rounds level.

Despite the loss Foster still had to fend off offers, but some were just too good to turn down. In 1936 McLarnin lost then won against Tony Canzoneri, and then on November 20 he gave the new lightweight champion, Lou Ambers, a severe mauling, but that would be his last fight.

Jimmy thought that his fine performance against Ambers would clinch a fourth meeting with Ross. He desperately wanted to retire as an undefeated champion, but Barney was holding out for too big a slice of the action, and so Pop and his protégé decided that enough was enough. The pair had travelled a long way from the ramshackle gym in Vancouver.

Baby Face was still not thirty; he had retained both his marbles and his money and could look forward to a wonderful future. And that is exactly how his life worked out. He married Lilian and they raised a son and three daughters, and then there were the grandchildren. His business ventures all made considerable money and he bought a luxury home in Glendale, California; and when he had the time he could be found on the golf course with his pal, Bing Crosby. Not bad for the little guy who started out fighting for just one dollar.

Nor did the great Benny wind up a charity case. Leonard could never be forgotten in New York and was kept busy. He was a frequent guest on sports shows, and whenever there was a major fight the newspapers sought him out for an expert analysis. At the age of forty he married his secretary, and when the US joined the war he was commissioned as a lieutenant commander in the navy, teaching physical fitness and boxing to the sailors at the Hoffman Island Training Station.

He also took out a licence as a referee, so once again the fans saw The Wizard glide across the canvas. And that is where the story ends: on April 18, 1947 at the old St Nicholas Arena, Benny Leonard suffered a fatal heart attack while handling a preliminary bout between Mario Ramon and Bobby Williams. He was only 51, but for a man who had lived and loved boxing the setting was appropriate.

Benny would have had just one beef. The venue should have been the Garden, never St Nick's.

CHAPTER TWENTY

Jimmy Carter *v* Ike Williams

FRIDAY, MAY 25, 1951

Let us begin at the end. On a summer day in 1960, and five years after his final fight, former world lightweight great Ike Williams tendered a last hurrah to the sport which he had graced for nearly half his lifetime. There were no cheering crowds, no gloves or gumshield, and Ike would much rather have been staring down a Bob Montgomery or a Kid Gavilan than those stony faces in the suits, leaning into their microphones, desperate to come across dignified and concerned for the TV cameras. But he was a champion and he had never ducked a challenge.

Williams was just one of the many big names who were called that year to testify in Washington before a senate committee investigating corruption in boxing, chaired by Senator Estes Kefauver. Sonny Liston was on the bill, vainly trying to explain his complex managerial arrangements; Jake La Motta finally confessed to going into the tank against Billy Fox; and Frank Carbo was a most reluctant participant, making liberal use of the Fifth Amendment, as was his custom.

For two hours boxing's czar stonewalled until an increasingly frustrated Kefauver asked him, 'You look like an intelligent man. Are you understanding the questions I am asking?'

Carbo never faltered, 'I respectfully decline to answer the question on the grounds that I cannot be compelled to be a witness against myself.'

Kefauver, however, attracted the headlines as he always knew he would, although there were a few negative reactions. The revered sportswriter Red Smith, for one, dismissed the senator's committee with scant regard, making its members appear like a gang of publicity joyriders. And he had a point. But Red's credibility went out the window when he referred to Carbo as 'the more or less benevolent despot of boxing's Invisible Empire'.

Benevolent? Carbo? Or his good buddy, Frank Palermo? Little Blinky managed Ike Williams during Ike's golden years and, as the former champ related to the senators, Mr P indulged in some extremely weird business practices. In fact, on two occasions, according to Williams' testimony, Blinky did not even pay him one thin dime from his purses. A not inconsiderable matter of $65,000.

But the committee was not really interested in such fiscal aberrations: the senators were looking for admissions of dives; Ike could only tell them about turning down bribes. In his hour in the spotlight, however, Williams succeeded in painting a picture of a fighter's life under 'the more or less benevolent despot' and his trusty aide, and all the colours were dark and depressing. His title successor, Jimmy Carter, could have told a similar story.

There were no shady deals done on the night of 1951 when the pair met for the title but there could have been, had Williams listened to a suggestion from his manager. Instead, the occasion marked the last championship appearance of a lightweight who must be ranked alongside Gans, Leonard and Duran as the finest 135lb boxers of all time. It was also the first title shot for Carter, who would reign on no fewer than three different occasions, and whose career must be reviewed with suspicion, even a benevolent suspicion.

Following Joe Louis, an increasing number of black fighters were being given their chance, but with the exception of a choice handful – Beau Jack, Montgomery, Williams, Gavilan and, of course, Sugar Ray – they were by no means champions at the box-office. Ezzard Charles, Archie Moore and Sandy Saddler were three terrific performers but the public remained cool; Jimmy Carter, much less talented than that trio but still very good, could never muster a following, and that was mostly down to his wildly inconsistent form. In a career that spanned fifteen years, Carter's longest unbeaten streak stretched to nine fights, and that was back in his early days. After that, it became a case of win some, lose some.

Jimmy had the familiar black boxer's beginning. He was born on December 15, 1923 in Aiken, South Carolina, and when he was very young the family moved north to New York to find a better life, settling in Harlem. A quiet, well-behaved youngster, he started boxing in his teens but was never regarded as a future champ, and did not make the switch to professional until after his army service when he was a 22-year-old. That was back in 1946 – the same year that the NBA champion, Williams, was beating Johnny Bratton in New Orleans, Enrique Bolanos in Los Angeles, and Ronnie James, in a title defence for Jack Solomons, in Cardiff.

Jimmy Carter's four rounds points win over Clifton Bordies on March 14 in Newark barely warranted a line, but before the end of the year, he was a twenty-fight veteran, upped to eight-rounders, and already with three losses on his record. His manager Willie Ketchum was one of New York's well-connected, but at that stage he had no great plans for his lightweight other than keeping him earning. Jimmy had to make up for lost time, and although he was improving fast in the gym under Teddy Bentham, then one of the top men at Stillman's, Ketchum believed that the best place to learn was in the ring.

And so in his second year Carter was sent down to New Orleans where he was outpointed by another future lightweight champion, Joe Brown. Carter and Brown were at about the same stage of development, but Sandy Saddler was far more experienced. True, Saddler was just a featherweight but he was already a leading contender, and Carter did well to earn a draw in Washington. The New Yorker was paying his dues, developing into a seasoned pro, but there were so many other black lightweights just like him: Brown, Bud Smith, Tommy Campbell, Freddie Dawson and Luther Rawlings – all accomplished performers who, on their best night, were well capable of beating one another . . . beating Ike Williams was an entirely different proposition.

Ketchum kept Carter on the road and in 1949 Jimmy fought in Detroit, went west to San Francisco, then sailed off to Australia for three bouts, before winding up in Los Angeles, dropping a points verdict to Rudy Cruz. A hard way to earn a living, and the money was never sensational, but the lightweight had few options. He was either booked as the opponent for a local attraction or pitted in dog-eat-dog matches with the likes of Campbell, a fine fighter with a high rating who was treated like a serf by his managers out on the West Coast. Carter and Campbell boxed a draw in New Orleans, but by then Tommy had all but given up hope of ever getting a title shot and Jimmy could only dream about one.

Hopes were revived not long after their Louisiana stalemate. Champion Ike had not defended since outpointing Dawson in December 1949, had been boxing against welters, and as the months passed, the NBA began hassling him to make a defence. Dawson and Campbell still outranked Carter, and the New Yorker seemed to have eliminated himself when he dropped decisions to Calvin Smith and then to featherweight Percy Bassett. He should have had more faith in his manager.

Now was the time when Ketchum's cosy connections paid off. To the complete indifference of the boxing media, the word went out that James Carter was going to get the next shot at Williams.

Few of the New York writers knew Jimmy personally and, although he was articulate and approachable, he rarely offered any worthwhile quotes. As for his ability, the experts ran a fast finger down through his record, spotted the eleven losses and the seven draws, and agreed that this was just a body being delivered for Ike's benefit. Blinky Palermo did nothing to hype the challenger's chances, probably because he was already contemplating some business being done, and Carter would be a great price.

That was Blinky. He had been at the ringside in Philadelphia when Carter was beaten by Bassett and had been unimpressed. But with an eye to attracting a decent crowd to the Garden he should have kept his opinion to himself; instead, he smugly explained to his newspaper cronies, 'If I thought Carter had a chance, do you think I'd let him have the match?'

Those words of wisdom may have lengthened the odds against the challenger, but they also effectively killed the Garden gate on May 25. A crowd of only 3,594 turned up, paying a derisory $13,260 – a record low attendance for an MSG title bout, although live television coverage guaranteed wider exposure and the important money. And bigmouth Blinky was miles off the mark when he claimed that there could be only one outcome. His champion was having serious weight problems, and would meet with further set-backs before fight night.

Palermo was aware that Williams had not scaled anything near 135lb for seventeen months, but that was not his concern. As usual he was embroiled in schemes and at the training camp he approached Ike with a $50,000 offer to throw the fight and win

back the title in a rematch. Blinky's offers were always relayed
from a mysterious 'they' as if he, himself, had no mob ties. His
sensitivity was wasted on Williams who had long become disillusioned with his manager. In fact managers had never been
Ike's favourite people.

Like Carter, Ike Williams came from the south, being born on
August 2, 1923, in Brunswick, Georgia. And like Carter, he
journeyed north, accompanying his mother to a fresh life in
Trenton, New Jersey, after his parents had separated. Unlike
Carter, however, Ike Williams never became your average Mister
Nice Guy.

Ring columnist Jersey Jones, usually an affable sort, delivered
the following blast back in 1949. 'First impressions of Ike,
personally, are not exactly flattering. The dour-faced Trentonian
seems surly, nasty, antagonistic. He seldom smiles, and when he
talks, he appears to be lacking in even the basic fundamentals of
tact and diplomacy. Generally, Williams leaves a sour taste in the
mouths of those meeting him for the first time.'

Wow! Obviously, Jersey J had suffered a traumatic encounter
with the champ. But in fairness, his article went on to praise Ike
for an exceptionally generous donation to charity out of his
purse from the second Enrique Bolanos title fight. Jones,
however, was far from the only writer to describe Williams as
sullen and uncommunicative.

Perhaps Ike never got a look at life's sunny side. He was nine
when he headed north, and could vividly remember the strict
segregation enforced in Brunswick. Trenton proved no picnic
either, with his mother being forced to take on all sorts of menial
work for miserable money. And his experiences in boxing might
have soured a saint.

Williams stood out in his early teens as a hot amateur prospect,
and he won several titles around New Jersey but when he turned
sixteen, his trainer, Jesse Goss, decided that it was time to start
earning. Usually when a fighter turns pro, his manager allows him
to keep the entire first purse as a symbolic gesture. But on March
15, 1940, after Ike won his four-round debut against Carmine
Fatta in North Brunswick, NJ, he received only six bucks from
the $10 purse.

Goss chose Connie McCarthy to manage Williams while he
stayed on as trainer. The new team did not hold back with their

protégé. Despite his youth, Ike was regularly overmatched early on, and in the circumstances the 5ft 9″ feather did well to drop only four decisions in a hectic eighteen-month apprenticeship before setting off on an extraordinary streak which saw him climb high into the lightweight ratings. Starting with a humble six-rounder against Vinnie De'Lia in Newark on November 3, 1941, the teenager won 31 fights on the trot, beating increasingly testing opposition and gaining a reputation as a fearsome puncher. In 1943 alone he scored ten stoppages from his eighteen wins and now Connie McCarthy was talking titles.

No blame to McCarthy: his fighter's progress had been electrifying, and he was not acting the over-brave manager when he agreed to a match against Bob Montgomery in Philadelphia. The Bobcat had held the title, was gearing up for a March return with Beau Jack, and McCarthy, not unreasonably, figured that an impressive victory would see his man jump the queue. An equally attractive persuader was the money – their best purse yet – and the upcoming contest stirred up huge interest throughout Philly. Unfortunately for Ike, this was one fight too far at that time.

The fans always turned out for a genuine grudge match, and they were aware that Montgomery harboured a beef. Just over two months earlier Williams had dealt out a cruel beating to The Bobcat's friend, Johnny Hutchinson, stopping him in three rounds, and Bob had sworn vengeance. In a packed Convention Hall on January 25, 1944 the Philadelphia favourite produced one of the great fights of his career, outclassing the twenty-year-old who performed heroics just to survive until the twelfth and last round when Montgomery at last put him out of his misery.

Such a savage battering might have caused irreparable harm, both physically and mentally, but Williams quickly shook off the effects. Just over a month later he was back in the ring, as sprightly as ever. But he was never going to forget such a painful lesson, and filed Montgomery away under 'unfinished business'.

The Bobcat and Beau Jack were thrilling huge crowds in the Garden, passing the New York version of the lightweight belt back and forth, while a heavy hitter from Guadalajara named Juan Zurita was recognised by the rival National Boxing Association after a victory over Sammy Angott. The revived Williams twice outpointed Angott, did a number on quality opponents such as Cleo Shans, Freddie Dawson, Lulu Constantino, and a Palermo hopeful,

Dorsey Lay, and although tricky Willie Joyce twice outsmarted him, Ike was now an outstanding contender for either title.

With both Montgomery and Beau Jack about to join the army, manager McCarthy set his sights on Zurita's NBA belt, but to clinch the title shot he had to agree to travel to Mexico City, which was to prove an unnerving experience. On April 18, 1945 Williams knocked out 138-fight veteran Zurita in the second with a right hand to the body followed by a left hook to the jaw. But as the triumphant 21-year-old was presented with the prized belt all hell broke loose when a mob invaded the ring. McCarthy's head was split open by a missile and a hooligan snatched the belt from the new champion. Williams never saw the trophy again, but right then reaching the dressing rooms safely before escaping back over the border was of far more importance.

Following their adventures in Mexico, the relationship between Ike and his manager took a turn for the worse.

Their association had survived six years, and McCarthy had played a major role in guiding Ike to the championship, even shed blood shielding his fighter in Mexico City. But according to Williams, McCarthy was an habitual drinker and had been drunk in the corner for the Zurita fight. That was Ike's side of the story; no doubt Connie had a different version, but soon open warfare broke out and McCarthy sought recourse from the Managers' Guild, an upstanding body of men, and the brainchild of Carbo.

Having a manager who belonged to the Guild guaranteed a boxer plenty of work and all the prime opportunities. Carbo had a tidy mind, and there was a certain sense of order, even logic, to his Guild but, of course, he was just tightening the squeeze, constructing a monopoly, as Williams quickly discovered when he tried to break with McCarthy.

The Guild blackballed him: no fighter managed by a Guild member would fight him; no promoter could hire him. Ike tried to fight back by forming a boxers' union, but that proved hopeless. He approached such successful independents as Jake La Motta and Ray Robinson but, while sympathetic, they were not about to sign up for a rebellion. Ike was in a bad jam, until Frank Palermo happened along.

The diminutive numbers racketeer had a simple solution: sign a contract with him and all Ike's problems with the Guild would vanish overnight; not only that, but he would guarantee Ike a unification fight against his old enemy, Montgomery. Years later, Williams claimed that he had no knowledge of Palermo's dodgy reputation, and we will give him the benefit of the doubt, but the bottom line was that Blinky was in, Connie was out, and the lightweight was about to reach a marvellous peak in the ring. Outside the ropes it was an entirely different story.

Ike was a magnificent all-round performer. He was a patient, brainy boxer and a terrific puncher with either hand; he was brave and could take a serious belt on the chin and second time around Montgomery was no match for him. On August 4, 1947, again in Philadelphia, Williams was masterful, handing out a severe beating before winning in the sixth. The Bobcat never won a fight after that, while the new undisputed champion seemed unbeatable.

In 1948 the stony-faced champ reached heights that had the old-timers comparing him to Benny Leonard, and the ancients coupling his name alongside Joe Gans. He outpointed Kid Gavilan in a non-title contest, then in quickfire succession defended against Enrique Bolanos, a huge attraction in Los Angeles, Beau Jack, and then Jesse Flores, who took six counts before being stopped. The Bolanos fight drew a gate of more than $150,000 and Williams enjoyed a big paynight; he also should have earned handsomely from the Jack and Flores defences, but swore that not only did he not receive a cent, but he had to pay taxes on the $65,000 which he had been promised for the two fights.

He told Peter Heller, author of *In This Corner*, 'I fought those two fights for nothing and paid taxes on them! I knew I was going to have trouble with the government, so I said suppose we leave the money with the promoters and pick it up in 1949, because I knew I wouldn't make that kind of money in 1949. But Palermo stopped by and picked the money up. So then I went to him about the money, he started crying about he's broke, and he's going to get his brains blown out if he doesn't pay some people, he said he needed my purse to pay off some old debts.'

The sheer scale of Palermo's embezzlement must have brought a warm glow to the heart of the other Frank. Whether he was bribing or borrowing, Blinky always insisted he was doing it on somebody else's behalf.

The incorrigible Palermo had failed to interest Ike with a bribe to lose his first meeting with Gavilan, and so the little man registered no surprise, only disappointment, when the champion turned down the fifty grand on offer to fold against Carter. Much later Williams would rue his decision, because by the day of the fight he was convinced that, even giving his all, the odds were stacked heavily against him. He had refused $50,000 to lose a fight that he did not think he could win.

The pounds had been so difficult to work off. The previous June he had scaled 144lb – 9lb over the lightweight limit – when outpointing Lester Felton in Detroit; arriving at his training camp for this defence, he discovered he had blown up as high as 156lb – almost a middleweight and for the final few days he had spent long sessions in the sweatbox. On the day of the fight he took more than an hour to shed the last, stubborn ¾lb before weighing in – totally dried out – right on the button.

If that was not handicap enough, he was also carrying an injury. For quite some time he had been suffering, off and on, from a shoulder injury sustained sparring a year earlier. The torn muscles had never healed properly and in the lead-up to Carter the trouble had flared up once again. Williams fretted that he would have to box one-handed.

Had the gamblers been aware of that snippet, then Jimmy Carter may well have started favourite. As it was, there had been late money for the challenger following the news from the weigh-in, but at the opening bell Ike was still a solid 2/1 on chance to retain his title for the eighth time.

There was an eerie atmosphere in the sparsely populated Garden and the sporadic shouts of encouragement echoed throughout the vast arena, the smack of leather on flesh quite audible many rows back.

Most of those early smacks were delivered by Carter. He started cautiously, chin well covered, scoring with left leads and hooks, moving the champion around the ring, and Ike was content to conserve his energy, fighting in spurts, using the old dodge of finishing a round with a flourish to impress the judges. Later, we would discover just how impressed the judges had been.

But this was far from the confident, aggressive champion who had annihilated Montgomery and Bolanos and Beau Jack: he was only 27, just months older than his challenger, but the long hours in the sweatbox had aged him, and as the rounds passed Carter became bolder. Now he was scoring inside, hurting the champ to the body, growing stronger as Williams visibly grew weaker.

After the fight Jimmy Cannon, one of America's best-read boxing experts, wrote off Carter as 'a fighter without class' and certainly the challenger would never possess the flair of a vintage Ike Williams. But if Jimmy was unspectacular, he was also very effective and by the tenth he had softened up the champion sufficiently to bang home a cracking left hook which lifted Williams off his feet, sending him flying through the ropes and on to the ring apron. Ike did well to beat the count, and he called on all his skills to frustrate the New Yorker, countering as best he could, but by now he was totally drained.

Years later, he remembered, 'I was so tired from losing weight that the last two or three rounds, I couldn't even throw a punch.'

By round fourteen he had been on the deck three times, and the fans who recalled the glory days were urging him to last the distance. But once more Carter knocked him down and referee Pete Scalzo, the former featherweight champ, deciding that Ike had suffered enough, called a halt. The weight-weakened champion had been comprehensively beaten, and yet at the stoppage one judge had the fight level at 6–6–1; his colleagues had Carter ahead, but by only 7–5–1.

The reception for the new lightweight boss was muted; the following morning's newspaper reviews voted unanimously that the scales and not Carter had licked Ike; and Jimmy's take-home cheque of $3,627 (including his TV fee) was scarcely designed to make him feel like a world beater. In fact, he soon discovered that his new status could not even gain him entry into Stillman's gym without stumping up the required 50 cents admission.

On that embarrassing day the champ was not even planning a workout, just a quick word with Ketchum, who was holding court inside but Jack Curley, who was Lou Stillman's factotum and the guardian of the door, barred the way until Carter produced the half buck. What Jimmy should have done, of course, was walk away and then return five minutes later: he invariably did better the second time around.

Even in his first year at the top a disturbing pattern began to emerge, one that earned him considerable notoriety which he always strongly resented. Time and again, the New Yorker would lose an upset decision – and twice the title! – then comfortably win the rematch. The charitable will say that Carter was always an in-and-out performer, often a reluctant trainer, and could only produce the goods when he was psyched up for a battle. The cynics, taking a good look at the guys who were pulling the strings back then, remain convinced that every now and then Jimmy did a favour for the boys. Never any concrete evidence, but the statistics will never look good.

By 1951 Art Aragon had taken over from Bolanos as the Golden Boy in California, having been steered a cautious course through the ranks. Three months after becoming champion Carter journeyed to Los Angeles and lost a ten-rounder to Aragon, which prompted a rematch for the title. On November 14, again in LA, the Golden Boy was badly banged up, twice knocked down and outpointed by huge margins. Major turnaround, but both fights pleased the fans, and everybody cleaned up.

There was more big money to be made out west. The following year Carter returned to Los Angeles to defend against Lauro Salas, a crude but exciting puncher from Monterrey. Carter won a unanimous decision, but Salas had the clout to get a second chance just six weeks later, and this time he copped the decision and the title. Huge surprise. For the inevitable third fight the circus moved back east, but Chicago offered a cool welcome.

Only 5,283, a record low attendance for a title fight in Chicago Stadium, saw Jimmy outpoint Lauro The Lion to become champion for the second time. The judges' cards – 84–66, 82–68, 81–69 – give an indication of how easy it had been.

There was never any doubt Carter could turn on the style, and in 1953 he performed like a true champion when successfully defending against Tommy Collins in Boston, George Araujo in the Garden, and the French-Canadian Armand Savoie in Montreal. All three failed to last the distance, but on the down side, earlier in the year Savoie had beaten him in a ten-rounder, and so too had Eddie Chavez and Johnny Cunningham. Extremely weird.

His erratic form continued into the following year, when Paddy De Marco, a light-hitting Brooklyn veteran, contrived to borrow Carter's title in the Garden, only to be stopped in the San Francisco return on November 17, 1954. Jimmy Carter was a three-time champion, but his public was underwhelmed and perhaps there was a sense of relief when Bud Smith twice outpointed him in 1955 and Jimmy was a champ no more.

He would box on, but now he was losing more than he was

winning and he retired in 1960 with a career record of 81 wins from 120 bouts: a record that will forever be shrouded in mystery and controversy.

If Carter harboured any regrets about his roller coaster career, they never surfaced. While still champion, he explained, 'As long as I win and I know I can beat the guys around, then I don't mind if they underrate me or if they say I have no colour or if they remember my name. They can say what they want, but I think I'm a pretty good champion.'

He was at least that, but we will always wonder if he could have been much more. Jimmy died penniless, back in his birthplace of Aiken, on September 21, 1994, aged 70.

Ike Williams had died just two weeks earlier in Los Angeles and, like Carter, he had suffered a heart attack and finished up broke. But, unlike Jimmy, there is no dispute about Ike's place in boxing history. He was an all-time great, and retired with a record of 125 wins from 154 fights. Out of the ring, he had shown his stubborn streak when he tried to form a boxers' union, and then his courage when he testified before the senators.

He never managed to change the murky system, but at least he gave it his best shot. No champ could do better.

CHAPTER TWENTY-ONE

Jose Torres *v* Willie Pastrano

TUESDAY, MARCH 30, 1965

A quote. 'Fear is like a fire. If you control it, as we do when we heat our houses, it is a friend. When you don't, it consumes you and everything you do and everything around you.'

The wisdom of Constantine D'Amato who for many years preached his unique brand of psychology on the streets of Manhattan and from his rundown Gramercy gym on East 14th Street and then, until his death, in the cleaner air of his training hideaway in the Catskills. The idiosyncratic Cus was a one-off, denounced as a nut and a charlatan by his many enemies and critics, but remembered as a genius by those whom he allowed closest to him, particularly the three young men that he fashioned into world champions . . . Floyd Patterson, Jose Torres and the teenage Mike Tyson.

Those three did not learn only to keep their bodies in mint condition, their gloves high and their chins low; or how to double up on a left hook or put together a blistering combination. D'Amato also lectured them on fear, and how they must grow to accept that sinister sensation as part of every good boxer's working day. He taught them that they must control the demons who are constant visitors to the dressing room on fight night and turn them into allies.

Old Cus believed that fear made a good boxer more focused on the task in hand, and he was forever assuring his protégés that every worthwhile fighter experienced the slight tremble down the arms and legs, or the butterflies deep in the stomach, or the parched mouth, during the final countdown. Nothing to be ashamed of, and the guys who denied ever feeling extreme anxiety as the minutes ticked away were either brilliant liars or were about to get flattened in the first round.

Very few boxers are willing to discuss this apprehension: somehow, such feelings do not go with the territory patrolled by a tough guy. But Jose Torres, an extremely bright sort both in and out of the ring, readily admitted to those moments of dread in the dressing room and on the march to the ring, and he was proud of the manner in which he could keep his fears in check. In fact, by the time the first bell rang Jose felt he already had won one victory.

Torres must have been even more uptight than usual on the Tuesday in March 1965 when he prepared himself to face Willie Pastrano in the Garden. Not that Pastrano was a destructive puncher, but this was Jose's big shot, the opportunity to become a world champion and thousands of his fellow Puerto Ricans had wagered heavily on him and were now waiting to cheer him on. Heavy pressure.

He could console himself, however, with the knowledge that Pastrano would also be feeling the heat. Everybody knew Willie was always wisecracking about the scary guys he was going to fight. He had collected enough material for a nightclub routine, but this was just Pastrano's way of dealing with his demons, and no braver boxer ever ducked through the ropes.

Wilfred Raleigh Pastrano spent a lifetime masking his anxieties. He was born on November 27, 1935 in New Orleans, and from when he was just a little boy – an extremely fat little boy – he became accustomed to battling the terrors, both those inside his head and those planning actual bodily harm on his chubby person. A no-win situation: either fight his gang of tormentors or suffer a belting from a father who worked in the shipyards and had no time for wimps.

A pal, Ralph Dupas provided a solution to the trauma. Ralph was a month older than Willie and was already boxing at a gym run by a character named Whitey Esneault, a well-known face in Louisiana fight circles. He urged Willie to join him for workouts, if only to get rid of the blubber. The keep-fit guys proved as cruel as the schoolkids and enjoyed a good laugh, but overnight Willie had been bitten by the boxing bug and he persevered. Esneault gave him his own key to the gym so that he could train on his own or just with Dupas, and after one year of incredibly hard graft thirteen-year-old Wilfred Raleigh had transformed from a roly-poly light heavy figure of fun into a fourteen-year-old sleek featherweight with dancing feet and a beautiful left hand.

At that stage, however, he was nowhere near Ralph's class. Many years later Dupas would lose in challenges for the lightweight and welter belts before winning the junior middleweight title and even back then he was considered a phenomenon in New Orleans.

Whitey had him boxing professionally before he was fifteen, and by the time Pastrano was deemed ready to join the pros his friend had lost only once in 21 outings. On September 10, 1951 the two fifteen-year-olds were featured on one of Esneault's New Orleans shows, Dupas topping the bill and outpointing Noel Humphreys, Willie calming his nerves enough to win a four-rounder against Domingo Rivera.

Pastrano would often recall how terrified he had been throughout his first amateur bout (he had won easily) and how he fought the Rivera debut over and over in his head before entering the ring. He was becoming a man, but after four wins the Louisiana commission discovered that he was still a boy – sixteen was the minimum age in the state – and he did not fight again for five months. Esneault was fined $100, but the equally young Dupas somehow slipped through the net, continuing to box while Willie was laid up.

The situation was bizarre. Come the school holidays other kids went off to camp or spent their vacation with their parents: Pastrano and Dupas travelled to Miami Beach to fight for promoter Chris Dundee. The age limit in Florida was eighteen, so some imagination was obviously required when applying for the licences, and there was also significant business done backstage. Dundee's younger brother Angelo was brought in as co-manager of the teenagers, along with Esneault, whose health was failing. Later Angelo would become the outright boss, but in the meantime the two hot prospects alternated between New Orleans and Miami Beach.

Willie was still growing. Four days before his nineteenth birthday he outpointed the former welterweight contender Bobby Dykes. That was his 35th contest; he had been beaten only four times, and now he was a middleweight, bordering on light heavy. But by the end of the following year – 1955 – he was a fully fledged heavyweight, outpointing the veteran Rex Layne in New Orleans.

Champion Rocky Marciano made his official retirement announcement the following April; D'Amato's Floyd Patterson won the vacant title, and Pastrano reckoned he could beat him, and any of the other contenders. For the next four years he was never ranked worse than fifth best heavyweight in the world.

Willie had a terrific chin and most heavies were too slow to land a clean shot on it, but in turn, he was never a knockout puncher. In fact in his entire career, from featherweight all the way up, Pastrano won only fourteen fights inside the distance. He relied on his brilliant boxing skills to beat fair fighters such as Johnny Arthur, Pat McMurty, Charlie Norkus and Johnny Holman, but Europe was the setting for his most spectacular heavyweight triumphs.

The British could never see enough of the silky smooth, handsome American, who in one purple patch repaid their generous hospitality by outpointing Dick Richardson, Brian London and Joe Bygraves before slipping over to Italy to beat Franco Cavicchi in Bologna. True, London gained a degree of revenge, winning a rematch – the only cut-eye loss in Pastrano's career – and he was outpointed by the Welshman, Joe Erskine, as clever as Willie, but also a non-puncher. The money in Europe was excellent, and the social life even better.

The American was a hit wherever he went. He was warm and witty and patient with the demands of both the press and the public. He had married Faye, had fathered four sons and a daughter, and always wore his wedding ring laced to his boxing boot as a lucky charm. The newspaper boys loved that one. But Willie could not resist a pretty face, and some that were not so pretty and little Angelo was forever having fits trying to track down his fighter. In the 5th Street gym, packed with champions and contenders, Willie was one of the hardest trainers; getting him there was as different matter.

By now Sonny Liston was beginning to bludgeon his way through the heavyweight ranks, and Dundee wisely decided that the smart move would be to return to the light heavies. The money would be less, but so too would the risks.

Willie was still only 24, but he had packed in 67 bouts in his ten years campaigning when he flew to Glasgow in September 1960 to face the local hope, Chic Calderwood, in a match which promoter Peter Keenan billed as a world-title eliminator. Calderwood was awarded a disputed verdict, but before the end of the year there was an even bigger set-back, when a listless Pastrano was beaten by Jesse Bowdry in Miami Beach. His motivation had vanished and, aside from boxing a draw against Lennart Risberg in Stockholm, he disappeared for seventeen months.

Lack of funds dictated that he must fight again; a high-profile draw with Archie Moore rekindled his ambition; and a tough three-fight series against Wayne Thornton brought him back to peak fitness. And then, incredibly, he was offered a title shot against Harold Johnson from Philadelphia.

He had been neither the first nor the second choice to challenge Johnson. Mauro Mina, the original opponent, had cancelled because of a damaged hand; his replacement, Henry Hank, burst a cheekbone in training; Pastrano was a last resort for the promoters, and he was not going to come cheap. Johnson was an intelligent counter puncher who could finish an opponent with a single shot, and Willie held out for a purse of $21,500 – three times the original offer – before he decided to risk his well-being.

Nobody gave him a chance. Johnson had not been beaten for eight years and was installed a 6/1 on favourite, but on June 1, 1963 at the Las Vegas Convention Center Pastrano conned him out of the title. He refused to lead, and a frustrated champion was forced to abandon his normal tactics and began chasing the fight. Had he not done so there would have been no action. As it was there was little excitement as Willie used the ring and his left hand to steal the points. He was given the majority decision, but nobody could convince Johnson that he had not been robbed.

A tearful Willie was in wonderland. This was the climax of a long, hard journey, and he was determined to cash in on his good fortune. The following year he made two defences and, curiously enough, won both inside the distance. The Argentinian Gregorio Peralta, who had beaten Pastrano in a non-title affair, was halted in the sixth, and then the champ and Dundee headed one last time for Britain to face the former middleweight kingpin Terry Downes at Belle Vue, Manchester.

Once again Willie proved the perfect ambassador, a delight to all who met him, but as far as the fight was concerned he might as well have been back in Miami. By the end of round ten Downes was ahead, and the situation had reached crisis point for the lethargic American. During the minute's break a furious Dundee slapped him hard, at the same time yelling that he was tossing away the title and at last Pastrano became focused. He walked out in the eleventh to do a number on the gutsy Londoner, flooring him and forcing a stoppage. But this had been a very close squeak, and back in the States the word went out that the champion was now boxing from memory.

The 28-year-old Jose Torres was easily the most colourful of the contenders. He had been beaten only once – a stunning knockout by the Cuban Florentino Fernandez back home in San Juan; had flattened the old middleweight holder Bobo Olson on his latest appearance; and most important from Pastrano's angle, Jose had a tremendous following amongst New York's Puerto Ricans. Willie was looking for a major paynight.

Today, Don King could probably scrape together one hundred grand if he dug deep through all his pockets, but back in 1965 $100,000 was mega money for a light heavy, and that was the sum Pastrano had set as a guarantee. There would be considerable soul-searching before Team Torres came up with the readies.

Financially, D'Amato was on the ropes. He was engaged in an ongoing war with the IRS and all his funds were tied up. Cain Young, an affluent real-estate developer with aspirations to break into boxing, came up with a deal. He offered to put up the $100,000 provided Torres could get a release from D'Amato, and he (Young) could become the manager of record. Jose turned him down; he thought far too much of Cus, who had never taken a percentage from any of his purses. Instead, the fighter approached his friend, the author, Norman Mailer, who said he was willing to lodge up to $60,000 of his own cash to secure the title shot.

D'Amato, rather nobly, decided that the wise move was to go with Young, and he gave Torres the necessary release from his contract. There were many who claimed that Jose's career had been put on the back burner when Cus was feuding with the International Boxing Club during his time managing Patterson. To some extent that may have been the case, but now he was making amends bigtime. His fighters had never been mere commodities as far as D'Amato was concerned: their welfare always came first, second and third.

Now, after seven years as a pro, Torres, the one-time idol of New York's small club circuit, was finally going to get his big chance in the Garden, and nobody could say that he did not earn his shot. For all too long Jose had worked in the shadow of his friend, Patterson, and a few years earlier he had been denied a crack at a version of the middleweight title when a proposed match with Paul Pender fell through because his team failed to put together a suitable financial package. He knew that this time failure was not an option.

Jose Luis Torres was born on May 3, 1936 in Playa Ponce, Puerto Rico, the second oldest of seven children. He was a bright and happy child, an excellent high school student, but then he surprised everyone by enlisting in the army. And that is when he first pulled on a boxing glove.

Torres had no burning desire to become a champion boxer. Like so many other future stars who emerged from the forces, Jose much preferred sparring a few rounds to cleaning out latrines or standing guard, and the food for the fighters was in a different class. But he quickly discovered that he was far better than the average army scrapper, soon collecting a truckload of trophies. The Puerto Rican teenager became the Maryland State AAU champion, the All-Army champion, then the All-Services champion, before coming out on top in the Olympic trials. All systems go for Australia!

The 1956 Melbourne Olympics opened in November with the shockwaves still reverberating around the world in the aftermath of the Hungarian rebellion, which had been crushed so ruthlessly by the Soviet tanks. In Australia, all Hungarian competitors were acclaimed as heroes, but none more so than the marvellous Laszlo Papp who had already won Olympic gold in London and Helsinki. Tough luck on the twenty-year-old Torres that in the light middleweight final he had to face not only a legend, but also a pro-Hungarian crowd. After a terrific fight, Laszlo's ringcraft gave him the narrowest of edges, but Jose had let nobody down, and always remembered Melbourne as his favourite sporting experience.

His fine showing prompted a flood of offers to turn pro and he opted to sign with D'Amato, who had just steered Patterson to the heavyweight championship. Typically, Cus was in no hurry for Torres to begin earning: there were long schooling sessions in the Gramercy gym, and Torres won the 1958 Golden Gloves title and an important inter-city tournament in Chicago before his manager decided he was ready.

D'Amato was an extremely cautious matchmaker, and on May 24, 1958 Gene Hamilton failed to last a round when the prospect made his debut in Brooklyn and by the end of the year Jose had extended his unbeaten run to nine.

Right from the off, the middleweight was attracting sell-out crowds to the Sunnyside Gardens in Queens, and more than 4,000 packed into the St Nicholas Arena in Manhattan on the night he stopped the big Canadian, Burke Emery, in the fifth. He also made a fleeting appearance in Los Angeles, beating some-body called Benny Doyle in one round on the Patterson–Roy Harris championship undercard, and a story that he had knocked down Floyd in a sparring session did no harm to his reputation. Everyone agreed that Jose's first eight months as a pro had been an unqualified success.

But trouble was looming. In 1959 Torres boxed only five times, and the following year the total dropped to three. The reasons were not hard to find. In a sensational upset in June 1959, Ingemar Johansson took Patterson's title and overnight, D'Amato became a target for all sorts of investigations and allegations. When Cus controlled the heavyweight championship, he was often seen as a dictator rather than a crusader, and no better than the IBC which he had sworn to bring down. Time and again he ignored the claims of deserving contenders in favour of hand-picked challengers for Floyd, and this was payback time.

The columnists lined up to take their best shot, claiming that D'Amato was a hypocrite who had ruined Patterson by feeding him a series of poor opponents; some, who were really out for blood, went further and alleged that Torres was also getting a kid glove build-up. As Cus ducked and dived, for a time the fighter was caught in the fall-out, and his career stalled quite dramatic-ally. But by 1961 he was back on track, heading for a crack at the middleweight title, but significantly, for three years he had no fights in New York.

And then, on May 26, 1963 he lost for the first time, and once again his career was under threat.

Florentino Fernandez was another Angelo Dundee fighter, not much of a boxer, but a ferocious puncher who fell just short of the top grade. Torres had home advantage in San Juan, but the mere fact that D'Amato had accepted the match rather dispelled the cotton wool theories: anyone facing the wide-shouldered Cuban was at risk, and Jose got caught in the fifth. All over, and once again the critics got on his case, but the Puerto Rican listened only to his own thoughts and those of his manager: after a four-month break he returned with a points win over Don Fullmer, his confidence intact.

Torres had always been a big middleweight, and now he had options in the light heavy division. He was back fighting in New York, his fans were as loyal as ever, and he stayed unbeaten through 1964, finishing the year with the one-round demolition of Olson. True, Bobo was an ancient, but he had lost only three times from his last nineteen fights and had been beating decent opposition. The win was enough to make Jose a live challenger for Willie P's title.

March 1965 was a troubled month for Americans. The war was escalating at an alarming pace in Vietnam: previously the American soldiers had been described as 'advisers' but now Lyndon Johnson was taking off the gloves and sending in the Marines. And back home a month of civil rights protests in Alabama climaxed with Dr Martin Luther King leading 25,000 marchers to the steps of the state Capitol in Montgomery.

The march came only two days before the Garden showdown, but history tells us that sport always provides huge comfort in times of great crisis. Escapism, perhaps, but on the night of March 30 the Garden was packed to overflowing to see Pastrano defend against Torres, and welterweight champion Emile Griffith face Jose Stable from Cuba. Gate receipts swelled to a record $239,556.

The experts were unsure. Pastrano's jab could steal the points, but would the legs that once were such marvels let him down? Torres was the fresher and had the better variety of punches, but Willie had never been on the canvas. This one could go right down to the wire. Not so.

The pattern was set in the very first round when a confident Torres hurried out of his corner behind the trademark peekaboo guard, and right away began to outjab the jabber. And not just token shots either. Three great left hands banged into the champion's face without reply, and Pastrano prepared himself for a long and stressful evening.

Recalling the fight to Peter Heller, Torres said, 'It was a psychological thing. When he tried to jab me, I made him miss and I jabbed. I outjabbed him and that was his best punch. I took his best punch away. Then he was concentrating mostly on defence with me. And then, every time he stopped and tried to throw punches, there was no confidence behind the punches.'

In his corner at the end of those opening three minutes a jubilant challenger, the man who had to control his fear in the dressing room, told trainer Johnny Manzanet not to worry: the fight was in the bag.

Across the ring not much was being said. Willie had worked hard in the gym, but the snap was missing from his punches, the bounce from his legs, and by round three the Garden was witnessing a first: Willie Pastrano bruised and banged up, blood trickling from his nostrils. Willie's classic good looks were being vandalised.

He was being made to box a rearguard action, bravely but not very successfully and in the sixth came another landmark, as Pastrano dropped slowly to the deck for the only time in 84 fights. A hellish left hook to the body had done the damage, and Willie had never experienced such pain.

There was no air in his lungs, no feeling in his legs, but he listened to the unfamiliar count and somehow struggled to his feet. Referee Johnny Lo Bianco anxiously asked him if he was all right, but for once no wisecrack came to mind. He was busy watching the challenger stalk towards him, and then another vicious hook to the liver doubled him over but this time he stayed upright, covering up as Torres pounded him with both hands until the bell.

Willie had always made light of his profession and his talent; had cracked gags about his being scared of the big punchers and his dread of taking severe punishment; but behind the jester's mask there was a proud, serious pro who was determined to bow out like a true champion.

For the next three rounds Pastrano soaked up a terrible beating as Torres, urged on by his ecstatic support, pot-shotted with more hooks and straight rights that sent the spray flying. But the champ refused to take the easy way out and go down for the full ten. He kept telling himself that there was always the chance that Jose might punch himself out; that he might magically turn the fight as he had done against Downes in Manchester; but Willie was kidding himself.

By the end of the ninth he was totally used up and taking a needless hammering and as he tried to rise off his stool for round ten, Lo Bianco told him that he had suffered enough and the fight was over. Pastrano's loud protests were not for the benefit of the ringsiders.

Party time in the Garden, as the Puerto Ricans began their celebrations. Pastrano offered his congratulations to the new champ then disappeared, almost unnoticed, to the solitary quiet of the loser's dressing room. But for Torres the journey from the ring was that of a conquering hero, as his delighted countrymen lifted him on their shoulders and carried him out into the crowd, who passed him up and down the aisles, everybody wanting to touch the new light heavyweight champion of the world.

Few champions have been granted such a joyous coronation, and for a time Torres gloried in his new status. In 1966, despite being hospitalised because of a pancreas condition, he boosted his bank balance with successful defences against Wayne Thornton, Eddie Cotton and Chic Calderwood, but even before his final big test of the year – against the two-time middleweight champion Dick Tiger – the Puerto Rican had discovered another exciting world outside of boxing.

He had become a close friend of Norman Mailer, the pair often indulging in sparring sessions, and through Mailer he got to know other writers such as Budd Schulberg and Pete Hamill. Torres found that there were other ways that he could express himself, aside from through his fists. Boxing was no longer occupying his mind full time.

And that just might have been one of the reasons why on December 16, 1966 he lost his title to Tiger, being outpointed by clear margins. In the February return Jose did much better, but two judges voted 8–7 for the Nigerian, the third scored 8–7 for Torres, and for twenty minutes the Puerto Ricans threw bottles and chairs. Their demonstration, however, was not going to change anything.

Torres drifted into semi-retirement. The following year he boxed only once, travelling to Australia to stop Bob Dunlop in six rounds, and then on July 14, 1969 he fought for the last time, getting off the canvas to beat Charlie Green in round two. He finished with a career record of only three losses from 45 bouts, and immediately looked around for fresh challenges.

Encouraged by his literary friends, Torres became a writer and, soon, a very successful one.

He became a much-read columnist for the *New York Post*, wrote acclaimed biographies of Ali (*Sting Like a Bee*) and Tyson (*Fire and Fear*), and remains a regular contributor to a number of publications. He developed an interest in politics, knew Bobby Kennedy as a friend, and for a time held down the post as chairman of the New York State Athletic Commission. Channelling his fears has paid off handsomely for Jose Torres, and long may he prosper.

Civilian life was not so kind to Willie Pastrano. Angelo Dundee had wanted Willie to have a few more fights and gradually ease himself out of the business, but he was adamant: his gallant last hurrah in the Garden was definitely a farewell appearance.

Since his early teens Pastrano had known nothing but the boxing life, and he drifted from one job to the next: selling insurance with Bobby Dykes, selling cars, working on construction sites, then youth projects, appearing in some terrible movies. He sank into the dark world of drugs and inevitably, Faye, his wife of fifteen years, divorced him, and there were other failed relationships. Eventually he conquered his booze and drug habits, only to die of liver cancer on December 6, 1997. He was 62.

Willie P was boxing's Prince Charming, a wisecracker who could always keep his demons in check. Away from the ring, however, he was just another troubled soul.

The Night of Nights

On March 25, 1916 a sell-out crowd turned up to celebrate the first heavyweight championship battle ever staged in the Garden, with giant Jess Willard pocketing $47,500 to defend against rugged Frank Moran. New York had been buzzing for weeks, and on the night thousands were locked out of the spectacular building on Madison Square.

The actual ten rounds, however, proved a dreadful anticlimax as Texan Jess fumbled his way to a dreary no-decision. A money maker, but a flop.

Two new Gardens, and 55 years to the month later, New York was again going bananas over a heavyweight title fight. And not just in the Big Apple but throughout America and the rest of the world everyone, it seemed, wanted to see Ali and Frazier earn their $2.5 million apiece.

The fight of the century? This was going to be the greatest sporting occasion ever. And this time the fight lived up to the superhype.

CHAPTER TWENTY-TWO

Joe Frazier *v* Muhammad Ali

MONDAY, MARCH 8, 1971

Looking down from that great Stillman's in the Sky, Tex Rickard would have beamed approvingly as the beautiful people poured out from the endless caravan of limos that snaked back for blocks from the Garden. Designer gowns and elegant tuxes: Rickard's kind of customers. Peeking over Tex's shoulder, Mike Jacobs would have been zapping the throng with his professional eye on the scalpers, still conducting late business and now demanding a grand for a $150 ringside seat. Hustlers and hardcases: Mike's kind of guys.

Those thousand dollar rip-offs would be many rows back from the action, behind the cameras set up for the closed circuit transmission and the pews packed with bigshot politicians and movie icons and the 750-strong media army lucky enough to have been granted accreditation. The Garden had been forced to knock back another five hundred applications from all over the world, but there was always the closed circuit.

Dan Parker had passed on and Nat Fleischer would die the following year, but tonight the press benches were being graced by the super heavies: Budd Schulberg was on assignment from *Playboy*; William Saroyan was writing for *True*; *Life* had snapped up a terrific double act: Norman Mailer providing the prose, Frank Sinatra snapping the pictures. And there was Burt Lancaster, with Archie Moore on board as back-up, supplying a colour commentary.

This was m-a-s-s-i-v-e, baby: P T Barnum jumbo and Cecil B De Mille colossal, all expertly packaged by a Hollywood agent and bankrolled by a multi-millionaire who had started out life as a

293

lowly salesman in Canada. Two former Olympic champions, two undefeated heavyweight champions, clashing head to head for the richest prize in sport, and in the traditional home of boxing. After Joe Frazier and Muhammad Ali were done with one another, the fight business would never be the same again.

Back in 1938 Joe Louis had united his nation when he knocked out Max Schmeling in a round – a so-called jab, hook and right cross for good ol' democracy over the scumbag Nazis. This time, however, America was torn right down the middle: black against black, white against black, white against white. Only the reddest of rednecks could feign indifference about the outcome. Muhammad, the great crusader, was back from his three years' banishment, bigger and brasher than ever, demanding what was his. And Joe Frazier, much less mouthy but every ounce as proud, could not wait to ram a left hook down his throat.

A showdown had been inevitable ever since The Lip from Louisville had been allowed back in the ring in October 1970 – in Georgia, of all states – stopping Jerry Quarry on cuts in three rounds in Atlanta. And less than two months later, following his last round knockout over Oscar Bonavena in the Garden, the only real question remaining was not when or where he would fight Frazier, but how much they would be paid.

Ali has been credited with raising the earnings of not only fighters but of all athletes to heights never previously imagined, and his extraordinary charisma did open the floodgates. But it was a hardcore, blue-collar boxing man called Yancy Durham who did the bargaining for this fight – and not just for his man, Frazier, but also for Ali.

Yank Durham had been an amateur fighter whose career came to an abrupt halt during the war, when a jeep ran over his legs while he was serving in the army in England. He started working as a welder for the railroad, trained boxers in Philadelphia, but Yank had not discovered a decent prospect until the young Joe Frazier, a country boy from Beaufort in South Carolina, walked into the gym. They immediately struck up a relationship, and while Ali was in exile Durham steered Smokin' Joe first to the New York version of the title by beating Buster Mathis, and then to the undisputed championship, after stopping Ali's sparring mate, Jimmy Ellis.

By then Yank knew the value of his fighter and exactly how much each fight was worth. A natural negotiator, he met up with

Herbert Muhammad – Ali's business manager and the son of Elijah Muhammad, leader of the Nation of Islam – and the pair reached agreement that there should be purse parity for the big fight. Already Durham's idea of a purse was a million, and then some.

The front runners in the bidding were Madison Square Garden, who had done a lot of business with Frazier, and the Houston Astrodome, which had hosted Ali against both Cleveland Williams and Ernest Terrell. Fred Hofheinz, son of the owner of the Dome, was confident that $1,100,000 to each boxer would be the magic number to secure the signatures. Then Harry Markson and Teddy Brenner, the Garden's main men, arrived in Philly with an offer of $1.25 million apiece. Durham was impressed but not overwhelmed. The New Yorkers returned to their hotel, confident, but still with no firm agreement.

And that is where they received the call from Frazier's lawyer, Bruce Walker, which blew all their hopes out of the water. There was a new player, a man called Jerry Perenchio, and he had just tabled an offer of $5 million for the two fighters. Two million five hundred thousand bucks each! Who was this guy?

The forty-year-old Perenchio may have been Jerry Who in the world of boxing, but he was no starry-eyed novice when talking major deals. He spearheaded Chartwell Artists, a showbiz management agency which represented such earners as Marlon Brando, Richard Burton, Elizabeth Taylor, Jane Fonda and many other Grade A clients; he had brokered the sale of Caesar's Palace in Vegas for $83 million; and just to show he was serious about his bid, Perenchio deposited $200,000 cash. Now all he had to do was find some fellow with five million.

Perenchio had never met Jack Kent Cooke, but they talked the same language. A Canadian, Cooke was a hard-headed multi-millionaire who was a partner with Lord Thomson in newspapers, radio and cable television. He was also heavily into sport, owning the Los Angeles Lakers basketball team, the Los Angeles Kings ice hockey squad, and a 25 per cent share of the Washington Redskins footballers. For good measure, he also owned the Inglewood Forum where the Lakers and the Kings performed.

He was intrigued by the challenge and the potential profit, and decided to put in $4.5 million. The final $500,000 came from the Garden. Both Cooke and Perenchio had wanted the superfight to go to California but Durham and Frazier had hung out doggedly for New York, and finally got their way. Perenchio demonstrated footwork worthy of a vintage Fred Astaire.

He told the media, 'I'm a traditionalist. I'm a cornball. I believe if you have the biggest fight in history, you should have it in the greatest boxing arena in the world.'

The investors met the boxers for the first time on December 30, 1970, when Frazier and Ali came face to face to sign the contracts in New York. Jack and Jerry may not have been steeped in boxing lore but they knew how to squeeze every cent from a transaction: the contract stated that even the fighters' gloves, boots, trunks and robes would become the property of the partners after the fight.

There also would be the dough from souvenir programmes and posters, a proposed book and a planned documentary: petty cash, given the scale of the production, but still accumulating a big bundle of money. The Garden was a guaranteed sell-out (in fact all the tickets had vanished a month before the fight) and on the night a crowd of 20,455 returned receipts of $1,352,961. That money belonged to MSG, and Harry Markson was tearing his hair that he had not charged $250 ringside instead of $150.

For Perenchio and Cooke the deal hung on the closed-circuit figures, and those two master salesmen got to work. During the countdown everyone was feeling the pressure, aside from Ali who had never looked up the meaning of the word.

Durham was under fire from black activist groups for selling the fight to white promoters – wily old Elijah Muhammad probably anticipated such a reaction and distanced Herbert from the negotiations – but Durham rode the attacks like an old pro. Yank was doing the right thing for his fighter, and that was all that mattered.

Cooke was panned for pricing the closed circuit seats (some prime locations charged as high as $30) out of the reach of many fans, especially black fans. Even the outlets were up in arms; the exhibitor and the promoter usually split 50–50, but Perenchio was looking for 65 per cent. The partners were scathingly dismissive of the persistent sniping.

The final figures were astonishing. An estimated 300 million people in 46 countries around the world watched the fight. Revenue reached somewhere in the region of $25 million – a very pleasant region just south of heaven. In Pittsburgh a 5,000 outdoor crowd endured sub-zero temperatures and a 30mph wind. In Britain, cinemas charging five pounds a skull were packed out at three in the morning. Wild!

The boxers had no incentive to boost the closed circuit takings as they were on that flat guarantee of $2.5 million, but that did not stop Ali launching into a sales pitch as if he had a 10 per cent interest in every cinema seat. There was the old stuff: the poems ('Now this might shock and amazya, but I'm gonna retire Joe Frazya') and the rants on TV, and how he was too pretty and Joe was too ugly, and how he was the real champ. Harmless and even humorous at times, but somewhere along the line Ali's routine switched to seriously nasty, and when he labelled Frazier an Uncle Tom, he was punching way below the belt.

Even all these years later Joe bristles when he recalls the slander. Back then he was furious and hurt, his wife Florence was stunned and young son Marvis suffered verbals from his classmates. Uncle Tom. Just about the worst slur that can be pinned on any black American. And how, Frazier wondered, could Ali have the front to tag him with such a name?

Muhammad had been raised in a comfortable home in a safe neighbourhood in Louisville; Joe, the youngest of twelve, had been brought up on a dirt farm in South Carolina. Muhammad had turned pro sponsored by a group of white millionaires and had white Angelo Dundee and white Ferdie Pacheco running his corner. Joe relied on black Yank Durham and black Eddie Futch. How could he be the Uncle Tom?

Across the States, black Americans took sides. Muhammad had turned down the army, risked a five-year stretch, and had dropped millions when his licence was revoked. He was a standard-bearer, a proud disciple of Elijah Muhammad who had no truck with whitey. But other blacks felt more comfortable siding with Smokin' Joe. Here was a guy who had toiled on a farm in Beaufort, sweated in a slaughterhouse in Philly, and sang the oldtime gospel songs on a Sunday. Joe had become a champ without bad-mouthing anybody.

White America was equally divided. The campus kids were solidly behind Muhammad as were the loyal literary set who continued to champion his cause, but for many – particularly the Vietnam vets – Ali remained that draft dodger, Clay. Nobody was neutral, but some saner heads took time out to argue the respective merits of the fighters, and in bars and cocktail lounges left jabs against left hooks was the favourite topic.

Las Vegas was reporting unprecedented betting action, forecasting a billion-dollar turnover. Ali money claimed that The Greatest would be too fast, too classy, just too smart for a rumbling tank like Smokin' Joe. Frazier fans were banking on his pulverising left hook, an extraordinary workrate, and that unquenchable will to win. Joe predicted that he would do the business in the tenth; Ali, producing a sealed envelope for the closed circuit cameras, nominated round six as the grand finale. Take your choice, and get the money down.

Hassle everywhere as the weeks dwindled down to the last madcap, nail-biting days. New York's couturiers had never known such a last-minute scramble. What should one wear to the Garden? Senators and congressmen and mafia dons and pillars of Wall Street scrambled to get on the VIP list. Markson, Brenner, and the Garden's publicity guru John Condon were under round-the-clock siege.

And so too was Frazier, who was getting grief and not only from Ali. In the build-up he had received a number of death threats, taken seriously enough to warrant a five-strong police bodyguard. When he arrived in New York another three cops were added to the payroll, following a bomb threat phoned to his hotel. Crazy, but Durham was taking no chances, and Joe was moved secretly to fresh quarters.

And finally the great day. First the weigh-in, a meaningless exercise for heavyweights who can scale whatever they wish, but traditionally a last look at the opposition before the gloves go on. There would, however, be no eyeballing today as the commission officials, wary of an ugly confrontation, weighed the fighters separately. Frazier was first, bursting with energy and exuding menace, hitting the scales at 205½lb and then quickly departing with his entourage. Ali stepped on and off at 215lb and everyone applauded. But by now there was no safe way out of the building!

The Greatest had been made to fight through the crowds to get into the Garden, but the throng had swelled alarmingly and pandemonium reigned in the streets. Markson feared that Muhammad might come to harm and offered to set up temporary quarters inside the arena. Herbert Muhammad and Dundee weighed up their options, but the decision was down to Ali, and he chose to stay indoors. A bed, chairs and TV sets were organised; a regular supply of choice food was arranged; Bundini Brown was detailed to fetch the boxing equipment from the hotel; and Muhammad spent the afternoon taking a nap. Nothing seemed to bug him.

Markson was kept on the hop. Not too long before fight time, when Bundini eventually arrived back with the gear, he was accompanied by about 200 brothers, all looking to get through the employees' entrance. Ali's soulmate figured that he had bargaining power: 'We got the champ's stuff. We don't get in, he don't fight.' No way. Markson eventually allowed twenty through the door although he had no seats for them.

What further hassle? Diana Ross being removed from the press benches could hardly be described as an incident and, at last, all was set up for the fifteen rounds.

A library of books and a zillion words have been written describing The Fight, but permit us to add just a few more personal observations from more than thirty years after the great event.

First off, Hubert Humphrey, Teddy Kennedy, Mayor John Lindsay and the rest of the bluebloods were privileged to sit ringside for such a marvellous 45 minutes of skill and courage. The Garden's greatest fight? Possibly. But remember all the other fabulous nights in all the other Gardens, every one memorable for some different reason. Frazier–Ali, however, must be included on every shortlist of five.

And yet, four years later Joe and Muhammad actually surpassed their Garden heroics when they squared off for the third and deciding time. The Thrilla in Manila . . . for drama, guts and gore there will never be a fight quite like that one.

But back to New York, and back to Joe Frazier. Smokin' Joe will live out his life remembered mostly as one of the principal supporting players during the Ali era. But that night in the Garden Joe Frazier was a great heavyweight champion, a heavyweight who could have beaten Dempsey or Marciano or Louis or Tyson . . . on at least that one night.

He never stopped trundling forward, bobbing and weaving, never stopped throwing punches, never allowed Ali a moment's respite, never flinched as the left side of his face ballooned grotesquely, and never had the slightest doubt that he would come out on top. That night Smokin' Joe was a 205lb Henry Armstrong.

There were two key rounds when the Garden threatened to explode; defining rounds in which the fight was won and lost.

Round eleven. Ali had been showboating earlier, playing games against the ropes, shaking his head to the fans as he absorbed Frazier's shots. Mocking. Cunning. Then Joe landed flush with a terrific left hook and Ali lurched into the ropes, kidding no longer and in dire trouble. Joe charged in, throwing more dynamite hooks and uppercuts and Muhammad's brains were scrambled, his legs gone, but he refused to take a count. At the bell he somehow made the journey back to his corner unaided.

For the first time in his life Ali had taken a sustained battering and he had passed the test, colours flying. In contests to come he would time and again demonstrate his extraordinary powers of recovery and his willingness to accept the brutal punishment that would later cost him so dearly. But the Garden crowd was first to see this new Muhammad.

He gave an encore in round fifteen. Frazier, his features horribly bruised and swollen, continued to press forward relentlessly through Ali's stinging counters. Then Joe glimpsed an opening, and again launched the left hook which crashed off Muhammad's jaw, lifted him off his feet and deposited him on his backside in a neutral corner. Amazingly, he was upright at four and prepared to resume when referee Arthur Mercante completed the mandatory eight count. Quite remarkable that Frazier, after fourteen exhausting rounds, still had the strength to throw such a devastating shot. Equally astonishing that Ali had the reserves not only to rise, but to box his way through to the end of the round.

The final bell rang out through the thunderous cheers, and Mercante quickly stepped between the totally drained warriors, who exchanged insults instead of the congratulations they owed one another.

A quick plug for Mercante, who aside from one freak moment in the tenth (he accidentally poked a finger into Frazier's eye!) handled the contest superbly. Through the fifteen rounds he was always the boss, but was never obtrusive and decades later he remained the best referee in the world. Mercante's score of 8–6–1 Frazier, was just about right; judge Artie Aidala made it 9–6 for Joe; and it was just as well that Johnny Addie's final announcement was lost in the roar of the crowd. Judge Bill Recht had somehow made Frazier the winner by 11–4.

Both boxers required urgent medical attention. The right side of Ali's face had blown up to frightening proportions right after the knockdown and his handlers were convinced that the jaw was broken. He was rushed to the Flowers Fifth Avenue Hospital where the X-ray plates showed no fracture. But the madness was not yet over for the day: somebody pinched the pictures!

For several weeks after the fight Frazier holed up in St Luke's Hospital in Philadelphia. The first few days he could not stand up, much less walk; he was unable to eat, drink or urinate; and his swollen eyes hurt in daylight. The price of victory that only a special few fighters are prepared to pay.

Meanwhile, up in the celestial Stillman's a rueful Tex Rickard paid over a few grand in bets to the ever-hungry Mike Jacobs. Those two Garden legends had enjoyed a marvellous fight and an even more wonderful night in the house where their ghosts will always be welcome.

Tex and Uncle Mike . . . if only. The shows those guys would have dreamed up had closed circuit and pay-per-view been invented back when!

Bibliography

Anderson, Dave, *Ringmasters*, Robson Books 1991

Andre, Sam, and Fleischer, Nat, *Pictorial History of Boxing*, Hamlyn 1975

Arnold, Peter, and Mee, Bob, *Lords of the Ring*, Hamlyn 1998

Astor, Gerald, *Gloves Off: The Joe Louis Story*, Pelham Books 1975

Berger, Phil, *Blood Season*, Macdonald Queen Anne Press 1989

Birtley, Jack, *The Tragedy of Randolph Turpin*, New English Library 1975

Buchanan, Ken, *The Tartan Legend*, Headline 2000

Calder-Smith, Dominic, *Tarnished Armour*, Mainstream 2000

Doughty, Jack, *The Rochdale Thunderbolt*, Pentaman Press 1991

Dundee, Angelo, with Winters, Mike, *I Only Talk Winning*, Arthur Barker Ltd 1983

Frazier, Joe, with Berger, Phil, *Smokin' Joe*, Robson Books 1996

Fried, Ronald K, *Corner Men*, Four Walls, Eight Windows 1991

Grombach, John V, *The Saga of the Fist*, A S Barnes 1977

Gutteridge, Reg, *The Big Punchers*, Stanley Paul 1983

Hauser, Thomas, *The Black Lights*, Robson Books 1987

Hauser, Thomas, *Brutal Artistry*, Robson Books 2002

Hauser, Thomas, *Muhammad Ali*, Robson Books 1991

Heller, Peter, *In This Corner*, Robson Books 1985

Hughes, Bill, and King, Patrick, *Came Out Writing*, Mainstream 1999

La Motta, Jake, with Carter, Joseph, and Savage, Peter, *Raging Bull*, Bantam Books 1980

Lawton, James, *Mission Impossible*, Mainstream 2000

Lewis, Morton, *Ted Kid Lewis*, Robson Books 1990

Mead, Chris, *Champion Joe Louis*, Robson Books 1986

Mee, bob, *Heroes and Champions*, Colour Library Direct 1998

Mullan, Harry, *Illustrated History of Boxing*, Hamlyn 1990

Newfield, Jack, *The Life and Crimes of Don King*, Virgin 1996

Norton, Ken, with Terrill, Marshall, and Fitzgerald, Mike, *Going the Distance*, Sports Publishing Inc 2000

Pep, Willie, with Sacci, Robert, *Friday's Heroes*, Frederick Fell 1973

Remnick, David, *King of the World*, Picador 1998

Sugar, Bert Randolph, *The Great Fights*, Gallery Books 1984

Torres, Jose, *Fire and Fear*, W H Allen 1989

Weston, Stanley, and Farhood, Steven, *Chronicle of Boxing*, Hamlyn 1993

Record Books

Boxing News Annuals, International Boxing Register, Ring Record Books, Boxing Yearbooks (Barry Hugman)

Magazines

Boxing Digest, Boxing Illustrated, Boxing Monthly, Boxing News, Boxing Outlook, Boxing Yearbooks (1958–60), *Championship Boxing Annual* (1964), *Fight Game, K.O., Ring, World Boxing*

INDEX